L to R: Andy Warhol, Nico, Danny Williams,
Sterling Morrison, Maureen Tucker,
Mary Woronov, Paul Morrissey, Lou Reed,
Gerard Malanga and John Cale.
(Malanga Archive)

We would like to specially acknowledge the contributions of the following people: Philip Milstein was President of The Velvet Underground Appreciation Society when we began writing this book and his untiring and generous assistance helped us more than any other single factor. He gave us free access to his archives, allowed us to quote at will from his magazine and gave his time to advise us throughout the project. He also read and criticized the finished manuscript. Phil is no longer publishing his excellent magazine *What Goes On,* The Velvet Underground Appreciation Society's newsletter which he issued three times. He is now in a band tentatively called *Disneyland.* Sterling Morrison contributed his archives and advice throughout the project and read the manuscript for accuracy as well as contributing the introduction. We could not have written this book without his aid. Andy Warhol kindly allowed us to quote from his book *POPism,* which covers the Sixties and his collaboration with The Velvet Underground extensively. Most Warhol quotes come from this source. He also advised us on some of the visual material. Nigel Trevena's pioneering book on The Velvet Underground was an invaluable aid to us at the beginning of this project. We salute him for his groundbreaking research. Nat Finkelstein returned to New York in the middle of the project and assisted us with his vitality and visual memory. Price Abbott supported our efforts with her constant care and presence. We thank her for her great meals, encouragement and patience. Miles contributed throughout with his encouragement and clarity. His was the third mind on this project. Allen Ginsberg blessed us. Danny Fields, Maureen Tucker, Henry Geldzahler, Billy Linich, Tony Conrad, Al Aronowitz, John Wilcock, Betsey Johnson, Ed Sanders, Wayne Kramer, Chris Stein, Debbie Harry, Jonathan Richman, Jim Condon, Pinkie Black, Allen Reuben, Leslie Goldman, Karen Rose, Paul Bang, Ralph Perri, Fayette Hickox, Jed Horne, Steven Sesnick and Mark Saunders were most helpful. We thank them for all their time and memories.

In our research on this book we have drawn on interviews with or about The Velvet Underground by Jim Condon, Allan Richards, Nigel Trevena, John Wilcock, Glenn O'Brien, Mary Harron, Philip Milstein, Lester Bangs, Lenny Kaye, Richard Goldstein, Nat Finkelstein, Giovanni Dadomo and Jean Stein. We acknowledge and thank these pioneers for their reports which were published in the following magazines: *What Goes On, Little Caesar, High Times, New Musical Express, Melody Maker, Sounds, Record Mirror, Trouser Press, New York Rocker,* and from the following books: *POPism* by Andy Warhol (New York, 1980), *Edie* by Jean Stein, edited with George Plimpton (New York, 1982), *The Sex Life and Autobiography of Andy Warhol* by John Wilcock, (New York, 1971), and *No One Waved Goodbye,* (London, 1974).

The update section of this edition of *Uptight* draws on interviews by the following: David Fricke (*Rolling Stone*), Lisa Robinson (*New York Post*), Roger Morton (*NME*), Adam McGovern (*Cover*), Jon Pareles (*New York Times*) and Matt Snow (*Vox*). Discography for 1995 edition compiled by Peter Doggett.

Dedicated, with thanks, to Andy Warhol

First Cooper Square Press edition 2003

This Cooper Square Press paperback edition of *Up-Tight* is an unabridged republication of the edition first published in London in 1995. It is published by arrangement with the authors.

Copyright © 1983, 1995, 2003 by Victor Bockris and Gerard Malanga.

Book design by Neville Brody, copyright © 1995 by Omnibus Press
Cover photograph from the Malanga Archive
Picture research by Victor Bockris and Gerard Malanga
Update picture research by Nikki Russell

Published by Cooper Square Press
An imprint of The Rowman & Littlefield Publishing Group, Inc.
200 Park Avenue South, Suite 1109
New York, New York 10003-1503
www.coopersquarepress.com

Distributed by National Book Network

The Library of Congress cataloged a previous edition of this work as follows:

Bockris, Victor, 1949–
    Up-tight : the Velvet Underground story / by Victor Bockris, Gerard Malanga.
        1st Quill ed.
            p.   cm.
        Discography: p.
        1. Velvet Underground (Musical group).   2. Rock musicians—United States—Biography.   I. Malanga, Gerard.
    ML421.V44 B6   1983   84062398
    784.5 '4 '00922   CIP

978-0-8154-1285-4

♾ ™The paper used in this publication meets the minimum requirements of American National Standard for Information Sciences—Permanence of Paper for Printed Library Materials, ANSI/NISO Z39.48-1992.

Manufactured in the United States of America.

up-tight

THE VELVET UNDERGROUND STORY

BY VICTOR BOCKRIS/GERARD MALANGA

Cooper Square Press

● INTRODUCTION

● I like Victor Bockris and Gerard Malanga's book and am impressed by the scope of it. What I would change, and clearly which cannot be changed, is the overall *tone* of the work, starting with "uptight" in the title, and proceeding to recount the disintegration of first the show, and then of the band. It becomes a chronicle of doom (sort of). What has been buried is the laughter and happiness that attended all of this; the jokes; the parties; the zany adventures. We were serious about what we did, but not grim (very often).

I'm probably picturing something other than a factual account of what went on, and what happened later. I suspect that my main fear concerns my final comment about the experience being *fun*. In the light of all that is described, my comment seems insensitive and shallow. Nevertheless, as serious as I was as a "crusader", I had no desire to become a martyr. The fun and enjoyment of the people and things we were caught up in sustained me in no small measure. I was having, shall we say, the time of my life, and I savored it, knowing full well it couldn't last. In fact, "exploding", "plastic", and "inevitable" sum it all up from an apocalyptic perspective – the origin of the universe and its contents, the mutability of form, and the inescapable decline, entropy, the end.

Against this backdrop, how can a handful of artists, dancers, and musicians hope to fare any better?

Sterling Morrison,
Dept. of English
The University of Texas at Austin
March 10, 1983.

● CONTENTS

PART ONE

● ANDY WARHOL UP-TIGHT (1965-1966)

The Formation of The Exploding Plastic Inevitable

FREDERIC VIGNERON: If you were to compare The Velvet Underground to an ice cream flavour, which one would it be?
ANDY WARHOL: Aaaah. . . white.

● MAKING ANDY WARHOL UP-TIGHT

If you had been in New York City in February 1966, you would have been one of a thousand people who received this flyer in the mail.

If you'd gone to the new location of the Film-Makers Cinematheque on West 41st Street, you would have sat in this audience.

Henry Geldzahler in center in dark glasses. Factory photographer Stephen Shore second from right.
(Nat Finkelstein)

They are about to see *Andy Warhol, Up-Tight*, a multimedia rock show formed out of a combination of films by Andy Warhol, lights by Danny Williams, music by The Velvet Underground and Nico, dancing by Gerard Malanga and Edie Sedgwick, slides and film projections by Paul Morrissey and Warhol, photographs by Billy Linich and by Nat Finkelstein who had a show of his super enlarged contact sheets of The Velvets at the Factory in the foyer of the Cinematheque all week, movie cameras by Barbara Rubin, and the audience by themselves. Donald Lyons and Bob Neuwirth (Dylan's roadie and confidant), listed in the ad, came as Edie's escorts. The Cinematheque was a small avant-garde movie house. The show began with a film called "Lupe" starring Edie Sedgwick. The second to last film she and Andy made together, it details the last night of the Mexican Hollywood star Lupe Velez, who planned the perfect suicide by dressing up, lighting candles all around her bed and taking a big dose of barbiturates, but ended up drowning in her own vomit in the toilet bowl that nausea had made her crawl to. The parallels between Velez and Sedgwick are inescapable.

After two 35-minute reels of "Lupe", The Velvet Underground and Nico walked onto the stage in front of the movie screen and began to tune up in the dark. Andy, who was working one movie projector, now trained a silent version of "Vinyl", his interpretation of "A Clockwork Orange", starring Gerard Malanga as a juvenile delinquent, on the screen. Superimposed on this by another movie projector run by Paul Morrissey were close-up shots of Nico singing "I'll Keep It With Mine" by Bob Dylan. Looking ghostly in the flickering movie lights, Nico on stage picked up the song from Nico on screen and the band joined in behind her. Then, as The Velvet Underground went into "Venus in Furs", Gerard Malanga and Edie Sedgwick moved to centre stage and began gyrating in a free form dance pattern. The whole ensemble was now playing in front of two movies "Vinyl" and "The Velvet Underground and Nico: A Symphony of Sound" being shown silently next to each other. While Nat Finkelstein circulated taking uptight photographs ("Maybe I worked so well with the uptight series because part of my own technique was to move in as close as possible so everybody knew there was a camera there"), Danny Williams, the Factory's Harvard grad electrician, began to project color slides over the band and the films. Suddenly and unexpectedly, a huge spotlight came crashing down and shone directly on the audience, as Barbara Rubin rushed down the aisle with her sun-gun glaring into their faces screaming questions like "Is Your Penis Big Enough?" and "Does he eat you out?" It was Barbara who had suggested the *Andy Warhol, Up-Tight* name and developed the concept of making people uptight rather than relaxed by filming their responses with her movie camera. As The Velvets went into "Run Run Run", Lou leaned into his guitar grinning maniacally in black dungarees, a rumpled black jacket over a black t-shirt and high-heel boots. John Cale was hunkered over his viola in a black suit with a rhinestone choke necklace designed by Kenny Jay Lane in the shape of a snake, while Nico, tall, thin, hauntingly beautiful, stood silhouetted alone in a chic white pants suit. Maureen Tucker, the innocent looking drummer whose sex nobody could at first discern, stood behind her bass drum using tom tom mallets to hit it with a machine-like precision, while rhythm and lead guitarist extraordinaire Sterling Morrison, all in black, stood rock still in the midst of this terrible discordant-chaotic-flashing commotion of light, sound, and sight. For the most part the audience sat there too stunned to think or react. The music was supersonic and very loud. The Velvets turned their amps up as high as they could go. The effect vibrated all through the audience. To some it seemed like a whole prison ward had escaped. Others speak of it today as hypnotic and timeless.

HENRY GELDZAHLER: As far as I can remember the presentation was thrilling but the music was to me much more romantic and melodic. Andy Warhol – Up Tight was explosive and abrasive but I kept finding the traditional, almost folk substructure of The Velvets music. I was more impressed with the music than with the other effects, but it was enhanced by the combination.

Lou began to sing "Heroin". Gerard slowly unwound, came to rest on the floor of the stage, and proceeded to light a candle and, in a kneeling position, slightly bent over, undid his belt. He pulled out a spoon from his back pocket, rolled up his sleeve, heated the spoon over the flame of the candle, touched the spoon with what appeared to be a hypodermic needle (actually a lead pencil), wrapped the belt around his arm tightly, and began to flex his arm in a sweeping up-and-down motion. Then he pressed the "needle" into his arm, slowly rose and began to whirl frantically around the stage. Lou was in the high-pitched middle instrumental

Andy Warhol and Paul Morrissey at The Factory, 1965.
(Nat Finkelstein)

segment of the song. Behind the projector in the audience Paul Morrissey was explaining to a reporter that this is "a completely different kind of rock and roll". Behind the other projector in the projection booth Andy Warhol was explaining the simultaneous showing of the movies to another reporter: "On the one screen you have a movie that takes an hour and a half. On the other screen you have a movie that takes an hour and a half.Except that . . . it takes longer than an hour and a half".Below them, Gerard was lying full length on the stage staring blankly up at Lou Reed.

This was the beginning of a one-and-a-half year collaboration between Warhol and The Velvet Underground that would shortly result in *The Exploding Plastic Inevitable*, a twelve person group (or team, as they saw themselves) that toured the States from 1966 halfway through 1967 changing the way people saw, heard and felt rock & rock in the U.S. and subsequently the world. This first half of our book – "Andy Warhol, Up-Tight" – is the story of the formation of *The Exploding Plastic Inevitable*, which introduced The Velvet Underground in the States, and constituted Warhol's major contribution to rock & roll. Before delineating its details, let's step back and take a look at where the different members of the group came from and how they got together, since what each brought to the project puts the overall effect of the team into perspective.

In the winter of 1965 Andy Warhol was working very fast and accurately through a series of changes that had made him into a media superstar. There wasn't a week that went by that the newspapers or magazines didn't carry a story about him. Already famous for his pop paintings and his revolutionary movies, he was reaching a watershed in his highly successful collaboration with Edie Sedgwick. They had made eight movies together and Edie was the envy of every girl in town, but the pressures of the life she was leading weighed heavily upon her exotically unstable character. A growing involvement with Bob Dylan's circle, where the manipulative use of acid and amphetamine did little to bolster her ego, was further debilitating her, and Warhol was finding it hard to continue the collaboration, even though he wanted to. Jonas Mekas had offered him a week at the Cinematheque and they'd decided to do an Edie Sedgwick Retrospective. Meanwhile Andy had temporarily stopped painting and was looking for new sources of income to support the movies which weren't making any money yet. Paul Morrissey, who had just joined the factory, worked the sound and lights.

PAUL MORRISSEY: Do you remember the details of why The Velvet Underground was brought to the Factory and we bought them amplifiers? For the record, a famous Broadway producer called Michael Myerberg, who'd just done "Waiting for Godot", invited Andy and I over to Sardi's one night to make a deal. He was going to open up the first discotheque with an enormous dance floor in an airplane hangar in Queens. And he said he would pay Andy to come out there every night, with as many people like Edie Sedgwick as he wanted, to bring it publicity. I immediately said, 'I have a better suggestion. There's no real reason to just come out and sit there and get paid.' (It wasn't much money anyway). 'The only reason Andy will go is if he could be like Brian Epstein and present a group he managed.'

Myerberg liked this idea and said if we did that he might even use Andy's name in the title of the discotheque. It turned out he was bullshitting us but he seemed sincere at the time and Andy said 'Why don't we call it Andy Warhol's Up.' And I said, 'Not only will Andy's presence be justified because his group is there, but behind the group we'll be projecting two or three images of film footage,' because we were making all these movies that we'd been showing at the Cinematheque that had no commercial value, and I thought this would be a good way to have them generate some money too. This was agreed upon and I was set to go out and find a rock & roll group. I didn't know what group it was going to be.

As Morrissey began his search, Barbara Rubin, a boyishly attractive, precocious 21-year old art groupie, came to the Factory and invited Gerard Malanga, who was Andy's Prime Minister without portfolio, to go with her to see a group called The Velvet Underground. Malanga had been a dancer on Alan Freed's *Big Beat* TV show when Freed got busted in a payola scandal (that also affected, among others, Dick Clark) and the show got closed down. Rubin was an intimate of, among others, Allen Ginsberg, William Burroughs, Bob Dylan, Jonas Mekas and Andrei Voznesensky, who had, according to Ginsberg, "dedicated her life to introducing geniuses to each other in the hope that they would collaborate to make great art that would change the world". It was the middle of December 1965.

GERARD MALANGA: She asked me to bring my whip and suggested I dance

while the group performed, as Barbara knew how much I enjoyed it, having already seen me dance to Martha and The Vandellas in Andy's film "Vinyl". On the following day, Barbara and I entered Cafe Bizarre to the glaring sounds of what appeared to be a rock & roll group, but there all resemblance ended. The stage was level with the rest of the floor, so the group was right up against the tables and chairs. I waited for about 20-minutes before getting up to dance. I was tentative at first because no one else was on the dance floor at the time and I thought my participating would be an intrusion since the musicians were in such close proximity to the audience. I did, finally, make my way to the front of the audience – a few scattered customers – and was joined minutes later by a young girl who quickly retreated back to her seat. During intermission Barbara introduced me to Lou Reed and John Cale. Lou said how much he enjoyed my getting up to dance to the music. I told him I felt a little self-conscious because I was intruding, but he assured me I wasn't, and both he and John said I should come back and dance again. They really wanted people to dance to the music and not just to sit and listen to it. The music was very intimidating.

MORRISSEY: The next day you told me The Velvets were interesting, you and Barbara wanted to film some footage of them, and you asked me to come along to help with the lighting. I thought they were fascinating. The first thing that registered to me, and I think to Andy later, was the drummer Maureen, because you could not tell whether she was a boy or a girl. This was a first within rock and roll because The Beatles all looked like little girls but you knew they were boys. You had no idea what Maureen's gender was. The second thing was John Cale's electric viola. And the third thing was they sang a song called "Heroin". For some reason when I'm looking for something the first thing I see always works out for me. When I take an apartment it's always the first one. And usually casting actors in movies I always cast the first one that comes in front of my mind and I say that's right. I never fool around and change a person. I never saw any other rock and roll groups. They were a unique group and they were called The Underground. That's another reason I went down because you told me the name of the group. And this was the term always connected with Andy, too. I didn't say anything at the time, but the next day I said, 'Andy, I found the group to play at Michael Myerberg's UP'. So Andy came down the very next night.

The Cafe Bizarre was a long narrow room with sawdust on the floor and a number of tables with fish-net lamps ranged along the walls. The Warhol party, including Sedgwick, Morrissey, Malanga and Rubin, sat at a couple of tables against the wall in front of and to the left of the band. It was a Thursday night. Nobody paid any attention to their arrival. The art and rock worlds were still quite separate and the ten or fifteen people scattered among the tables didn't recognize the new arrivals. The silver-haired man in dark,glasses and a black leather jacket with his chin resting on an elegantly slim hand listened to the animated conversation of his companions, occasionally interrupting with a short, playful comment but remained for the most part silent. As soon as The Velvet Underground started to play however, Andy became quite animated, because he immediately recognized he could work with this band. The music was so loud it was impossible to talk while they were playing, but in a break between songs he asked Edie what she thought about having the band play in front of the movies during her upcoming retrospective. She was understandably unenthusiastic about a suggestion that would clearly have drawn a good deal of attention away from her starring role and got up-tight. But when Gerard got up and danced in black leather pants with his whip, eerily mirroring The Velvets' style with his sinuous, mesmeric movements, which resembled a cross between the Frug and an Egyptian belly dance, Andy saw Gerard become a part of The Velvets and had even more reason to feel that here was a rock band with whom he could really connect.

The Velvet Underground was little known outside their small circle but active on the same level of the underground movie scene that Andy was championing. Working more in tune with his own artistic approach than any other rock group he'd seen, they refused to accept any form of pre-conditioned order or restraint.

LOU REED: That was a very funny period with a very funny group of people. Everybody in a certain section was doing almost exactly the same thing without anyone knowing anybody else.

After the set Barbara brought The Velvets over to Andy's table. They were all in their early twenties and dressed from head to foot in black. John Cale's sonorous accent and dreamy deportment bespoke his Welsh background and classical music training. Curly

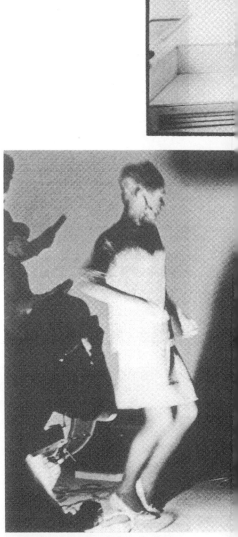

Edie Sedgwick in Andy Warhol, Up-Tight at The Cinematheque, February, 1966.
(Fred McDarrah)

Maureen Tucker, John Cale,
Sterling Morrison and Lou Reed
(Nat Finkelstein)

haired Lou Reed's shy gum-chewing smile identified him most closely with Andy, with whom he shared a similar temperament. They sat next to each other and immediately hit it off. Sterling Morrison and Maureen Tucker were quiet at this first meeting, but the vibes were good. They were all aware of who Andy was and gratified by his interest and compliments.

MORRISSEY: On the night Andy came to the Bizarre Gerard had invited Nico, who had just come to town, and that's when I met her. I think Gerard had already brought the record "I'll Keep It With Mine" up to the Factory. I felt that the one thing The Velvets didn't have was a solo singer, because I just didn't think that Lou had the personality to stand in front of the group and sing. The group needed something beautiful to counteract the kind of screeching ugliness they were trying to sell, and the combination of a really beautiful girl standing in front of all this decadence was what was needed. That very night, right away I said, 'Nico, you're a singer. You need somebody to play in back of you. You can maybe sing with this group, if they want to work with us and go in this club and be managed.'

ANDY WARHOL: The Pop idea, after all, was that anybody could do anything, so naturally we were all trying to do it all. Nobody wanted to stay in one category, we all wanted to branch out into every creative thing we could. That's why when we met The Velvet Underground at the end of '65, we were all for getting into the music scene, too.

Before leaving Andy invited The Velvets and Nico to come up to the Factory whenever they felt like it. He left before the second set, but at dinner afterwards kept saying to his friends "We have to think of something to do with The Velvets. What can we do? What could it be? WE HAVE TO THINK OF SOMETHING!" He had always been interested in rock music. The great "Sally Goes Round The Roses" by The Jaynettes was his favorite song, he played it non-stop. He was excited about the possibilities of combining The Velvets' musical with his visual sensibility.

The New York Times.

Music: A Long, Long, Long Night (and Day) at the Piano

John Cale, fresh in body, during his first appearance.

As he ends his 20-minute stint, Cale is relieved by John Cage, responsible for 18-hour-40-minute piano marathon.

Cale, seemingly hypnotized by the 80-second work of Erik Satie, tries to rest in theater basement in the morning.

So does Arthur Conescu, owner of Pocket Theater.

The end of the concert, which began 6 P.M. Monday, being applauded by the hardy audience at 12:40 P.M. yesterday.

Vexations

Work performed consists of 180-note passage to be repeated 840 times, as indicated by composer's instruction at top of score. A dozen pianists participated in the concert.

The New York Times (by Edward Hausner and Larry Morris)

Satie's 'Vexations' Played 840 Times by Relay Team

Whatever it was, it made musical history, from 6 P.M. Monday to 12:40 P.M. yesterday at the Pocket Theater, 100 Third Avenue near 13th Street.

In 18 hours and 40 minutes, the 180 notes of Erik Satie's "Vexations," an 80-second work, were played 840 times—a grand total of 151,200 notes that took 67,200 seconds to play, and took a relay team of 10 pianists, plus two pianists who made an occasional appearance, to play them.

The idea was John Cage's. He had located the music, and the result was conceivably the longest concert since Homer sang the entire "Iliad" and "Odyssey." As no one man could cover this heroic effort, a relay team of critics was formed, to pass the baton at, roughly, two-hour intervals.

6 to 8 P.M. Monday

By HAROLD C. SCHONBERG

Viola Farber led off. Before her was a photostat of the "Vexations" manuscript. On it were written, in Satie's hand, instructions to the effect that the music is to be repeated 840 times.

Why 840? It could as easily have been 1,000. Or 529. But he wrote 840, for reasons best known to himself. He was, after all, the great eccentric of French music.

"Vexations" was composed around 1920 (Satie died in 1925) and is a rather pretty, slow-moving, chordal piece of 13 rhythmic beats.

There were no program notes, thinking that a concert

lasting a day and a half might need some kind of come-on, the management did print some house rules: $5 for first admission, refund of 5 cents for each 20 minutes, and a 20-cent bonus to anybody who stayed the entire program. Time cards like these were issued at the beginning.

Miss Farber started promptly at 6, before an audience of seven persons, two of them critics and one a critic's wife. But everybody felt the hot breath of a historic event. The hall rapidly began to fill. By 8 there were 22 in the audience. They did not stay put; many moved in and out of the hall.

Behind the pianist were seated two others—one a score-keeper, the other the relief. At

6:20, Miss Farber rose as Robert Wood moved in. His left hand played the bass theme, and then he slipped behind the vacated

And so to the others—to Mac-Rae Cook, John Cale, John Cage, Christian Wolff, David Del Tredici, David Tudor, Philip Corner and James Tenney. Joshua Rivkin helped out one 20-minute spell.

Note succeeded note; implacably, doggedly, swinging back and forth like the windshield wiper of an automobile, and staying in much the same orbit. Base line, tritones, bass line, tritones.

Time meant nothing, and the listener floated in a suspended animation as seconds flowed into minutes with the idiot

repetition of beat after beat. Nirvana? Shantih, shantih, shantih. . . .

8 to 10 P.M. Monday

By RICHARD F. SHEPARD

"Vexations" still running strong on keyboard. Fireman drops in to check that audience doesn't exceed 197; 18 in sight, each in a silent cocoon of contemplation.

In locker room, John Cale, fresh from keyboard, says it's a tricky business playing the piece. Not so much on the hands but "the head goes first," he says.

At 8:40 Mr. Tudor still standing takes over from David Del Tredici in a neat changing of the guard in which the new man's left hand moves in while the other's right hand moves off.

Nobody onstage counts house, although audience has slipped to 13, all very quiet.

Survival rations in lobby — coffee, chicken broth, peaches and pastry—moving slowly but the night is young. In front of theater some off-duty pianists and friends talk music. Inside, "Vexations" is still returning. By now, as hard to forget as a television commercial jingle. At 9:20, big influx of audience; house now holds 32. Augurs well for the evening.

10 P.M. Monday to 12:45 A.M. Tuesday

By RAYMOND ERICSON

Everything quiet and proceeding on schedule. About 20 persons listening, some reading, some writing, a few whispering.

No one sleeps. One woman complains about the "terribly noisy" click of a photographer's camera.

The people drift out and back again slowly in the languorous rhythm of the music. The atmosphere is dreamlike and hypnotic, à la "Last Year at Marienbad."

The pianists are of all kinds; one is stiffbacked, using little motion of the hands; another is a keyboard wiper with limp wrists; one bends over the keyboard as if in prayer; another sits slightly sideways as if afraid of the piano.

Two of the pianists play gingerly, with an uneven touch; are they out of practice? There is an occasional wrong note and

Continued on Page 48, Column

● WHAT WAS THE MUSICAL SENSIBILITY OF THE VELVET UNDERGROUND?

● **JOHN CALE: I had a classical education in classical music playing the viola in youth orchestras. I heard rock & roll on the radio in the Alan Freed days, and it was exciting, but I never thought of playing.**

John Cale was born on December 5th 1940 in Crynant, South Wales where he went to school until he was seventeen. According to Nico, Cale's 'father is totally deaf and his mother is totally mute.'

John studied at London University Goldsmiths' College from 1960-1963. 'When I was studying composition I was completely oblivious to the fact that The Rolling Stones were playing in some nearby club.' At Goldsmiths he spent his time ostensibly working on a musicological dissertation, but was not oblivious to the latest trends in avant-garde classical music and performance art. He got involved with electronic music and performances with the British composer Humphrey Searle. One of his teachers, Cornelius Cardew, was an important booster of John Cage, La Monte Young and other avant-garde American composers. John Cage was the first major influence on John Cale.

CALE: Most classical musicians are really insecure about self-expression. The conductor always tells you how to play a piece. Then Cage comes along and gives you a sheet with dots and diagrams, and gives you the freedom to play what you'd like and most people goof off.

Cage's music can sound like anything – Mozart, Beethoven, Bach – anyone. It can sound like what any one individual wants it to sound like. You can find your own riff and do exactly what you want. Classical musicians however are not given this freedom in the system they play.

La Monte Young, the second major influence on Cale, is an important American composer whose work has been infrequently heard by his own choice. His 1958 "Trio For Strings", which inspired composers like Philip Glass and Steve Reich has, for example, never been recorded.

In 1963, under the aegis of Aaron Copland, Cale was awarded a Leonard Bernstein scholarship to study Modern Composition with the Franco-Greek composer, Iannis Xenakis in the Eastman Conservatory at Tanglewood, in Lenox Massachusetts. According to Copland they originally met in England where he saw Cale perform and subsequently made posssible his arrival in the States for that summer of study at Tanglewood. However, Copland later decided Cale couldn't play his work at Tanglewood because it was too destructive. 'He didn't want his pianos destroyed.' So John went to New York City and found La Monte Young, who was writing pieces in which the musician talked to the piano or, in one memorable incident, screamed at a plant until it died.

CALE: La Monte was perhaps the best part of my education and my introduction to musical discipline.

We formed The Dream Syndicate, which consisted of two amplified voices, an amplified violin and my amplified viola. The concept of the group was to sustain notes for two hours at a time. La Monte would hold the lowest notes, I would hold the next three on my viola, his wife Marion would hold the next note and this fellow Tony Conrad would hold the top note. That was my first group experience and what an experience it was!

It was so different. I mean the tapes are art objects. Some people who came to our concerts know what it was like, but it is the only example of that kind of music in the world. The Indians use the drone also, but they use a totally different tuning system and though they attempt a scientific approach, they don't really have it buttoned down like we did.

The members of The Dream Syndicate, motivated by a scientific and mystical fascination with sound, spent long hours in rehearsals learning to provide sustained meditative drones and chants. Their rigorous style served to discipline John and developed his knowledge of the just intonation system. He also learned to use his viola in a new amplified way which would lead to the powerful droning effect that is so strong in the first two Velvet Underground records.

CALE: When we formed The Dream Syndicate I needed to have a strong sound. I decided to try using guitar strings on my viola, and I got a drone that sounded like a jet-engine! Playing the viola in the just intonation system was so exciting. The

LaMonte Young and Marion Zazeela, Summer 1968 (Ron Zimardi)

John Cage (Gerard Malanga)

thing that really amazed me about it was that we played similarly to the way The Everly Brothers used to sing. There was this one song which they sang, in which they started with two voices holding one chord. They sang it so perfectly in tune that you could actually hear each voice. They probably didn't know they were singing just intonation, but they sang the right intervals. And when those intervals are in tune, as they were in The Everly Brothers and our group, it is extremely forceful.

While he worked with LaMonte Young, John Cale shared a flat with fellow Dream Syndicate member Tony Conrad on Manhattan's Lower East Side.

TONY CONRAD: In the Fall of 1964, John Cale and I were sharing an apartment at 56 Ludlow Street, which is now sealed up. We had been working with LaMonte for some time doing very austere regimented things which were pretty intense. We had been talking about serious things like intervals, and Indian music and theory and avant-garde music, but when John moved into my place on Ludlow Street it turned out that when I went home I sat around listening to Hank Williams records and was blasting a huge 45 collection. John started getting interested in rock & roll, although there was a great ambiguity in his mind about how somebody could be interested in both rock and classical music. But there was something very liberating about the whole rock thing, and in a sense 56 Ludlow Street came to stand for a lot in terms of some kind of liberating musical influence. There was a guy next door called David Gelber, who was playwright Jack Gelber's brother (wrote "The Connection"), and he had a lot of friends who were weird, dumpy, pasty, party chicks from Queens. He went to their parties, and one day he told us that we should come and meet these people because they owned a record company and they were looking for some people with long hair to form a rock band. We had hair that would now look suitable for business dress, but they thought we were the weirdest things in the world. The upshot of it was that we went to this chick's party and there were these creepos who we were introduced to. They asked us if we played guitar and were we interested in rock. These guys looked so alien to us we couldn't believe it. I mean this was the other side of the Queens Life Central. This guy Terry Phillips, who had slicked-back hair, a pencil-thin mustache, a real flaccid manner and weird distance from life, was interviewing us about whether we're interested in rock & roll and we naturally felt like rock & roll stars already. He was connected to this record company Pickwick, which is a big record company that would do re-issue albums like Bobby Darren and Jack Borgheimer where there'd be one Bobby Darren song and ten Jack Borgheimer songs. They said did we have guitars and we said no. Did we know a drummer, and we said yeah, so we got Walter DeMaria, who's done some great, great drum work, on this thing and we went out to this weird cinderblock warehouse which was the headquarters of Pickwick Records, in Coney Island. The place was packed floor to ceiling with records and in the back these sleaze-balls and weirdos wearing polyester suits had a little hole-in-the-wall room with a couple of Ampex tape recorders in it. What had happened was they'd got back there with one of their staff writers, gone crazy one night and recorded a couple of his songs. They'd decided they wanted to release them, but needed a band to cover, because the executives and creepos had made the record so there wasn't any band – it was a studio shot. The first thing they wanted to do was sign us up to seven-year creative contracts.

We realized after a narrow reading of the contracts that they would make all our artistic work actually owned by Lee Herridon Productions, which was the parent company that owned Pickwick, so we all refused to sign. But we went over and listened to the record. It was called "The Ostrich". They'd gotten together with this guy and spent the night taking, in their own words, "everything", gotten really wiggy and done this weird mix-down. We refused to sign the contracts, but we agreed to their proposal that we play some gigs to promote the record. Next weekend they came around and picked us up in a station wagon and John Cale, Walter DeMaria and I began going out on these gigs trying to break this record in the Lehigh Valley area. There were actually four people in the group because there was also the guy who'd actually written and recorded the song – that was Lou Reed. He was 22.

By the time Lou entered high school he'd already formed his first band and was playing professionally on weekends. At age fourteen, he released his first record "So Blue"

Lou Reed as a student at Syracuse University, c. 1963. (Malanga Archive)

(1957) in a high school group called The Shades on the Time Label. The flip side was called "Leave Her For Me".

REED: Our big moment came when Murray the K played it, but he was sick and someone else stood in. He played it once. I got royalties of 78¢. We were still in school. We'd open supermarkets, shopping centers, things like that. We had glitter jackets. It was what was called style – later on people would call it punk but

at that time what we meant by punk was a pusher, y'know, 'He's just a fucking punk!'

"So Blue" sunk into oblivion but has since been re-released on a bootleg collection of early Velvets material. Lou Reed always wanted to be a rock & roll singer, a rock & roll star. He was born March 2, 1942 in Freeport, Long Island, the elder of two children (a sister, Elizabeth) to a middle-income family. His father was an accountant. Ironically his first practical contact with music came from his parents who paid for him to have five years of training as a classical pianist. "They wanted me to do a scholarship and all that but no . . . no thank you . . . this is not my idea of what's exciting." He began to amass a vast collection of rock & roll 45s. Lou was a natural born rock & roll animal. Although it should be noted that his tastes in music have always been very Catholic: "When I started out I was inspired by people like Ornette Coleman. He has always been a great influence."

He seemed quite normal to his high school acquaintances, who remember him as a good basketball player and occasionally accompanied him on double dates or went along with him to one of his weekend shows. His parents, however, seem to have taken a very dim view of the direction their unfathomable son was developing in. "I went out and did the most horrifying thing possible in those days. I joined a rock band. And, of course, I represented something very alien to my parents." So alien that at the age of eighteen they took him to a hospital where he was administered a series of electro-shock treatments. "I didn't have the bad ones where they don't put you to sleep first. I had the fun ones where they put you to sleep first. You count backwards, then you're out. It was shocking, but that's when I was getting interested in electricity anyway."

In 1960 Reed left home to attend Syracuse University in upstate New York. His career at Syracuse does not seem to have changed the course he was bent on, although he picked up some influences, the major one undoubtedly being the legendary American poet Delmore Schwartz who became his mentor and drinking partner: "I was friends with Delmore. He wrote great poetry and was an incredible man. Once when he was on a drunken binge with me, he had his arm around me and he said, 'You know, I'm going to die one of these days'. He was one of the unhappiest people I ever knew. 'You can write – and if you sell out and there's a heaven from which you can be haunted, I'll haunt you.'" In fact Delmore Schwartz did return to haunt Lou on a Reed solo album called "The Blue Mask" released twenty years later, but in an affirmative, encouraging vein.

Sterling Morrison first met Lou when they were students at Syracuse living in the same dormitory. "The first sound I ever heard from Lou was when the ROTC (Reserve Officers' Training Corps) were marching in the field behind the dorm in their uniforms. First I heard ear-splitting bagpipe music from his hi-fi, and then he cranked up his electric guitar and gave a few blasts on that. So I knew there was a guitar player living upstairs." Lou had been thrown out of the ROTC Program when he'd put a gun to the head of his commanding officer. He had his own show on the campus radio station where he would play old rock & roll and R&B records, but Lou was thrown out of that position too, when he made fun of a commercial on muscular dystrophy.

Holmes Sterling Morrison Jr was born on August 29, 1942 at East Meadow, Long Island to a middle-class, two-car, small-town at first but later suburban family of Scots ancestry. He had two younger brothers – Robert and William; three younger sisters – Dorothy, Kathleen and Marjorie.

STERLING MORRISON: I began studying trumpet at seven, and continued until I was 12, when my teacher was drafted. Unable to find another good one, and in spite of my promise on the instrument, I switched to guitar, inspired by Bo Diddley and Chuck Berry. I liked the rockabilly form that was around (rockabilly WAS rock 'n' roll in the beginning) but was more interested in the guitar work of black musicians. Listened to Alan Freed and Jocko all the time; kept my honky ears open. Doo-wah music impressed me mightily. Later on liked Mickey Baker and T-Bone Walker; Jimmy Reed. Eventually caught up with acoustical blues aces like Lightnin' Hopkins, but always preferred electric guitar music and special effects. I got a flyer in the mail from Sam Ash Music in Hempstead inviting me to hear a demonstration of newly invented "fuzz-tone". I didn't have to go because my amp already was doing that on its own. I graduated H.S. with very high numbers and matching low esteem for just about everything but music. I was accepted at Syracuse along with Maureen's brother Jim, a friend since eighth grade. Regents Scholarships for us both. He went, but I headed west to U. of Illinois (major: Physics). Left there at request of Dean of Men after two semesters, mostly for not attending class and for having been drummed out of

L-R: John Cale, Angus MacLise, Sterling Morrison and Lou Reed – the original Velvet Underground line-up. New York, 1965. (Donald Greenhaus)

ROTC, which was compulsory. Good grades, bad attitude, 3.2 beer. Transferred to City College of New York but left after two weeks due to no place to live. Headed for Syracuse with intent to attend in January. Stayed the Fall term with Jim Tucker at Sadler Hall beneath Lou.

Lou Reed and Sterling Morrison were both great admirers of Delmore Schwartz, who'd had a tremendous early success marred by deep depressions, pills, booze and subsequent failure. "Delmore was a brilliant poet", says Morrison "but he had a clinical case of paranoia. He thought he was being investigated at the behest of Nelson Rockefeller, and eventually he decided that Lou and I and everyone around him were Rockefeller's spies."

There was a good music scene at Syracuse with Felix Cavalieri (of The Young Rascals), Mike Esposito (of The Blues Magoos) and Garland Jeffreys among other fellow students. Morrison and Reed played early Ike and Tina Turner numbers together in bands with names like Moses and his Brothers, Pasha and The Prophets, L.A. and The El Doradoes. L.A. stands for Lou Allen, the name Lou played under at the time.

MORRISON: I had gone home to the Island after meeting Lou at Syracuse to raise some money, and went back to City College in the Fall (major: English Lit.). Visited Syracuse frequently and played with Lou when I could; spring break; summers. I was always about to enrol but never did. Lou and I had some of the shittiest bands that ever WERE. They were shitty because we were playing authentic rock & roll. I was a very sensitive young person and played very unsensitive, uncaring music which is Wam Bang Pow! Let's rock out! What I expected my audience to do was tear the house down, beat me up, whatever. In the Sixties I had King Hatreds. I was a biker type and I hung around with nasty black people and nasty white people and I played nasty white and black rock & roll music.

After he graduated Lou moved back in with his parents in Freeport from where he began to commute to a job as a factory songwriter at Pickwick records, a company specializing in quickie albums, cashing in on popular trends such as hot rod, surf and Mersey Beat music.

REED: There were four of us literally locked in a room writing songs. They would say 'Write ten California songs, ten Detroit songs', then we'd go down into the studio for an hour or two and cut three or four albums really quickly, which came in handy later because I knew my way around a studio, not well enough but I could work really fast. One day I was stoned and (after reading in Eugenia Sheppard's column that ostrich feathers were big that season) just for laughs – I decided to make up a dance. So I said, 'You put your head on the floor and have somebody step on it!' It was years ahead of its time. And another thing called "Sneaky Pete". And when they heard it they thought it could be a single, so we needed people who could be a group to go out and promote it.

CONRAD: See, by the time they approached us, they had pressed the record already. "The Ostrich" was the A side and "Sneaky Pete" was the B side. We had nothing to do with making the record, we were just stringers hired to promote it. The impression I got was that Lou had a close relationship with these people at Pickwick because they recognized that he was a very gifted person. There was something really authentic about their understanding of his talent. He impressed everybody as having some particularly assertive personal quality, and it's certainly to their credit that they hung out and popped pills and goofed in the studio with him. Anyway, they made up this name for us The Primitives, and they thought "The Ostrich" would be a new dance craze, 'Do the Ostrich!' They said, 'Don't worry, it's easy to play because all the strings are tuned to the same note,' which blew our minds because that was what we were doing with LaMonte in The Dream Syndicate. It was pretty amazing, we couldn't believe it. They said, 'All you do is go Dun de Dun Dun/Dun de Dun Dun', and then we learned the breaks. The first couple of times we did this we hadn't even rehearsed, we just stepped out on stage. It was bizarre because they would say, 'And now, from New York City – The Primitives!' The kids would start screaming YAAAAAAAAAA and run up and we'd go Dun de Dun Dun. I remember we did a radio interview in Redding, Pennsylvania, played a high school gig in New Jersey, a supermarket and taped a TV show with Shirley Ellis who did "Name Game" and "Clapping Song". Lou was prepared to assume the role of director because he knew the tunes, so he told us what we had to do, but there was also the odd thing that Walter and John and I took all this with a grain of salt, especially at first, because we

knew they didn't really know who we were in the sense that we actually did have some particular powers and were not complete ingenues, which is what they had been looking for. They didn't know shit about who we were. Those gigs were completely mindblowing to Walter, John and me. I mean we're riding around in a station wagon goofing on the idea that we're going to be playing rock & roll music, then we're on this stage and we don't know what's going on and none of us have really played this kind of music before, and then there's all this hype and screaming kids and meeting other groups. The whole thing was absolutely unexpected and hypnotizing. We did it about half a dozen times on weekends. It was fun. There was even a flutter of interest including a photo in VOGUE, but the record died. After a point we said, 'We're not getting anywhere with this, we're not making any money, and the record isn't going to break'. They also kept pressing these contracts on us and it began to be kind of a turn-off, so we just didn't do it any more. The thing is, John was really impressed with Lou because Lou had this unique ability to sing lyrics. He would go out there without anything in his head at all and just sing songs. Lyrics would just come out of his mouth. You didn't know where they came from but suddenly he was doing rock & roll. It was obvious that Lou really authentically loved rock & roll, but he was wrestling with some kind of problems in his personal life and he was also living with his mother out on Long Island, so he was vanishing into Long Island at this point and not really furthering his scene very much. Then John started getting together with Lou. He was really attracted to Lou's whole approach.

CALE: When I met Lou, he was a staff writer for some publishing company. He played me the songs he'd written for them, but they were nothing new or terribly exciting. They were just like every other song on the radio. But then he played me several which he claimed they wouldn't publish. He played "Heroin" first and it totally knocked me out. The words and music were so raunchy and devastating. What's more, his songs fit perfectly with my music concept.

CONRAD: So Lou began coming into the city and began getting together with John. I took off, so there was more room in the pad and Lou soon moved in, which was great because we got him out of his mother's place. Lou was like a rock & roll animal and authentically turned everybody on. He really had a deep fixation on that and his lifestyle was completely compatible and acclimatised to it. He was definitely a liberating force for John, but John was an incredible person too.

He was very idealistic in the sense of putting himself behind what he was interested in and believed in in a tremendous way, and anytime you do that you wind up with fantastic abilities and experiences, so there was a tremendous amount of resonance going on there musically. Lou was definitely possessed by rock & roll. He was definitely a rock & roll punk straight from the books, but the books were only written twenty years later. On the other hand there was no group of people in music more sophisticated than the group we were involved with. This was an unbelievably alert group of people who were engaged in a way which was part of and in touch with everything, open to everything, particularly John – the way that he sought out LaMonte and engaged himself directly with the group and the way that he lived, which was extremely ascetic and barren and weird. John was a very interesting person in terms of his personal aura and the kind of creative presence that he brought about, and inventive in terms of ideas about techniques. In terms of musical influence what John was doing with the viola, which had grown out of the kinds of things we were doing in our group, was obviously tremendously important and yet it was extremely odd that we wandered into this group of people who tuned their guitars all to one note.

Rather than suggesting that there was an influence that flowed one way or another I'm trying to suggest that it seemed like a very powerful encounter in a sense, each of them moving in a direction which was daring and audacious for the other as well as themselves. John was moving at a very very fast pace away from a classical training background through the avant-garde and into performance art and then rock. It was phenomenal for Lou considering his interest in what would be referred to today as punk – somebody who is really living rock and is interested in an extremely aggressive assertive position – to discover that classical musicians and avant-garde artists were also engaged in that. There was a real bonding that occurred between John and Lou in that particular relationship.

L-R: Sterling Morrison, Lou Reed, John Cale and Angus MacLise when they were living on Grand Street and Ludlow Street respectively. Location: 450 Grand Street. c. 1965.
(Donald Greenhaus)

TOM WILSON: You and John were the original members then. Where did you find Sterling?

REED: I met him on the subway. I hadn't seen him in three years and he didn't have any shoes on and I had boots on and we took him home.

MORRISON: This account, though amusing, is preposterous. I did indeed run into Lou (and John for the first time) on the subway – on the "D" train at the Seventh Avenue stop or thereabouts. I was on my way up to school at City College. I have never, ever, gone shoeless on the dogshit streets of Manhattan. And, since it was January, I may be supposed to have been wearing my winter coat too. But meet we did. I hadn't seen Lou for almost a year. He invited me over to this guy Rick's place to get high and talk/play music. The three of us kept going from that moment. By then the whole thing with Pickwick had fallen through, so we sat around and said, 'Well, we're retired. There's no way we can put a band together

Tony Conrad

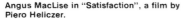
Angus MacLise in "Satisfaction", a film by
Piero Heliczer.

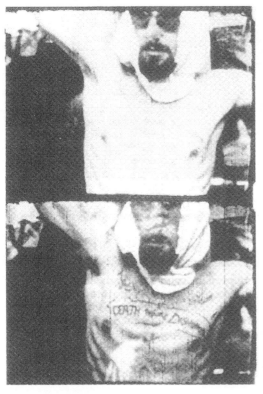

that can work in this city'. Because all that was going on in Manhattan in the early '60's were those slick midtown club acts like Joey Dee and The Starlighters who wore matching suits. So we decided to forget about competing and just play songs we liked.

CONRAD: By then, I'd stopped playing with them and Walter DeMaria had moved so John, Lou and Sterling started playing with Angus MacLise on drums. He lived in the same building and had also worked with LaMonte Young. A lot of people went through that building on Ludlow Street. Mario Montez (one of Jack Smith's and Andy Warhol's original Superstars) lived downstairs, Angus was living upstairs. John and I were there and Piero Heliczer (a poet and underground film-maker who would play a major role in the development of The Velvets' connection with multimedia presentations) had the apartment next door. They used a series of different names like The Warlocks and The Falling Spikes. Angus had some unique percussion equipment. When he played the bongos, it was just like poetry. He made a number of tapes with Piero, John and myself when we all lived in the same building on Ludlow.

REED: I first started thinking about "Metal Machine Music" as far back as when John used to work with LaMonte Young. It took a long long time. It's way more complex than people realize, but that's alright. I wasn't going to put it out even; I made it for myself. John and I were always making tapes. A lot are still circulating around. We made soundtracks for underground movies of the time. We always encouraged bringing tape recorders to our jobs.

CONRAD: The first thing I heard of what they were doing were those tapes. Angus used to make tapes so there would be these great tapes lying around in a pile and some of them would get erased. Who knew what happened to them. I wish I had copies because some of the stuff they did was very nice. The things they were into were ethereal and ornamental, very very free. In that sense the influence of Angus's personality was much more visible during that period. Anyway, Angus, John, Lou and Sterling started calling what they were doing a group.

It was 1965. They decided to follow Maupassant's dictum to "Do something beautiful in the form that suits you best according to your own temperament", and began composing some of the music that would eventually wind up on their first album. They also continued to evolve within the milieu of the downtown New York art scene which was developing rapidly. Angus had introduced them to Piero Heliczer who had been his classmate at Forest Hills High School in the mid-fifties. Piero had moved from Ludlow to a gigantic fifth floor walk-up at 450 Grand Street and was conducting a series of multimedia happenings involving films, lights, poetry and music at Jonas Mekas' Film-makers' Cinematheque in the basement of the Colonnades building, a New York Historical Landmark on Lafayette Street.

MORRISON: Whenever I hear the word 'underground', I am reminded of when the word first acquired a specific meaning for me and for many others in NYC in the early Sixties. It referred to underground cinema and the people and lifestyle that created and supported this art form. And the person who first introduced me to this scene was Piero Heliczer, a bona fide 'underground film-maker' – the first one I had ever met.

On an early Spring day in 1965 John and I were strolling through the East-side slums and ran into Angus on the corner of Essex and Delancey. Angus said, 'Let's go over to Piero's', and we agreed.

It seems that Piero and Angus were organizing a 'ritual happening' at the time – a mixed-media stage presentation to appear in the old Cinematheque. Naturally, this was well before such events became all the rage. It was to be entitled "Launching the Dream Weapon", and it got launched tumultuously. In the center of the stage there was a movie screen, and between the screen and the audience a number of veils were spread out in different places. These veils were lit variously by lights and slide projectors, as Piero's films shone through them onto the screen. Dancers swirled around, and poetry and song occasionally rose up, while from behind the screen a strange music was being generated by Lou, John, Angus and me.

For me the path ahead became suddenly clear – I could work on music that was different from ordinary rock & roll since Piero had given us a context to perform it in. In the summer of 1965 we were the anonymous musicians who played at some screenings of 'underground films', and at other theatrical events, the first of which was for Piero's films (I think that Barbara Rubin showed "Christmas on Earth" and Kenneth Anger showed a film also). Piero taped the music, and later played it at the other screenings of his films – especially for "The New Jerusalem".

In July they recorded a tape which included "Venus in Furs", "Heroin", "Wrap Your Troubles in Dreams" and "The Black Angel's Death Song" and distributed it as a demo to a few people including rock entrepreneur Miles Copeland in England.

MORRISON: This tape was often reproduced and widely circulated in England. It evidently aroused some interest in us, and John was going back and forth throughout 1965 to see what he could get going (and to pick up records – we were very impressed by the singles he brought back. Of course John's peculiar tastes determined what he brought back for us to hear, but we couldn't escape the conclusion that these obscure English bands were closer to our sensibilities than the 'pop' groups here in the US.) At the time when we met Andy we had all but actually packed up and gone to London. I feel certain that we would have been in London by Spring 1966, come what may, had not The E.P.I. happened. Cale knew his way around, had spoken to many people over there in preparation for us, and by his daily presence lessened any culture shock we might have experienced. If we could deal with him, there was nothing forbidding about the English.

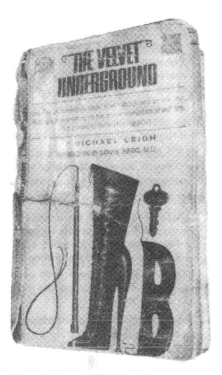

They were basically in limbo and looking for connections, believing strongly in their music, thriving on their collaboration and the milieu in which they found themselves appreciated by a small intelligent audience, but felt the chances of their breaking through in the U.S. were minimal. One day Tony Conrad, who was no longer living at Ludlow or playing with them but maintained a collaborative friendship with Cale, who was still peripherally involved in The Dream Syndicate, found a paperback lying on the sidewalk of the Bowery and brought it back to Ludlow Street where he was still keeping a lot of his stuff. It was called *The Velvet Underground*.

MORRISON: We had a name at last! And it was adopted by us and deemed appropriate not because of the S&M theme of the book, but because the word 'underground' was suggestive of our involvement with the underground film and art scenes.

Around this time, somehow, CBS News decided that Walter Cronkite should have a feature on an 'underground' film being made. By whatever selection process, Piero,was able to be the 'underground film-maker'; since he had already decided to film us playing anyway, we got into the act (and besides, we had 'underground' in our name, didn't we? Maybe someone at CBS reads Pirandello).

The actual copy of "The Velvet Underground" that inspired the name.
(B. Broughel from the Tony Conrad Archive)

Very shortly after this momentous event Al Aronowitz, the legendary journalist whose writings on pop music – featuring The Beatles, The Rolling Stones and Bob Dylan, all of whom he was personally acquainted with – were helping to break new ground in the cultural climate, heard about The Velvet Underground's performances behind the screens at the Cinematheque and Lou Reed's claim that he was 'the fastest guitarist alive', and took Robbie Robertson of The Band to inspect one of Heliczer's happenings. Robertson quickly grew bored and, turning to Aronowitz, dismissed Reed's performance with a 'he ain't nothin'', but Aronowitz, who had exceptionally good taste and was interested in getting involved in the music business from an entrepreneur's point of view in the hopes of making a buck – he was already managing a band called The Myddle Class – decided to approach The Velvets with an offer.

He went to the 5th floor Grand Street apartment where Sterling and Lou were now living and had a 15 minute meeting with them, leaving Brian Jones and Carole King waiting for him in a limousine below.

MORRISON: Al had brought Brian Jones around to Ludlow Street on an earlier occasion to score some acid. Brian stayed in the limo with two babes while Al came up to get us. We all wanted to meet him but since there was no room for the three of us in the car, and since John had the connection, he got to ride in the front seat. Lou and I followed in Lou's mother's car so we could get John and head elsewhere. We were interested in a guitar/organ made by Vox. The Stones endorsed Vox and Brian played a Vox Phantom, so we wanted John to ask him about it.

Al Aronowitz, 1967
(Aronowitz Archive)

John: Have you ever played one of those Vox Guitar/Organs?
Brian: Yes.
John: Does it work?
Brian: No.
End of conversation.

Aronowitz offered The Velvets a spot opening for The Myddle Class at Summit High School in Summit, New Jersey for $75.00. Angus said, 'You mean we start when they tell us to and we have to end when they tell us to? I can't work that way.' The other members were eager to accept the job and expand their audience, so he withdrew from the group. Desperate for a drummer to play the Summit gig, Sterling and Lou remembered old buddy Jim Tucker's sister Maureen, who always liked to play drums. Maureen Tucker was born in 1945 in New Jersey.

MAUREEN TUCKER: I always wanted to play drums. You know when you're in fourth grade and they sign you up for music lessons? Well, I picked drums, but I never went. Then rock & roll came around and I really wanted to get in on the creative end of that. I played guitar for a while, then tambourine, but that wasn't making it, so I got a really cheap drum set.

Maureen remembers Lou visiting her parents' house when he was a student at Syracuse and she was in the 12th grade, so he wasn't a complete stranger when he came over this time to audition her for the position.

TUCKER: Lou came over and we went up to the room where I kept my drums and he'd say, 'Can you play this?' which I could, so I was in. It wasn't as if I was a full-time member though. John was adamant about not wanting any girls in the band.

WILSON: And what about Mo?

REED: We needed an amplifier and she had one plus she's an out of sight drummer. She worked as a computer key-puncher and when she'd come home at five she'd put on Bo Diddley records and play every night from five to twelve, so we figured she'd be the perfect drummer and she was.

MORRISON: Maureen had been playing with a band on the Island. She had recently quit when the guitar player in the other band on the bill was shot onstage at a gig in Syosset.

WILSON: She has great time. And, like most things that we found out don't matter, sex doesn't matter anymore so far as musicianship is concerned and so far as the love of groovy music is concerned.

REED: I'd second that.

The Summit High School gig took place on November 11th 1965. It was the first time they used the name*The Velvet Underground* playing after a band called 40 Fingers and before The Myddle Class.

MORRISON: At Summit we opened with "There She Goes Again", then played "Venus in Furs", and ended with "Heroin". The murmur of surprise that greeted our appearance as the curtain went up increased to a roar of disbelief once we started to play "Venus", and swelled to a mighty howl of outrage and bewilderment by the end of "Heroin". Al Aronowitz observed that we seemed to have an oddly stimulating and polarizing effect on audiences.

Aronowitz recognized they had a future, but felt they lacked experience and needed, as he says today, "to acquire some chops. Like The Beatles got chops playing till 3 a.m. eight nights a week in Hamburg". To this end, he acquired a residency gig for them during December at the Cafe Bizarre, a relatively dead club on West 3rd Street just east of Macdougal Street in the heart of Greenwich Village.

CALE: When we first put The Velvets together we formed a group around the guitar, bass, drums and my electric viola. We wanted The Velvet Underground to be a group with a dynamic symphonic flair. The idea was that Lou's lyrical and melodic ability could be combined with some of my musical ideas to create performances where we wouldn't just repeat ourselves. We used to do "Sister Ray – Part Seven", in which Lou would personify this southern preacher, along with a series of different roles, all made up on the spot. In the beginning, when Al Aronowitz was managing us and we were playing at the Bizarre, we practised a lot and were pretty tight.

L-R: Lou Reed's ass, Nico, Sterling Morrison and John Cale rehearsing at The Factory together for the first time. Cow paintings by Andy Warhol.
(Nat Finkelstein)

● MAKING ANDY WARHOL, UP-TIGHT, CONTINUED

● By the time Andy Warhol met them at the Cafe Bizarre, The Velvets were doing a number of covers like "Carol" and "Little Queenie", as well as their own unmistakable material, some of which the Bizarre management found too disruptive for their establishment. The band were pretty much fed up playing there having been forced to work on Christmas Day and wanted to get fired, so when the manager told them that if they played the "Black Angel's Death Song" one more time they'd be asked to leave, they cranked out their best version ever. They were fired two days after they met Andy. At least Maureen gained tenure as a full-fledged member because, although the owners had refused to let them use drums saying they'd be too loud, the others had chosen to keep her on playing tambourine.

TUCKER: It was really a regression, but that's when it became kind of apparent that I was in the band.

MORRISSEY: After we met them they came to the Factory and right away I proposed that we would sign a contract with them, we'd manage them and give them a place to play. They said yes and Andy immediately bought them some new amplifiers and they started rehearsing at the Factory.

New Year's Eve 1965 The Velvets, Edie Sedgwick, her friend from Cambridge Donald Lyons, Andy and Gerard went to the Apollo Theatre in Harlem to see James Brown. After leaving the Apollo the whole crowd went in Edie's limousine over to Danny Field's apartment to watch the CBS Walter Cronkite show on Piero's film "Venus in Furs" featuring The Velvets playing "Heroin", then journeyed on to Sterling and Lou's apartment at 450 Grand Street where they just sat around. Andy was biting his fingernails and looking at a magazine. There was no heat and everybody had coats on. It was freezing. Edie was wearing her leopard skin fur coat. The atmosphere was weird. Hardly a word was spoken. Gerard seems to remember that John Cale and Edie were already involved in some kind of problem that may have contributed to the uptight feeling in the room. This was a complex group of people between whom there was immediately a lot of intrigue and rivalry for each other's attentions.

Most complex of all perhaps was Nico, who had come to New York from London, where she'd recorded a single on Rolling Stones' manager Andrew Loog Oldham's Immediate label, hung out with Brian Jones and attracted Dylan's attention in Paris where he'd given her the song "I'll Keep It With Mine". Nico was born of Spanish and Yugoslavian parents in Budapest, Hungary, March 15, 1943, although there's no way of confirming this date (she may, in fact, have been born as early as 1940). In the Second World War she took shelter during air-raids in the family bath tub in Cologne and always remembered the sound of the bombs. Nico has been very careful to conceal her real age. Educated first in France and then in Italy, she speaks seven languages.

At 15 while vacationing at a friend's villa in Rome, Nico was introduced to some young actors from "Cinecitta" (Italy's Hollywood), who invited her to the set of a movie they were making with an eccentric director named Federico Fellini. Claiming to be somebody's cousin, she was admitted on the set with instructions to keep to the sidelines. A party sequence was to be filmed in the exquisite remains of a Renaissance palazzo. The director was late and it was the cocktail hour. It was impossible to distinguish cast from crew. Her friend was dancing with a distinguished man in an elegantly cut suit (Marcello Mastroianni). Slightly bewildered by the noisy confusion Nico took shelter in a cobwebby corner and leaned against a carved marble table. The music died suddenly. A man in shirtsleeves, probably the prop man, yelled "Porte mi la candale".

Realizing he was addressing her, Nico picked up the large baroque silver candelabra from the table and walked slowly towards this man who took a step back with each step Nico advanced. Silence slowly overtook the room as people cleared a path. The jaded sophisticates were enchanted by the aloof elegance of the naive schoolgirl, as was Fellini, the man gesturing her towards him from across the silent room.

Still from "La Dolce Vita" by Federico Fellini, 1961.

Police breaking up the filming of "The Velvet Underground And Nico: A Symphony of Sound" at The Factory, January 1966.
(Stephen Shore)

Top: Danny Williams, Andy Warhol, Lou Reed, Sterling Morrison, John Cale.
Middle: Edie Sedgwick.
Bottom: Jason Collins, Barbara Rubin, Gerard Malanga, Martha Dargan, Donald Lyons. At Panna Grady's apartment during the shooting of "Lupe".
(Nat Finkelstein)

The movie? "La Dolce Vita". Nico got a sizable role. Her parents, enraged by a film in which their daughter certainly didn't do anything more offensive than walk up a staircase, prevented Nico from signing a contract with the great director.

Nico went to a private school in Germany where she says, 'They gave me a very hard time'. She also worked as a child model and studied acting and singing at the Lee Strasberg Method Studios. When she auditioned for a singing job a the famous Blue Angel in New York in 1964 she got so wound up she fainted immediately after the audition. She woke up to find she got the job.

NICO: I have a habit of leaving places at the wrong time, just when something big might have happened for me.

Persuading The Velvets to play with Nico was not as easy as one might imagine. First of all she really wanted a backing band so she could sing all the songs. The multi-talented Velvets had no interest in being a backing band. Anyway, some of their best songs, like "Heroin" and "Waiting for My Man", weren't as well-suited for Nico's voice as they were for Lou's. However, everybody was eager to do something and Andy was in a position to offer them a chance to become famous at his upcoming discotheque. Nico had already taken a shine to Lou, so they all agreed to Andy and Paul's proposal that Nico be allowed to sing some songs, and when she wasn't singing just stand on stage looking beautiful. Andy then persuaded Lou to write some new songs, like "All Tomorrow's Parties" and "Femme Fatale", specifically for Nico, and he even, indicating just how strong a will Andy's enthusiasm carries, persuaded them to change the name to The Velvet Underground and Nico, although that didn't sit so well with Lou and John, who saw their images as rock stars and positions as leaders of the group rapidly evaporating. However, they were all intuitive enough to realize that, at least for the time being, the direction he was pulling them in was basically right and they agreed to work together. The first evidence of this collaboration was a 70-minute black and white film Warhol shot of them rehearsing at the Factory in January 1966. Called "The Velvet Underground and Nico: A Symphony of Sound", it was broken up by the New York City Police, who came in response to complaints about the amount of noise the band was making, and was later used as a silent film backdrop to a number of their performances.

MORRISSEY: We used the week at the Cinematheque to experiment with what we were going to put into the Michael Myerberg discotheque with the movies behind The Velvets.

MALANGA: Everybody involved with the week at the Cinematheque was very excited about what we were doing together, although it was still more of an art than a rock event and there were a number of kinks to be ironed out before "Andy Warhol, Up-Tight" would bloom into the "Exploding Plastic Inevitable". We all went out to dinner after each show. Andy's question to everybody was always the same, 'How can we make it more interesting?'.

GLENN O'BRIEN: How did you meet Lou Reed?

WARHOL: He was playing at the Cafe Bizarre, and Barbara Rubin, a friend of Jonas Mekas, said she knew this group. Claes Oldenburg and Patti Oldenburg and Lucas Samaras and Jasper Johns and I were starting a rock & roll group with people like La Monte Young, and the artist who digs holes in the desert now, Walter DeMaria.

O'BRIEN: You started a rock band!?

WARHOL: Oh, yeah. We met ten times, and there were fights between Lucas and Patti over the music or something.

O'BRIEN: What did you do?

WARHOL: I was singing badly. Then Barbara Rubin said something about this group and mixed-media was getting to be the big thing at the Cinematheque, so we had films and lights, and Gerard did some dancing and The Velvets played.

O'BRIEN: Was that a light show before the San Francisco light shows?

WARHOL: Yeah, it was, sort of. Actually, the Cinematheque was really combining all the arts together.

REED: We worked with lights and stuff behind us before we met Andy. We did it in the old Cinematheque on Lafayette Street. It wasn't his original conception. It was a lot of people's conception. It was a natural step to meet Andy and say, 'Oh you've got a week at the new Cinematheque' so obviously since we combined

music with movies and everything it was just such an easy step to say, 'We'll play along with your movies'. Then we said, 'You've got all these things. Why don't we show lights?' It doesn't matter whose idea it was. It was just so obvious. It wasn't Andy putting it all together. It was everybody. It was just Andy had the week at the Cinematheque. That's what Andy had to do, and then everybody put it together. The thing was that the basic idea was so obvious that you would have to be a fool not to think of it. So everybody thought of it.

MORRISSEY: What really happened is I had this idea that Andy could make money not only from underground films but from putting the movies in some sort of rock & roll context. Discovering The Velvets, bringing them up the Factory and working with them was done for purely commercial reasons.

After their week at the Cinematheque word about *Andy Warhol, Up-Tight* began to spread. People were clearly confused about what to expect. Michael Myerberg began to cool off after seeing a night at the Cinematheque, but film departments were calling from colleges to book the show, which they, interestingly enough, took to be primarily an underground movie presentation. Warhol was invited to present the show in a film series at Rutgers University, New Jersey. By the time *Andy Warhol, Up-Tight* was ready to go out on the road in March, Edie Sedgwick, the first amputee, had definitely left the group in a stormy split that occurred one night at the Gingerman, a restaurant opposite Lincoln Center, shortly after the completion of the Cinematheque shows.

MALANGA: All The Velvets were there with Ingrid Superstar, Paul Morrissey, Donald Lyons, Danny Fields, myself, Andy and another of Edie's friends from Cambridge, the film-maker Chuck Wein. Edie began asking Andy, 'What's my place with The Velvets? I'm broke. I have no money. Why am I not getting paid?' And he said, 'You gotta be patient.'

Edie said, 'I can't be patient. I just have nothing to live on'. She told Andy that she had signed a contract with Bob Dylan's manager Albert Grossman and he'd said she shouldn't see Andy so much because the publicity that came out of it wasn't good and she didn't want him to show her films anymore.

MORRISSEY: She said, 'They're going to make a film and I'm supposed to star in it with Bobby'. Suddenly it was Bobby this and Bobby that, and they realized that she had a crush on him. They thought he'd been leading her on, because just that day Andy had heard in his lawyer's office that Dylan had been secretly married for a few months – he married Sarah Lowndes in November 1965. Everything was secret in those days for some reason . . . all phoney secrecy, so Andy couldn't resist asking, 'Did you know Edie that Bob Dylan has gotten married?' She was trembling. They realized that she really thought of herself as entering a relationship with Dylan, that maybe he hadn't been truthful.

MALANGA: Edie got up and went to make a phone call, presumably to Dylan. When she came back to the table she announced she was leaving the Factory, or more specifically leaving Andy, since her diatribe was directed at him. And he was saying, 'But . . . but . . . Edie, you have to be patient, we're not making any money. I'm not making any money from the movies, you just have to be patient'. But Edie wasn't buying it. She left and everybody was kind of quiet. It was stormy and dramatic. Edie disappeared and that was the end of it. She never came back.

Andy may have been surprised, shocked or hurt by Edie's defection to the Dylan camp, but he had little time to sit around thinking about it. Throughout 1966 he would make the *Exploding Plastic Inevitable* more and more interesting, changing the way people looked at rock & roll in tune with McLuhan's understanding in his book "The Medium Is The Massage" that "Electric circuitry has overthrown the regime of 'time' and 'space' and pours upon us instantly and continuously the concerns of all other men. It has reconstituted dialogue on a global scale. Its message is Total Change, ending psychic social economic and political parochialism."

REED: Andy told me that what we were doing with music was the same thing he was doing with painting and movies and writing, i.e., not kidding around. To my mind nobody in music was doing anything that even approximated the real thing, with the exception of us. We were doing a specific thing that was very, very real. It wasn't slick or a lie in any conceivable way, which was the only way we could work with him. Because the first thing I liked about Andy was that he was very real.

Paul Morrissey, Andy Warhol and Lou Reed on the bus to Ann Arbor, Michigan, March 1966.
(Nat Finkelstein)

● **ON THE ROAD WITH "ANDY WARHOL, UP-TIGHT"**

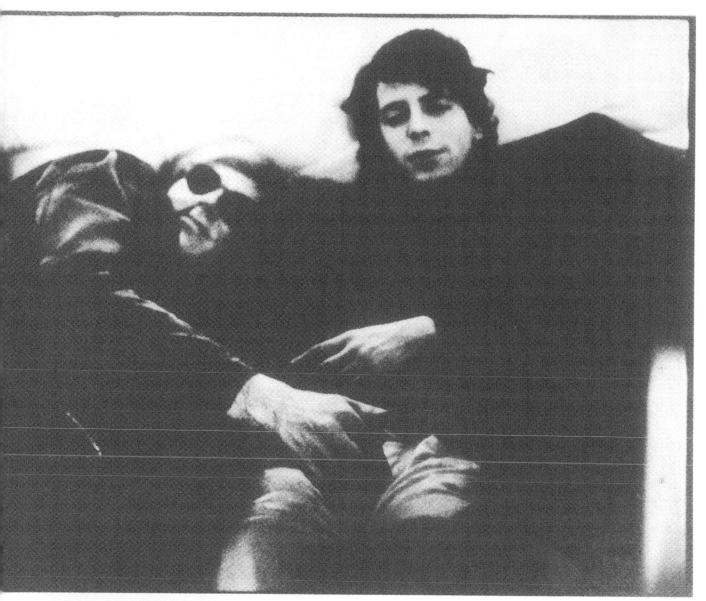

Ondine leaving The Factory.
(Billy Linich)

Andy arrived at Rutgers on the afternoon of March 9th with an entourage of thirteen people and went straight to the student cafeteria where the boys and girls flipped out gawking at Nico while Barbara Rubin filmed their reactions and Nat Finkelstein took photographs. When campus guards told him he couldn't, Nat punched one of them in the nose and the next thing he knew sixteen cops arrived. They asked Andy for his cafeteria pass (which he never had). Gerard and Paul started screaming, and everyone got thrown out.

MORRISON: Ondine, who played the Pope in Warhol's "Chelsea Girls", was part of the ensemble at Rutgers. He insists that Paul Morrissey forced him out of the show from then on, to his grief. He had always been our close friend, in or out of the show. We had no hand in, or knowledge of the machinations that removed him.

The show, which hadn't been selling too well prior to their arrival, sold out in the next two hours and 650 students packed the auditorium to see what would happen next. It was a perfect example of the effectiveness of making everyone uptight. Uptight meant interesting. Uptight meant something, as opposed to the perennial nothing, would happen.

Apart from The Velvets, Nico, Andy, Gerard, Barbara and Paul, the other integral members of the team were Danny Williams, a friend of Chuck Wein who had come down

Nico was a very good driver.
(Nat Finkelstein)

Clockwise from top left: Ingrid Superstar,
Andy Warhol, Gerard Malanga, Barbara
Rubin, Lou Reed, Maureen Tucker and
Suzanna a/k/a Tinkerbell on the bus to Ann
Arbor, Michigan, March 1966.
(Nat Finkelstein)

from Cambridge and worked at the Factory as an expert electrician. If it could be done with
wires, Danny would do it. Nat Finkelstein was a free-lance photographer, connected with
Black Star Photo Agency, who had come to the Factory in the Fall of '65 to take pictures for a
week and stayed for a year. Dave Faison was The Velvets' trusty equipment manager, who
stayed with them throughout the Warhol period, driving the van that carried their
equipment which he single-handedly cared for and set up. Faison was very important to the
show.

**MORRISON: At Rutger's we were all dressed entirely in white. The effect, with
all the films and lights projected on us, was invisibility.**

A few days later the same entourage, including Ingrid Superstar, the new girl at the
Factory who had replaced Edie Sedgwick, jammed into a mobile van and headed out to Ann
Arbor where another performance was booked at the University of Michigan Film Festival.

**MORRISON: We rode to Ann Arbor in some kind of 'recreational vehicle'. The
thing was big! It had a 120 volt A.C. generator on the back that supplied power to**

the inside. We could play our amps as we rolled along.

Andy remembers the drive in *POPism*: "Nico drove, and that was an experience. I still don't know if she had a license. She'd only been in this country a little while and she'd keep forgetting and drive on the British side of the road."

NICO: Oh my God! He was the only one who wasn't scared. He just couldn't care less. He figured that if I could take charge of 15 people on the bus I have to be a good driver not to land in a ditch.

WARHOL: Nico's driving really was insane when we hit Ann Arbor. She was shooting across sidewalks and over people's lawns. We finally pulled up in front of a nice big comfortable-looking house and everyone started unloading the van.

Ann Arbor went crazy. At last The Velvets were a smash. We had a strobe-light with us for the first time. The strobes were magical, they went perfectly with the chaos music The Velvets played. I'd sit on the steps in the lobby during intermission and people from the local papers and school papers would interview me, ask about my movies, what we were trying to do. 'If they can take it for ten minutes, then play it for fifteen,' I'd explain. 'That's our policy. Always leave them wanting less'.

INGRID SUPERSTAR: I remember in Ann Arbor part of the audience went a little berserk, and there were a few hecklers. They're all a bunch of immature punks. Like we have these problems with a very enthusiastic audience that yells and screams and throws fits and tantrums and rolls on the floor, usually at colleges and benefits like that for the younger people. So, anyway, the effect of the music on the audience is like the audience is just too stunned to think or say anything or give any kind of opinion. But then later I asked a few people in Ann Arbor, who had come to see the show a couple of nights in a row, what they thought, and they formed an opinion slowly. They said that they thought the music was very way out and supersonic and fast and intensified, and the effect of the sound it produced vibrated all through the audience, and when they walked out onto the street they still had these vibrations in their ears for about 15-minutes, especially from that last piece "Nothing Song", which was just noise and feedback and screeches and groans from the amplifiers.

The overall effect created by this bombardment of images and sound, with The Velvets often turning their backs on the audience throughout the entire performance, was the opposite of the accepted rock mores of the time. This may have had something to do with the fact that a number of the people involved in the production were on amphetamine, a drug which, among other effects, influences consumers to respond to everything with its mirror, or exactly opposite, image.

JOHN WILCOCK: I was on the bus with Nico and everybody. What do you remember most about that?

MALANGA: That we became a gypsy band.

WILCOCK: The eleven member Warhol group (supplemented by accompanying cars) had rented a microbus for the 1,500 mile round-trip to Ann Arbor ($50 per day plus 10¢ per mile) and although it offered some of the comforts of home – including a toilet that, like the one in the 47th Street Factory, didn't work – it proved to be far from the most reliable mode of transportation. The most chaotic moments came on the way back when a stop was made in the parking lot of a pop art monstrosity called the White Hut Superking for everybody to order hamburgers. Even before Nico, blonde locks falling about the shoulders of her black leather jacket, had brought the bus to a halt, a police patrol car came snooping around to see what else it contained.

MORRISON: The AC power came in handy, because we blew the alternator on the engine outside of Toledo on the way back to N.Y. The police so despised us that they insisted we get out of city limits at once. It was night, and we had no lights, but Danny cranked up the generator on the back, and ran extension cords from inside to photo floodlamps clamped to the bumper. The police followed us all the way to the line. I began to think that it was dangerous to cross the Hudson. I was a full-time student at City College at the time, but I was seldom seen, and ended up 6 credits shy of graduating. Good grades, in spite of all. I picked those up in the summer we played Max's.

● **THE DOM**

● Back in New York the group played at Paraphernalia, the ultra hip clothes store featuring the fashion designs of Betsey Johnson, who would later marry John Cale. The models could hardly gyrate through the mob which glutted both floors of the chic boutique. As Nico danced with Gerard, Andy's films bounced off the walls and Brian Jones, among others, looked on. Actually the best view was from outside, as bopping spotlights illuminated the models on the platform in the huge second-storey glass front. It drew a crowd and eventually the police. "Wow!" said Andy, "a policeman".

Paul Morrissey was trying to close the deal on *Andy Warhol's UP* so The Velvets and Nico could have their own place to play every night and become famous.

MORRISSEY: I kept trying to press Myerberg, through our lawyer Sy Litvinoff, to sign an agreement that Andy's group would open and be paid a certain amount of money. What happened is there was let's say an Italian influence in this club and I think they had their own plans for the opening. Somehow, even Myerberg lost control of it a little bit. About a week before they were scheduled to open, this lawyer said, 'They've changed their mind, they're going to open this weekend with The Young Rascals' starring Felix Cavalieri of Syracuse managed by Sid Bernstein who promoted The Beatles in the US.

MORRISON: Murray Kaufman ("Murray the K") was involved in this thing too – if not initially, then certainly at the end. The place was full of gangsters; one night we all went out there to look at the place and a limo full of them spilled out to challenge our right to enter. I'd seen enough already, and perhaps they had too. Inside, for an awkward moment, Lou and I ran into Felix Cavalieri, who must have known what mischief was afoot, but said nothing. The Rascals were a better band to open the place anyway, especially since it was closed down on opening night for liquor violations and never reopened. Eventually the club, which had finally been called "Murray the K's World", burnt down under the usual mysterious circumstances. Still, the price offered us to play there and hang out was $40,000 for the first four weekends. That would have been good pay for one night if we had collected it in advance. I don't know whether The Rascals got any money out of it.

MORRISSEY: I remember going down to the Cafe Figaro in the Village where Gerard had taken Andy to see Allen Ginsberg, who was about to go to Europe. I said, 'Andy, they're not going to sign the agreement, we don't have a club for The Velvets'. Andy had already invested this money in their equipment. I think we even got a management contract out of them.

MALANGA: What were the stipulations?

MORRISSEY: For presenting them and financing their equipment and support-ing them and making them famous we got 25% of their earnings.

MORRISON: Our agreement with Warvel, Inc., which we set up with Andy, called for our sharing in his many sources of revenue. After the initial purchase of a Vox Super Beatle and a Vox Westminster bass amp, we soon were able to make an endorsement deal with Vox and got all of their stuff free (even guitars). I'm playing a Vox Phantom in the movie that Andy made of us. We were the first American band on endorsement to Vox, and in England they only had The Beatles, Stones, and Hollies. I always liked Vox. Later we endorsed Acoustic, and finally Sunn (very good equipment). Paul, in other words, is not talking about major expenditures.

MORRISSEY: The idea was that they could've become very famous from being presented in this night club. Now, suddenly, my plans for presenting them fell through. But, as I was telling Andy this at the Figaro, sitting at the table behind me was Jackie Cassen and Rudi Stern and they heard me talking. They said, 'You're looking for a dance hall to present a rock & roll group? We present dance concerts with light shows and we know a wonderful place'. I said, 'You're kidding, where?' They said, 'On St. Mark's Place'. I said, 'You're kidding, I know that street. I never knew there was a place there.' I went over with them and I saw the Dom and I came back and arranged a rental deal through Sy Litvinoff on Wednesday. It was only signed on Friday and that afternoon The Velvets and Faison moved their equipment in. They never saw the place before. We couldn't go in until the

lease was signed. It was very hard getting the lease signed. Andy paid the money for the lease for the month of April. We moved in on Friday. Gerard was up on the back painting the wall white. I had to put the ad in the Village Voice the previous Monday. It was put in on the deadline. It was some sort of miracle that within that short space Andy Warhol presenting the EXPLODING PLASTIC IN-EVITABLE was created. The term "Exploding Plastic Inevitable" came from sitting around with Gerard and Barbara Rubin thinking of a name. I picked up a record album with Barbara on the back massaging Bob Dylan's head ("Bringing It All Back Home"). There were some amphetamine Bob Dylan gibberish liner-notes. I looked without reading and saw these words appear: something was 'exploding', something was 'plastic', something was 'inevitable'.

I said, 'Why not call it 'Exploding Plastic Inevitable', The Velvet Under-ground and Nico?' We moved in on Friday afternoon at 3 o'clock and at 8 o'clock that night all these people showed up. It was packed. It was an enormous success from its very first night.

Gerard's new dancing partners were Mary Woronov, a tall, beautiful art student he discovered at Cornell University and brought to the Factory, Ingrid Superstar, and Ronnie Cutrone, a 17-year old super bopper, who hung out on the fast scene.

RONNIE CUTRONE: The great thing about the 'Exploding Plastic Inevitable' was that it left nothing to the imagination. We were onstage with bullwhips, giant flashlights, hypodermic needles, barbells, big wooden crosses. In a sense it controlled your imagination. That's what you saw. Before that when you heard music you drifted off and you associated the music with what you thought about. This time – make no mistake about it – there was a clear image of what the group was conveying, and so it left nothing to the imagination. You were shocked because sometimes your imagination wasn't strong enough to imagine people shooting up on stage, being crucified and licking boots.

WARHOL: The Velvets played so loud and crazy I couldn't even begin to guess the decibels, and there were images projected everywhere, one on top of the other. I'd usually watch from the balcony or take my turn at the projectors, slipping different-colored gelatin slides over the lenses and turning movies like "Harlot", "The Shoplifter", "Couch", "Banana", "Blow Job", "Sleep", "Empire", "Kiss", "Whips", "Face", "Camp", "Eat" into all different colors.

WALTER DE MARIA: There was a serious tone to the music and the movies and the people, as well as all the craziness and the speed. There was also the feeling of desperate living, of being on the edge. The present was blazing and every day was incredible, and you knew every day wasn't always going to be that way.

Brian Jones and Andy Warhol at
Paraphernalia, 1966.
(Nat Finkelstein)

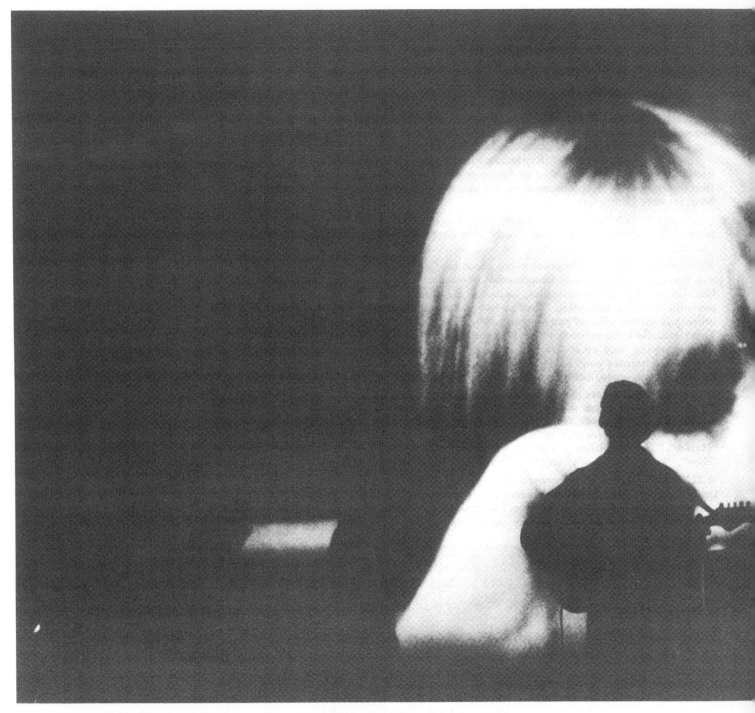

RICHARD GOLDSTEIN: The sound is a savage series of atonal thrusts and electronic feedback. The lyrics combine sado-masochistic frenzy with free association imagery. The whole sound seems to be the product of a secret marriage between Bob Dylan and the Marquis de Sade.

WARHOL: We all knew something revolutionary was happening. We just felt it. Things couldn't look this strange and new without some barrier being broken. 'It's like the Red Seeea,' Nico said, standing next to me one night on the Dom balcony that looked out over all the action, 'paaaaarting'.

DANNY FIELDS: It was an audience event to me, but it was also a musical event, because I preferred many times to close my eyes rather than see this psychedelic light-show travesty flashing on the group. To me it was the music. The great

Lou Reed in front of a projection of Nico at The Dom, April 1966.
(Nat Finkelstein)

credit due Andy is that he recognized it. He heard music when he first saw The Velvets. He thought that they were great. So, they were great before Andy. So, they were great during Andy, and afterwards, too. Andy may have created The E.P.I. but he didn't create the sound of the band. That was always there long before Andy found them. Lou's song-concepts were avant-garde and his lyrics were avant-garde, but I don't know if his melodies without John at that point would have been avant-garde. John really put a psychedelic air to it. I thought The Velvets were ahead of everybody. It's the only thing that ever, ever, ever swept me off my feet as music since early Mahler. They were a revolution.

Ed Sanders, the lead singer for The Fugs, another New York band that thrived on the Lower East Side in the same period, and with whom Gerard Malanga had originally danced before he met The Velvets, was taken by Barbara Rubin to see them at the Bizarre and remembers going to the Dom.

ED SANDERS: I liked that tune that started out real slow – "Heroin". I liked the drummer. I always liked Lou Reed's voice. The time was pretty good. Then it was more organic, yet within the organism it had certain time changes that were interesting. My wife Miriam seems to remember that the Dom gigs were crowded out by dopers. They had a kind of Allen Kaprow happening factor. I liked the show because it had a lot of energy. I liked the way everything was wrapped up in a good time-change. What The Fugs were doing wasn't exclusive nor were we competitive. There was plenty of room in the whole world for both The Fugs and The Velvets. I didn't feel competitive about anybody. I felt camaraderie towards The Velvets. We overlapped. So people would come to both shows. Nico used to come to my bookstore, The Peace Eye.

MORRISON: I agree with Ed completely. We often played together at shows and benefits, and liked and were liked by the same people. The Fugs, The Holy Modal Rounders and The Velvet Underground were the only authentic Lower East Side bands. We were real bands playing for real people in a real scene. We helped each other out if we could and generally hung out at the same places. I have a complete collection of Fugs albums and they bring me great joy.

MORRISSEY: Even at the first weekend, this horrible Charlie Rothchild came down. He said he was no longer working for Albert Grossman but I think he was. He said, 'You really have a great thing going here. You need somebody professional to manage it for you, and who's going to book The Velvet Underground?' He said, 'I did the bookings for Grossman, I could run the box-office here with a friend'. He had a kinda young blond partner who seemed rather on the up-and-up. I stupidly let them do it. They ran the box-office and collected the money.

MALANGA: Did you feel at that point that Nico would make it rather than The Velvets?

MORRISSEY: No, I thought they both would, really. I didn't think one more than the other. But I thought they really belonged together. Right after we opened and we had that success I told Andy, 'Now we have to make a record with them', and we went into a recording studio for three or four nights. It didn't cost that much. It was like a couple of thousand dollars.

MALANGA: Andy didn't go every night to the recording studio?

MORRISSEY: Maybe once or twice.

MALANGA: What were your impressions about what went down at the studio?

MORRISSEY: I thought what they were doing was good. All I remember is suddenly Nico had no material to sing. Lou didn't want her on the album. Lou was always jealous of Nico and he only let her sing little songs on the album and then he wrote a song for her called "Sunday Morning" and wouldn't let her sing it. You see Lou and John were such 'brothers'. They loved each other so much. Nico wasn't pure rock & roll or something.

As Andy was more involved with The Velvets than anything else, it was natural that he produce the album and continue to lend his name to their productions. People often ask exactly what did Andy do in the studio? He mainly contributed by having the vision to see how good The Velvets were and consequently encouraging them, he gave them confidence to follow their intuition and go to extremes to recognize and get their unique sound. He also suggested some ideas for songs (e.g. make "Sunday Morning" about paranoia), encouraged Lou to write others ("All Tomorrow's Parties") and discussed the merits of different tracks commenting on the way he liked the sound best. During this first recording session in a small studio on Broadway they only had time to do "All Tomorrow's Parties", "There She Goes Again", "I'll Be Your Mirror" and "I'm Waiting For My Man". The major conflicts during the sessions revolved around Nico.

MORRISON: Nico had two voices. One was a full-register, Germanic, gotterdammerung voice that I never cared for, and the other was her wispy voice which I liked. She kept singing "I'll Be Your Mirror" in her strident voice. Dissatisfied, we kept making her do it over and over again until she broke down and burst into tears. At that point we said, 'Oh, try it just one more time and then fuck it – if it doesn't work this time we're not going to do the song'. Nico sat down and did it exactly right. As for the haunting quality in her voice, it's not because she's singing to Bob Dylan or Lou Reed. Nico was just really depressed.

WARHOL: The whole time the album was being made, nobody seemed happy with it, especially Nico. 'I want to sound like Bawwwhhhb Deee-lahhhn', she wailed, so upset because she didn't. The Velvets didn't want to turn into a back-up band for a chanteuse, but ironically, Lou wrote the greatest songs for her to sing, like "Femme Fatale" and "I'll Be Your Mirror" and "All Tomorrow's Parties". Her voice, the words, and the sounds The Velvets made all were so magical together.

FIELDS: Andy had no influence on their sound whatsoever. Andy doesn't know how to translate ideas into musical terms. The songs on that first record sounded very much like the way I was used to hearing them live. What Andy was perhaps doing on the record was making them sound like he knew they sounded at the Factory. That's what I would do if I were an amateur at production, I would try and make them sound like the way I was used to hearing them. I think that's a great credit to the producer-artist relationship that you try to get them to sound like the person you fell in love with.

Back at the Dom, George English in an article in *Fire Island News* wrote, 'The rock & roll music gets louder, the dancers get more frantic, and the lights start going on and off like crazy. And there are spotlights blinking in our eyes, and car horns beeping, and Gerard Malanga and the dancers are shaking like mad, and you don't think the noise can get any louder, and then it does, until there is one big rhythmic tidal wave of sound, pressing down around you, just impure enough so you can still get the best; the audience, the dancers, the music and the movies, all of it fused together into one magnificent moment of hysteria.'

FIELDS: "The Exploding Plastic Inevitable" made a theatrical impact. We have very few records of that. But it was The Velvets who made the musical impact. If you were there the record will immediately bring it all back. But the show and the ambiance isn't on the record. You just have to rely on the music and that's all that's left. And especially as history goes further away and as witnesses die there's no one really to remember it and that record is all that will be. So, you have to say yes, it was that music. Also out of respect to the people in the band. It

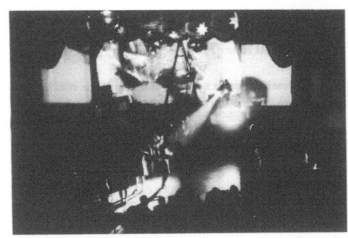

Danny Williams running the lights at The Dom.
(Nat Finkelstein)

Lou Reed, John Cale and Sterling Morrison in front of John Cale portraits at The Dom, April 1966.
(Nat Finkelstein)

was the house band of that scene and everybody danced to them. I was a big critic
of not showing the band. I always thought that was retarding their popularity.
You had to watch a fucking psychedelic light show! All these fucking plaids and
watercolors and drippings. I thought The Velvets were fabulous-looking people
and there they were drowned out by this god-damned psychedelic mediocrity. I
complained all the time about that. I said this may be art or a happening but I
love the band. I thought then that if this light and movie show wasn't happening
more people would see them and come to be intrigued with them, because I was so
in love with Lou. I thought he was just the hottest looking sexiest person I ever
have seen. The Velvets are an enormous influence on the music of today. And if
their influence lives on it's going to be as a musical group because rock groups
with light shows on top of them never became a very big thing. It was an
experiment that didn't work, because audiences really went to see the band. They
didn't go to see a live movie.

The Exploding Plastic Inevitable at the Dom provides a perfect example of how Andy
Warhol works so successfully with so many different people's talents and ideas. He has
always been a conduit through which multi-talented people who didn't know quite how to
use their talents could find a way to express themselves succinctly. Sterling Morrison has
said that Warhol was the most important influence on his life: 'It sounds crazy, but on
reflection I've decided that he was never wrong. He gave us the confidence to keep doing
what we were doing.'

Andy the movie-maker became here Andy the conductor of an orchestra, 'but having
at his fingertips,' as Jonas Mekas pointed out, 'not only many different creative components
– like sound control, a rock band, slide projectors, movie projectors, camera and lighting –
but also all the extreme personalities of each operator of each piece of equipment. He was
structuring with temperaments, egos and personalities.' The group was all the people
contributing to the show and everybody was paid the same amount for each night's
performance, i.e., Lou Reed received the same amount for playing and singing as Gerard for
dancing or Danny Williams for working the lights. On an average night at the Dom they
would be paid a hundred dollars apiece. During their first week there they took in $18,000.
According to Sterling Morrison they kept all the money in brown paper bags and used it to
finance some of the upcoming recording sessions and later their trip to California.

None of the ideas being used were Andy's more than anybody else's, but it was
undoubtedly his presence that gave the discordant production cohesion. It was also a
marvelous extension of his work as a portrait artist for here one had a multi-dimensional
living portrait operating once a night for a month. The movies were portraits of the people on
stage. The people on the stage were portraits of themselves. The songs The Velvets were
singing were portraits of people. And the audience, who were being photographed, filmed
and sung about as they watched the show, were being portrayed and becoming part of this
giant exploding plastic inevitable tableau too.

The Velvet Underground were intrinsically related to Andy Warhol. Between them
they reflected both the concept of rock & roll and the time in which it was happening more
accurately than any other performers that we know of. Picking up on the current
temperament, expressing uptightness and making the audience uptight is remarkably

Sterling Morrison, Lou Reed and John Cale
on stage at The Dom.
(Nat Finkelstein)

Jonas Mekas and Andy Warhol at The
Factory, 1966.
(Stephen Shore)

John Cale with bass guitar at The Factory.
(Nat Finkelstein)

accurate. We may think of the Sixties as a "groovy" time of peace and love, but the international rock scene out of which The E.P.I. grew was an extremely uptight scene. Just consider how uptight the stars in this constellation were: Bob Dylan and Brian Jones, who should be credited for their preparation and introduction of Nico and their catalytic presences on the scene, were both extremely uptight about their positions in the rock hierarchy. Nico was uptight because she wanted to sing all the songs and sound like Bob Dylan and because Bob had given "I'll Keep It With Mine" to Judy Collins to record. The Velvets were uptight because they saw that Nico could easily upstage them and they didn't want to sound like Bob Dylan at all.

MORRISON: We most certainly did not want to be compared with Bob Dylan, or associated with him. We did not want to be near Bob Dylan, either physically or through his songs. When Nico kept insisting that we work up "I'll Keep It With Mine", for a long time we simply refused. Then we took a long time to learn it (as long as we could take). After that, even though we knew the song, we insisted that we were unable to play it. When we finally did have a go at it on stage, it was performed poorly. We never got any better at it either, for some reason.

Gerard Malanga was uptight about maintaining his position as the star dancer, and his standing within the group's hierarchy. Paul Morrissey was uptight about Barbara Rubin's *Up-tight* approach, which he couldn't tolerate so Barbara was uptight with Paul. In fact the only person in The E.P.I. who may possibly not have been uptight was Salvador Dali who was advertised as part of it and appeared on a number of occasions to support it with his presence and reap the free publicity. Andy really loved the multimedia show, but he was uptight about whether Picasso had heard of him yet.

As far as relations between The Velvets were concerned there was some friction between the group and Nico because there were only so many songs that were appropriate for her and she wanted to sing them all. Whoever seemed to be having more influence, whether it be Lou or John, you'd find her closely involved as she went from one to the other, manipulating one or the other with sexual politics, but neither of these affairs lasted very long. For their part John and Lou resented Nico and – without being fully aware of their acts – would play little tricks on her. Maybe a page of her music would be missing or her microphone wouldn't work – prankster stuff just to fuck her up a little bit. All in all, however, they could be pretty pleased with themselves at this point. They were getting an unprecedented amount of critical attention and had a great advantage in being able to play at one place nightly. They were attracting a very electric crowd of people and their music was definitely having an impact. True, a great deal of the attention had been drawn by Andy Warhol's *Exploding Plastic Inevitable*, but the music was being written about increasingly.

MORRISON: It was at this time that The Velvets started wearing dark glasses on stage, not through trying to be cool but because the light-show could be blinding at times. Anyone in the audience could come up and work the lights. We never had things like 'When we do this ten second break, then hit me with the blue spot'. That's what I hate about modern rock & roll shows. They're so regimented. We just played while everything raged around us without any control on our part.

It's no wonder Jonas Mekas saw Warhol as a conductor, for it was Warhol, as Mekas wrote, who "manoeuvred it all into sound, image, and light symphonies of tremendous emotional and mental pitch which reached to the very heart of the New Generation. And he, the conductor, stood always there, in the balcony on the left corner, next to the projector, somewhere in the shadow, totally unnoticeable, but following every second and every detail of it, structurewise, that is.

"The Velvet Underground performances at the Dom during the month of April provided the most violent, loudest and most dynamic exploration platform for this new art. Theirs remains the most dramatic expression of the contemporary generation. The place where its needs and desperations are most dramatically split open. At the Plastic Inevitable it is all here and now and the Future."

McLuhan's statement, "In an electric information environment, minority groups can no longer be contained-ignored. Too many people know too much about each other. Our new environment compels commitment and participation. We have become irrevocably involved with, and responsible for, each other" – could almost work as a formal definition (which Andy Warhol would never make) of the aims of The E.P.I.

Maureen Tucker contributed her own individual drum sound by using unorthodox materials.

MORRISON: We felt that one reason why all bands sounded the same was because all the drumming was the same. In Angus we had a most unusual drummer, who played all sorts of weird drums and other percussion instruments. We wanted Maureen to play differently too, and she was willing to experiment. Her first departure was to play standing up.

TUCKER: What I'd always wanted to do was get an African drum sound, so I got a bass drum and turned it on its side, so I'd sit on the floor and play that. Then I got a cymbal, and I'd really play the hell out of the cymbal. After a while Faison built a stand to put the drum on, and then a box for the pedal so that I could use it horizontally. After that I got a floor tom. However, when we were playing at the Dom, somebody stole my little $50 drum set, so Lou said, 'Go out and get some garbage cans'. We went out, and whoever was with me grabbed the first ones we saw and I looked inside and said, 'No, too dirty'. So, we went around and finally we found some that had just been emptied and we put them in the truck, but they fell off and got bashed on the sidewalk. Eventually we found some more and took them back, stood them up on stage, and put some mikes under them. That's what I played for a week or so. The audience loved it. At the end of every night we'd have to clean up the little piles of garbage that got shook loose during the set. I remember one of the reviewers called it 'garbage music'. The reviewers didn't like it at all. But during this time the audience wasn't primarily there to see us. Andy was pretty much the focus of the whole thing, and they were there more to see what he was up to. We were getting an older artist-type of crowd.

Mo Tucker on the bus.
(Nat Finkelstein)

Allen Ginsberg was asked to join them on stage with Nico one night and he sang "Hare Krishna". Barbara Rubin's communal spirit, filtering through Andy's openness to anything, was clearly the basis of this collaboration. Ginsberg, who was himself first brought to the Factory by Barbara, remembers her as "a boyishly beautiful and very feminine art groupie, who was transfixed by star personalities. Being a groupie was honorable to her in the prophetic sense. Her insight into people's desires and motives, both political and spiritual, was quite correct. Everybody did have the ambition to have giant communal orgy revolution change of culture, and she worked directly on that principle of everybody's desire to get together to work with their fellow geniuses. She had a spiritual ambition in the best sense of uniting forces to work together to transform the culture."

"It was a rare thing," notes Ronnie Cutrone, "I don't think it'd happened before or has since that a rock group had been totally surrounded by this force of other people that then took on a whole other name."

In as much as Barbara was responsible for introducing The Velvets to Andy and encouraging them to work together, she was a driving force in The E.P.I., but Paul Morrissey hated her aspect of the act so much that he got on her case and kept on it until she threw up her hands in frustration and left the Factory one day screaming, never to return. Or, she left when her function – uniting the forces and creating the basis of the original *Up-Tight* series – was fulfilled, depending on your understanding of collaboration. The E.P.I. provides the perfect example for a study of spontaneous amputation.

MORRISSEY: The third week Charlie Rothchild said, 'I called California and got The Velvet Underground a four-week booking at the Trip in L.A.'. That was for May. We had only signed a lease for April and we couldn't sign one for May because there was some kind of Polish celebration going on there, so we decided to take the booking at the Trip and pick up the Dom lease when we returned.

PHIL MILSTEIN: What would you say was the general reaction of people to The E.P.I. show?

CUTRONE: If you could get somebody to see the show, nine times out of ten they would love it, simply because they'd be shocked and the look of the group was great. It was very severe. It scared a lot of people, too. Gerard and I got attacked by guys with beer bottles. They didn't know what the fuck we were. And when people don't know, sometimes they get frightened, and they react.

CALE: Andy's a good catalyst. He sort of had a way of picking out situations for us to appear in. He would almost invent places for us to play.

April 30th 1966 *The Exploding Plastic Inevitable* played their last show at the Dom. They didn't know it then, but they would never play in such a perfect art-rock cultural configuration time set again.

● ON THE COUCH AT THE FACTORY NO.1

Nat The Hat.
(Gerard Malanga)

This is an extract from a conversation between Ingrid Superstar and Lou Reed taped by Nat Finkelstein at the Factory, Fall 1966. Ingrid Superstar, one of Andy Warhol's most talkative superstars, is describing the members of The Velvet Underground. The couch referred to in the title is the famous couch on which so many films were made, including "Henry Geldzahler" and "Couch" (both 1964). The couch appears in groupshots which include Andy and The Velvets by Billy Linich, Nat Finkelstein and Stephen Shore.

INGRID SUPERSTAR: Lou Reed looks like a pretty little girl, with short hair. How tall are you Lou? About 5' 10", or 5' 11"?

REED: 5' 11¾".

INGRID: Oh, he's 5' 11¾" – being particular about ¼ of a fraction of an inch. Are you, Lou?

NAT FINKELSTEIN: Have you been trying to make Lou?

INGRID: Have I been trying to make Lou?! No.

FINKELSTEIN: Oh, come on, Ingrid.

INGRID: I don't make nobody, they make me. And he's got brown curly hair, he usually wears sunglasses. And he's slightly built and he's got a pug nose. That's about all I can say about Lou. Do you want me to describe Sterling Morrison? Sterling is very tall, and lanky, and slender and lean and he's got shaggy medium brown hair that looks like it's never been combed or washed. And he's got blue eyes, usually concealed by sunglasses, and he usually wears striped shirts and brown or white Levis and he's got a couple of faded blemishes on his face. Sterling's the friendliest. Sterling's always been a doll, he's a pussycat. I mean he'll talk for hours and make jokes. He can tell the funniest jokes. He'll have you in stitches, rolling, and yet he seems to be so quiet, sort of a Bill Wyman type. But Sterling is the biggest extrovert, the most open. He's a regular guy. He'll sit here with a beer and tell jokes and tell stories. John Cale. Good grief. I couldn't begin to describe him, he's just funny looking. He's got straight black hair, parted sometimes in the middle and sometimes on the side. When it's parted in the middle it gives him that bohemian Buffy St. Marie look, and he's growing a goatee with a matching mustache, which is really way out. All he needs is a pair of antennae – he can, you know, be an equivalent to a Martian. Yes?

REED: He looks very Mephistophelian.

INGRID: He looks very Mephistophelian. What does that mean?

REED: The devil.

INGRID: Oh, yes, he looks like a devil. The devil's disciple. He usually wears baggy pants and boots that are way too big for him, so he trips all over the place, and he wears a baggy shirt or a flower-print shirt, with puffed sleeves, Gerard Malanga-style. Well, that's what he was wearing in Chicago. And he's got black eyes, and he's very very relaxed, boring at times, but then aren't we all? And it's not an excuse. And he usually wears sunglasses. He's Welsh. One of the interesting characteristics about him is his little Welsh accent.

And then last but not least there's Maureen Tucker. The only girl in the band.

REED: She isn't a girl.

INGRID: Oh, she is too, Louis. Listen, I stayed with her the whole time in that hotel in Chicago and she is a girl, who was always the biggest mystery because nobody could ever figure out Mo. She's a beer drinker. She sits in the pub and knocks them back! She's absolutely straight – you keep on looking for the Buster Brown shoes! If something embarrassed her she just turns red! Maureen's very natural. She doesn't wear any make-up. She told me, I asked her. I even felt her hair. She's got freckles, and she's a cute little Irish girl, very religious, goes to church every Sunday...

REED: You know what her favorite expression is?

INGRID: Yeehaw.

REED: No.

INGRID: Ho hum.

REED: No.

INGRID: What?

REED: You piece of shit.

INGRID: You piece of shit. I thought that was Faison's expression.

REED: No, it's Mo's.

INGRID: Well, then Mo must have plagiarized it from Faison. She's got average build. She never wears a skirt, except when she works or goes to church. She's a very sweet. . .

REED: She doesn't wear a bra.

INGRID: She wears a bra.

REED: She doesn't have to.

INGRID: I think every girl has to, or every girl should. So, anyway she's a very quiet calm sweet person. And very easy to get along with.

REED: She's no virgin.

INGRID: Oh, yes she is.

REED: Oh, get out of here. She wouldn't be in the band if she were.

INGRID: I don't believe anything Louis says. He's crazy. Like the rest of us. But, what would this world be if it weren't for us crazy people?. Oh, and last but not least, I must describe the road manager, Faison. Oh, God. Oh, well you could call him like Captain Kidd, because he looks like a pirate, he's got real, real curly almost kinky brown hair, level with the bottom of his ears, and he's got a full beard with a mustache, and like the front of his beard curls up, and he wears one earring, pierced in his ear. Probably sterling silver earring, similar to the one that Edie used to wear, only much shorter. He can be a bitchy person, but so can everybody. He's a real pool shark, along with the rest of The Velvets. He's got a mean temper, and he says he's a Scot but I don't believe him, because he looks more Jewish. All he needs is a pole, you know, and he'll look like Moses, oh, but that's Allen Ginsberg's award.

Now, last but not least, we come to the beautiful flawless, chanteuse, Nico. She's got blonde hair, sort of Jane Asher style, down to her shoulders. She's got blue eyes, and she's about 5' 9", 5' 10". A very good photographic model, and actress, and she's got great potential. She could be like 5 or 50, like being an actress in a movie, and she could make it in Hollywood any day.

Her voice is very bland and calm and low and smooth. Some people mistake it like for a boy's voice. And she sings sort of like in one tone mostly. She doesn't have too much modulation, which is groovy, it's like a new sound. She's just a very, very beautiful girl – a cool Dietrich for a cool generation.

REED: How old is she?

INGRID: She's 23. And she's got a very, very cute little German accent.

Ingrid Superstar at The Factory, 1966.
(Nat Finkelstein)

Dave Faison, equipment manager.
(Sterling Morrison Archive)

A SHORT ESSAY IN APPRECIATION OF NICO

(This piece was written by Gerard Malanga in early 1967 for the magazine Status & Diplomat.)

If there exists beauty so universal as to be unquestionable, Nico possesses it.

The face is perfect. Impeccable features – mouth precise, nose straight and finely-chiseled, eyes limpid in delicate balance, visage framed by a curtain of pale shining hair. No feature dominates Nico's face; all is in improbably perfect proportion. Nothing is outstanding, yet everything is. Symmetry tends to boredom, but Nico arrests, startles, seizes. The appearance of a smile, a pout, a tear, thoroughly assaults with incongruity. But the most incongruous is the look of the eyes, focused most frequently on the imperceptible.

As superstar and chanteuse, Nico is unceasingly noted for the paradox of her beauty and its function – the contrast between Nico, on screen behind The Velvet Underground, languidly munching a Hershey bar or casually combing her hair in "Chelsea Girls" and Nico, on stage, who "hovers over a microphone, cupping her voice in an endless groan, the sound of an amplified moose." More apparent evidence in the dichotomy is Nico as "Nico", frolicking and giggling through "La dolce vita" or smiling malignantly from an *Esquire* cover, and Nico as Nico, walking with detachment after a performance, laughing vaguely. Yet, the critics' discovery of the paradox of effortless innocence on film and macabre, death-like stage presence is only a secondary manifestation of the real enigma: the eyes.

Because of her impact as a three-dimensional whole, Nico would be most effectively represented in sculpture, but not even the most profound artist could capture the strange and unexplainable quality of her eyes. They captivate, but do not beckon; they ignore, but cannot be forgotten; they reflect the inner reality, but leave no clue to its contents. Their expression, or lack of a comprehensible expression, does not relate to the thoroughly comprehensible phenomenon of her beauty. Nico's eyes seem to guard a great mystery which, hidden in aloofness, they do not want anyone to know exists. Whether or not a mystery is there, the eyes with the enigma of their absence from what surrounds them eclipse the perfection of features and form to add great magnetism. It is this magnetism, cool and inviolable, which enhances Nico's identification with the Garbo-Dietrich tradition, which elevates her above the genre of uniform Nordic beauties to the elite of an unapproachable mystique.

Opening Thursday, December 19th
COCKTAIL HOUR
5 to 8 p.m.

The Blue Angel Lounge

featuring the intimate songs of

Nico

All drinks 85¢   No minimum; no cover

152 East 55th Street   PLaza 3-5998

Nico in Stephen Shore's parents' apartment on Sutton Place.
(Stephen Shore)

Maureen Tucker
(Sterling Morrison Archive)

LICKING LOLLYPOPS IN L.A.

Charlie Rothchild booked The Exploding Plastic Inevitable into the Trip May 3rd-29th. Fourteen of them packed their whips, chains, lights, guitars and drums and flew out to L.A. on May 1st. Most of them stayed at the Castle, a large imitation-medieval stone structure in the Hollywood Hills which rock musicians often rented for $500 a week. Dylan had just been there with Edie Sedgwick. Nat Finkelstein and Faison stayed at the Tropicana.

The Mothers of Invention opened at the Trip. The hometown crowd cheered them and booed The Velvets. Lou hated The Mothers. Of Frank Zappa he said, 'He's probably the single most untalented person I've heard in my life. He's two-bit, pretentious academic, and he can't play rock & roll, because he's a loser. And that's why he dresses up funny. He's not happy with himself and I think he's right.' On the second night they played L.A. they turned up all their amplifiers after their last number, walked off the stage and let the feedback play. The owners didn't like the music nor did the critics: 'Screeching rock and roll – reminded viewers of nothing so much as Berlin in the decadent 30's', said *Los Angeles Magazine*. 'A three ring psychosis that assaults the senses with the sights and sounds of the total environment syndrome. . . Discordant music, throbbing cadences, pulsating tempo', said *Variety*. *The Los Angeles Times* was less critical: 'Not since the Titanic ran into the iceberg has there been such a collision as when Andy Warhol's Exploding Plastic Inevitable burst upon the audience at the Trip, Tuesday. For once a Happening really happened, and it took Warhol to come out from New York to show how it's done. The Velvet Underground is so far out that it makes the tremendous thumping beat of the great groovy group which opened the program seem passé.'

The Medium is the Massage includes a photograph of the group performing at the Trip. At the heart of his thesis McLuhan describes what was happening here: "Time' has ceased, 'space' has vanished. We now live in a global village . . . a simultaneous happening. We are back in acoustic space. We have begun again to structure the primordial feeling, the tribal emotions from which a few centuries of literacy divorced us.

'Electric circuitry profoundly involves men with one another. Information pours upon us, instantaneously and continuously. As soon as information is acquired, it is very rapidly replaced by still newer information. Our electrically-configured world has forced us to move from the habit of data classification to the mode of pattern recognition. We can no longer build serially, block by block, step by step, because instant communication insures that all factors of the environment and of experience coexist in a state of active interplay. We have now become aware of the possibility of arranging the entire human environment as a work of art.'

Indeed it was the 'artist' who seemed most welcome in the land of the silver screen: "The arrival of Andy, the hippie's hippie, on the Sunset Strip, the hippies' paradise, makes for the most perfect combination since peanut butter discovered jelly," said *The Los Angeles Times* after The Velvets second night at The Trip.

WARHOL: I love L.A. I love Hollywood. They're beautiful. Everybody's plastic – but I love plastic. I want to be plastic. Nico could probably make it here tomorrow. She has that ability to be 5 and 50 at the same time, but actually, it's Gerard who wants to be the new pop girl. He tries very hard and the 'East Village Other' has already named him Slum Goddess of the Year. After The Velvets opened, a lot of people wondered if they could last the full three weeks, and critics wrote things like, 'The Velvet Underground should go back underground and practise.' But The Velvets in their wrap-around shades and tight striped pants went right on playing their demented New York music, even though the easygoing L.A. people just didn't appreciate it; some of them said it was the most destructive thing they'd ever heard. On opening night, a couple of The Byrds were there and Jim Morrison, who looked really intrigued (he was still a student at the UCLA Film School at the time), and Ryan O'Neal and Mama Cass were there, kicking up their heels. We read a great comment by Cher Bono the next day in one of the newspapers, and we picked it up for our ads – 'It will replace nothing, except maybe suicide.' But Sonny seemed to like it all – he stayed on after she left.

They needn't have worried about their ability to fill the club throughout their engagement because it was closed down by the Sheriff's office on their third day. The troupe stayed in L.A., hoping the club would re-open, and the musicians' union said if they stayed in town for the (union rules) duration of their engagement they would have to be paid the complete fee. They used the time to continue recording the first album. Nat Finkelstein left

"Out of sight" ... Sonny Bono, actor

"It's like eating a banana nut Brillo Pad" ... David Crosby, Byrd.

"It doesn't leave anything for the imagination" ... Tony Hicks, Hollie

A Happening!

What is it? It's Andy Warhol, it's The Plastic Inevitable, it's The Velvet Underground, it's Nico, it's a pair of dancers, a candle, two whips, a candy bar, a violin, a pop bottle and movies.

It's from New York and it's on the West Coast for the first time at The Trip in Hollywood. It's going to other parts of the nation soon.

It's drawing crowds of curious celebrities and it's confusing crowds of curious.

It's happening.

See it for yourself, no questions allowed.

BEAT Photos: Howard L. Bingham

"I'm glad I've got short hair" ... Ryan O'Neal, Rodney

"The Velvet Underground should go back underground and practice" ... Barry Mc-Guire, chicken rancher

"It's where entertaining's going" ... John Phillips, Papa.

the group because of an argument about money.

MORRISON: We had a horrible reputation. Everybody figured we were gay. They figured we must be, running around with Warhol and all those whips and stuff. One day Andy cooked eggs for everybody at the Castle. After about a week and a half waiting for the Trip to re-open I moved to the Tropicana. Los Feliz, the street that led to the Castle, was too far from the club scene on Sunset Strip. Faison and Danny were already there at the Tropicana and I had had enough of Patrick Tilden imitating Bob Dylan's grating speech patterns up at the Castle. There wasn't much partying at the Castle while we were there because of our reputation – rumors so sinister were making the rounds on the Strip that hardly anyone had the courage to visit. And those who dared come up at night found dark rooms and passageways, lit only by an occasional flickering brazier, strains of music from the acetates of the first album, mutterings, shufflings and an occasional human form, such as Severn Darden gliding by in his monk's attire. I do not exaggerate. At the Tropicana we partied with The Buffalo Springfield who were staying there too, and various others from the L.A. music scene. I rode all over the place on a motor cycle that Kurt von Meier lent me, and as often as not was at the Castle anyway. It's just that I wasn't stuck up there.

We made the album ourselves and then took it around because we knew that no one was going to sign us off the streets. And we didn't want any A&R department telling us what songs we should record. We took it to Ahmet Ertegun and he said, 'No drug songs.' We took it to Elektra, and they said, 'No violas.' Finally we took it to Tom Wilson, who was at Columbia, and he said to wait until he moved to MGM and we could do whatever we wanted with him on their Verve label, which turned out to be true and MGM did sign us. They signed The Mothers of Invention at the same time, trying to revamp Verve and go psychedelic, or something.

MORRISSEY: And then we sold the record to MGM but Lou, who was always conniving and trying to make a deal, said, 'We'll only make the deal if it's in my name. The money has to come to us and then we'll give Andy and you the percentage you're entitled to.' Not only for presenting them and inventing them, but for making and recording the album. He was just selfish.

MILSTEIN: How did Tom Wilson come to produce the "Sunday Morning" song on the Banana album?

WARHOL: He was a friend of Nico's. When they went with MGM, Tom Wilson was the person there. What is Tom Wilson doing now? Do you know?

MILSTEIN: He died in 1978 in California.

WARHOL: Really?!

MILSTEIN: I read about it somewhere.

WARHOL: Oh, well gee, I didn't know that. . .

While they were in L.A. The Velvet Underground met Steve Sesnick, who was to become their manager in 1967 and play a large role in the rest of their career.

VICTOR BOCKRIS: My understanding is that you met and became involved with the group when they were in L.A. playing the Trip. Is that correct?

STEVE SESNICK: Yes.

BOCKRIS: Were you involved with them in any practical manner?

SESNICK: The entire idea was mine.

BOCKRIS: To go to L.A.?

SESNICK: To start the whole Exploding Plastic Inevitable.

BOCKRIS: Maybe you could fill me in on that.

SESNICK: My room-mate at the time was Tim Hauser who was the founder of Manhattan Transfer. I told him I had come up with this space idea. All that was was an idea of film and dancing and music – space music – and he was working at the time on doing 30s and 40s so we were very diametrically opposed in our personal interests. I mentioned it to Andy at a party at the Factory and he said, 'Oh gee, Steve, that sounds great. Do you think we can do it?' I said, 'Yes', and we had a series of meetings with Brian Epstein on the telephone through Nat Weiss. Danny Williams was the only one I remember, besides Andy and Edie Sedgwick,

Maureen Tucker, Lou Reed, Sterling Morrison and John Cale at The Castle, Hollywood Hills, L.A., Spring 1966. (Malanga Archive))

Lou Reed and Nico at T.T. & G. Studios in
Los Angeles recording the first album.
(Nat Finkelstein)

Sterling Morrison, Nico, John Cale and Lou
Reed at T.T. & G. Studios in Los Angeles
recording the first album. May 1966.
(Nat Finkelstein)

Nico, Andy Warhol, Maureen Tucker, Lou Reed, Sterling Morrison and John Cale at The Castle, Hollywood Hills, L.A., Spring 1966.
(Malanga Archive)

who was in on the original meetings for this whole idea. Epstein and Nat Weiss were partners. Nat was his American attorney. I was very friendly with Nat for a number of years, prior to his even getting into music. So having access to him I went to speak with him about this idea and he passed it on to Brian, and Brian went nuts over it. He said it really is fantastic and they did want to get involved. But their idea of what it was and mine and Andy's were just really different.

BOCKRIS: So how come you were out in L.A. when they played at the Trip?

SESNICK: It was related to the project. I was looking for an act.

BOCKRIS: I was under the impression that you helped in some capacity on the deal between The Velvets and MGM whilst in L.A.

SESNICK: I did, but I didn't initiate that relationship.

BOCKRIS: What was your perception of The Velvet Underground that made you feel they were the right group for you to work with? Was the music they were making purely the right kind of music, or was the image they were projecting the right image? When you saw them, what clicked in your mind?

SESNICK: I didn't see them at first, I just heard the music playing in the Castle. My immediate feeling was the words – somebody was putting out messages that I found interesting. Which turned out to be a fellow by the name of Lou Reed.

BOCKRIS: What was your age at this point?

SESNICK: 22. We were the same age.

BOCKRIS: And what was your background?

SESNICK: I was a basketball player. I played for St. John's University of New York. Freshman Year.

BOCKRIS: Lou was heavily into basketball too, right?

SESNICK: Oh, yeah.

BOCKRIS: Had you done anything in the music business?

SESNICK: I coached my mother. That was about all. No, in fact, I don't like music.

In L.A. Sesnick began to become involved with The Velvet Underground on a loose free-lance basis since they already had a managerial contract with Morrissey and Warhol. According to him he arranged for them to play at Bill Graham's Fillmore in San Francisco at the end of May, although in *POPism* Warhol says it was Graham who kept calling Morrissey in L.A. trying to book The Velvets into the Fillmore on the same bill with The Mothers of Invention and The Jefferson Airplane.

REED: We had vast objections to the whole San Francisco scene. It's just tedious, a lie and untalented. They can't play and they certainly can't write. I keep telling everybody and nobody cares. We used to be quiet, but I don't even care anymore about not wanting to say negative things, 'cos things have gone so far that somebody really should say something. You know, people like Jefferson Airplane, Grateful Dead are just the most untalented bores that ever came up. Just look at them physically, I mean, can you take Grace Slick seriously? It's a joke! it's a joke! The kids are being hyped.

By the time their three weeks in L.A. were up *The Exploding Plastic Inevitable* capitulated and agreed to play two nights at the Fillmore. The feeling of alienation between their party and the West Coast groups seems to have been mutual, and a lot of friction developed between Bill Graham and The E.P.I. Neither group could connect with the other.

Nico, Sterling Morrison, Maureen Tucker, Lou Reed and John Cale at The Castle, Hollywood Hills, L.A., Spring 1966. (Malanga Archive)

MORRISON: We actually built the light show at the Fillmore Auditorium. Bill Graham didn't, nor did any San Francisco entrepreneur. When we showed up Graham had a slide projector with a picture of the moon. We said, 'That's not a light show, Bill, sorry.' That's one of the reasons that Graham really hates us.

Marshall McLuhan gave us credit for inventing the light show in "The Medium is the Massage". There's a photo. He's the only one. It was nice of him. He showed the group that did it all. San Francisco was rigged. It was like shooting fish in a barrel. The fish being the innocent heads prowling around Haight-Ashbury. We came out there as an unshakable entity. I'd never heard of Bill Graham. In fact, I've never heard of him since. I don't know who he is. I just thought he was an insane slob, totally beneath my abilities to observe. He just didn't exist as far as I was concerned. An absolute nonentity. He knew what we thought of him. The day I arrived at his club, I was thrown out. I just walked in with my guitar and he said, 'You, get out of here.' They told him, 'You've lost your mind, he's playing here tonight.' He said, 'Get out, get out you s.o.b.' I wish I had.

When we arrived it was an attack against their way of life. The Mothers were following us around California. They also had an audition group perform. During the show Zappa would keep putting us down, like on the mike, he would say, 'These guys really suck.' So, The Mothers were chasing us around California so we arrived in Bill Graham country. He always had an audition group. The reason for this was they didn't get any money. He would say, 'If you're really good I'll let you play.' This guy's an operator. The audition group that night happened to be The Jefferson Airplane whom he was managing. They wanted publicity and The Mothers wanted publicity because there were so many people capitalizing on our show that night. We were just a neutral party. Graham made so much money that weekend we played at the Fillmore, that he didn't believe it. That's what blew his mind. We arrived at a time before Jefferson Airplane was known to anyone. They didn't even have Grace Slick yet. Everyone was nowhere at the time, The Mothers and, of course, ourselves. Warhol was the name that made the impact with the public.

Things finally fell apart completely when Paul Morrissey made Bill Graham get really uptight! The scene is recounted in Warhol's *POPism:* 'Why don't they take heroin?' Paul suggested, pointing to the group on stage. 'That's what all the really *good* musicians take.' Graham didn't say anything, he just fumed. Paul knew he was driving him good and crazy so he kept it up. 'You know, I think I'm really all for heroin, because if you take care of yourself, it doesn't affect you physically.' He took a tangerine out of his pocket and peeled it in one motion, letting the peels fall on the floor. 'With heroin you never catch cold – it started in the United States as a cure for the common cold'.

Paul was saying everything he could think of to offend Bill Graham's San Francisco sensibility, but in the end it was dropping the tangerine peels on the Fillmore floor – which he had done totally unconsciously – that brought on the showdown. Little things mean a lot. Graham stared down at the peels, and he got livid. I don't remember his exact words, but he started yelling – things like 'you disgusting germs from New York! Here we are, trying to clean up everything, and you come out here with your disgusting minds and *whips!*'

After the second night, Gerard Malanga was arrested in an all-night cafeteria in the North Beach area where he had gone with Lou and a friend of Andy's, an actress named Nancy Worthington Fish who was performing with The Committee. He was charged with carrying an offensive weapon (his whip) by the San Francisco police and thrown into the can where he spent an anxious night. The city clearly felt the same way about the 'disgusting germs from New York' as The Velvets felt about the capital of the hippies.

BOCKRIS: So you wanted to work with them, but apart from arranging the occasional show on a free-lance basis, you weren't actually working with them.

SESNICK: No, they really didn't want me. Well, Lou did after San Francisco.

BOCKRIS: What happened in San Francisco that led him to want to work with you?

SESNICK: Oh, I predicted a number of things and they all worked out that way and he realized they needed a manager. Everyone else was well-meaning; there wasn't anything naughty going on particularly, except they weren't managers. That was my interest.

BOCKRIS: After the end of the West Coast scene in May, did you all return to New York and then go out to Chicago from New York?

SESNICK: That's a long story; there's a lot of confusion there. There was a tremendous amount of confusion as to where anything was happening because of the money needed to keep the group together. The expenses were a real problem and everybody went in different directions. All sorts of problems happened in San Francisco while we were there.

MORRISON: Danny Williams stayed behind to design a light show after we went back to NY. He went from there directly to Chicago to set up our show at Poor Richards.

Danny Williams graduated from Harvard.
(Nat Finkelstein)

Maureen Tucker, Sterling Morrison
Lou Reed, and John Cale at The Castle,
Hollywood Hills, L.A., Spring 1966.
(Malanga Archive)

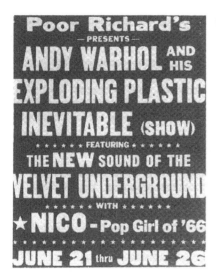

CHICAGO

At the beginning of June Nico took off for Ibiza. Lou contracted hepatitis and went into Beth Israel Hospital in New York. Andy and Paul were shooting the footage which became "Chelsea Girls." So when Steve Sesnick arranged another booking for the group, June 21-26 1966 at Poor Richard's in Chicago, some changes had to be made.

MALANGA: Just before the Chicago gig, Andy, Angus MacLise and I went to visit Lou in the hospital, because Angus was going to play with the group in Chicago. I distinctly remember Lou telling Angus, 'Just remember you're only coming back for two weeks. You're on a temporary basis. I don't want you to get any idea that you're coming back into the group again.'

MORRISON: Lou always was nice like that.

With Angus on drums subbing for Lou, Maureen switched to bass and Sterling and John took over the lead vocal spots. Ingrid Superstar replaced Mary Woronov as Gerard's dancing partner. Andy, Nico and Lou were absent. Danny Williams flew in from San Francisco to work the lights.

FINKELSTEIN: Everybody was on Danny's case. You could watch him disintegrate. He came in as a clean-cut preppy and left looking like a real seedy character. The silver dust at the Factory just coated his skin. The image I have of Danny is that he went out with his eyeglasses patched together with masking-tape.

MORRISON: Danny was involved in a Factory power struggle with Paul Morrissey, and Paul won. At issue was who was going to be Andy's 'technical' advisor. The struggle was so intense by Chicago that Danny and Paul actually came to blows over an extension cord – Danny wanted it for the lights, and Paul wanted it for the projectors. The only way I could deal with that was to laugh at the absurdity of it all, but perhaps Danny felt that he had no support in the group either, which wasn't the case. Danny was excellent at what he did, and a very hard worker.

Angus had originally left the group because he anticipated all kinds of compromises that would have to be made and then when he finally did play with us out in Chicago he realized that that was not true. We were as careless as ever.

BOCKRIS: At this point did he want to come back into the group?

MORRISON: Yeah, evidently.

Poor Richard's was inside an old church. Without ventilation the temperature was 106 degrees. The Velvets arrived just after the Chicago race riots. Andy had been promised by the promoters to do a series of interviews for radio and TV stations but sent Brigid Polk instead. All the local press and *Playboy* people were there to inspect Warhol's latest, and when the group went on without both lead singers the media were acutely disappointed. Other witnesses in the audience and on stage say that it was just as good as ever.

MORRISON: Everybody thought we'd be a flop without Lou but we were great. We just had to work a lot harder. In fact, we were held over for a second week, which was at least as successful as the first. We had a lot of fun there: Gerard and I went to a beach in Winnetka, an affluent suburb of Chicago, and were run off by the police (Gerard was wearing a novel Rudi Gernreich bikini which exposed the top 3 inches of his ass, and plunged even lower in the front); while I was staying at the Commonwealth Hotel I met a dwarf in the elevator who said he had a gun and would kill me with it if I ever got in there with him again. Is it because I'm tall, I wondered, or because I look happy? I later met another dwarf in Boston and he, too, had a gun that he said he would kill me with. I don't know what the pattern is to all this, but I'm still working on it. And for a long time afterwards, when attending large indoor gatherings, I would immediately upon arrival move quickly through all the rooms, peeking into the closets and behind the drapes. At outdoor events I would peer intently into the shrubbery before joining the throng. Now I'm sure that many people consider this to be odd behavior, but I didn't think I was acting oddly at all. Just checking for dwarfs. Anyway, I left the Commonwealth and joined Angus over at the Hotel Lincoln. Safer there. As for "Playboy," they hired us to play in the club at a noon fashion show – the clothing was given to us by a mod shop in Old Town. It was written up with a picture in their VIP magazine. We went on Studs Terkel's TV show, did a couple of radio

Sterling Morrison in West Allis, Wisconsin,
July 1966.
(Sterling Morrison Archive)

shows, and all that sort of on-tour stuff. We didn't lay low just because we didn't
have Lou, Nico, or Andy. On the contrary, I would say we made ourselves rather
conspicuous.

Chicago Daily News: Warhol has indeed put together a total environment, but it is an
assemblage that actually vibrates with menace, cynicism, and perversion. To experience it is
to be brutalized, helpless – you're in any kind of horror you want to imagine, from police
state to madhouse. Eventually the reverberations in your ears stop. But what do you do with
what you still hear in your brain? The flowers of evil are in full bloom with the Exploding
Plastic Inevitable.

One night Angus arrived half an hour late for the show so he made up for it by
continuing to drum for half an hour after the set was over.

'This show is a new phase for Andy,', Malanga explained to a reporter from the
Chicago Tribune between sets. 'It has no message. It's just entertainment. Yes, the films, the
lights, the music are all parts, but the main thing is the music. Andy is the catalyst for this,
but he has no part in the show itself.'

Was Warhol beginning to lose interest in The EPI as its personalities continued to
fragment and become increasingly difficult to conduct? "Andy was reportedly 'uptight' with
nerves in New York," said the *Chicago Daily News*. "A condition one would expect to be
normal judging by the corners of himself he reveals in The Exploding Plastic Inevitable."

The Velvets played part of the gig with their backs to the audience, a practice they
would increasingly use as they played to less and less acceptance. "Let's hope it's killed
before it spreads," the *Daily News* concluded their lengthy putdown. Ron Nemeth filmed one
of the shows. The Velvets hardly appear in it, but the film does have an unreleased live
sound-track. Two young kids called Susan Pile and Ed Walsh attached themselves to the
group in Chicago and later followed them to New York where they ended up working for
Warhol.

**INGRID SUPERSTAR: I remember when I was in Chicago there was one last
song they did in the show, and they had the feedback from the guitars which
sounded like 12 million guitars going at one time with these amplified,
intensified screeches that really hurt the ear drums, and it was nothing but a
chaotic confusion of noise. You couldn't even make out any distinction or
hesitation between the notes. I wouldn't call it beautiful and I don't know what
I'd call it. It's different. And I'm sure the audience readily would agree with me.**

**And, like we seldom got any applause, maybe one or two claps here and
there and when the audience walked out they just walked out struck in a daze and
a trance because they were just so shocked and amazed they didn't know what to
think. They didn't know whether they were being put on or being put out or being
put in or whatever you want to call it.**

**I must say the band did quite well without Lou Reed and Nico in Chicago,
and they created their own little variations on "Heroin" and "Waiting For the
Man" and "Venus in Furs". Well, some of their sounds I must say, like that . . .
those last two real, real fast songs are sort of like, I wouldn't call them music
Louis, I just call them noise. I hope I . . . did I hurt your feelings on that? Well is it
supposed to be that, I mean are you doing that intentionally?**

REED: (indistinct)

INGRID: You know, making all those noises and feedbacks and everything.

REED: (indistinct)

**INGRID; Well, it's something different to everybody. Everybody has their own
opinion, but most of the people I've talked to at the shows, you know, I've asked
them what do you think of the show, what did you think of the music? And they
just scratched their heads, shook their heads and . . . in awe . . . and shock, and
said I don't know I can't describe it, it's just different psychedelic music. It's
associated to sort of like a very intensified LSD trip.**

REED: (indistinct)

**INGRID: Oh, well, it is. A lot of people have told me that it does sound like that.
It's very fast and speeded up and intensified and hypertensial and hyper-
sensitive . . .**

REED: (indistinct)

**INGRID: I think those last two songs are very psychedelic. The other songs they
all tell a story, like "Venus in Furs", and "Waiting For the Man", and "Cast**

Your Troubles and Dreams Away", to which I often get misty. And one thing I must say, Louis is a very good songwriter. Like when we were in Chicago, we gave a reading, Gerard, me and Angus MacLise, who was like their fill-in drummer, and John Cale. And when John Cale read off "Venus in Furs", "Heroin" and "Wrap Your Troubles in Dreams", which is a very, very sentimental song. Well, Nico usually sings that song. And she usually sings it sitting down, while Louis has one leg perched up on a chair playing the guitar. And there are low lights, well there's hardly any lights, and like there's a big spotlight projected on Louis and Nico.

REED: (indistinct)

John Cale asleep at The Factory.
(Nat Finkelstein)

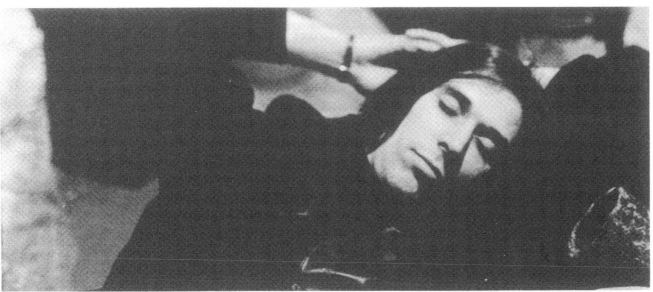

THE DEATH OF DELMORE SCHWARTZ

Delmore Schwartz in Washington Square
Park, 1961.
(Rollie McKenna)

In July Delmore Schwartz died in New York. Gerard took Lou to the open casket wake held at Sigmund Schwartz Funeral Home, 152 Second Avenue. They arrived in the middle of a eulogy being delivered by Dwight MacDonald. A few heads turned, including that of M.L. Rosenthal, upon their stumbling in and finding places to sit in the rear of the room. Gerard wore a black tie for the occasion, although they were both wearing black denim jeans. Lou was silent throughout the entire series of eulogies and prayers. Upon departing a former female classmate and student of Schwartz recognized Lou in the crowd and hustled him into one of the limos and off they went to the burial service, leaving Gerard to return to the Factory. At the end of July Bob Dylan had a motorcycle accident in Woodstock and broke his neck.

MORRISON: Dylan was always lurking around, giving Nico songs. There was one film Andy made with Paul Caruso called "The Bob Dylan Story". I don't think Andy has ever shown it. It was hysterical. They got Marlowe Dupont to play Al Grossman. Paul Caruso not only looks like Bob Dylan but as a super caricature he makes even Hendrix look pale by comparison. This was around 1966 when the film was made and his hair was way out here. When he was walking down the street you had to step out of his way. On the eve of the filming, Paul had a change of heart and got his hair cut off – close to his head – and he must have removed about a foot so everyone was upset about that. Then Dylan had his accident and that was why the film was never shown.

By August the album was ready and we all went crazy wondering what was happening with the tapes. Some recordings got lost. I know that Zappa and his manager wanted to be first with their release on Verve. And we were totally naive. We didn't have a manager who would go to the record company every day and just drag the whole thing through the mud.

● UP-TIGHT IN PROVINCETOWN

● At the beginning of September The E.P.I. entourage travelled to Provincetown, Massa-
chusetts, where Steve Sesnick had arranged for them to play on two consecutive days at
Walter Chrysler's Chrysler Art Museum. Apart from Mo, John, Lou, Sterling, Paul, Andy,
Gerard, Ronnie, Mary and Faison, the troupe now also included Susan Bottomly (a/k/a
International Velvet) and her boyfriend, fashion illustrator David Croland, as well as Eric
Emerson, a dancer and actor Andy and Paul had discovered at the Dom, who began living
with Nico in Provincetown. These excerpts from the previously unpublished *Secret Diaries of
Gerard Malanga* serve to illustrate the atmosphere within which The E.P.I. was working.

2 September 1966, Provincetown, Mass.

*Everyone is uptight for amphetamine. It's great to see everybody frantic when you can work on your
own juice and not have to think about where the next source of supply is going to come. We're all
waiting in front of the museum to go to the beach.*

Nico with Ari, her son by Alain Delon.
(Stephen Shore)

3 September 1966.

Early in the evening we did three shows at the Chrysler Art Museum. We wore mod fashions, got free flower print shirts. I adjusted the strobes to reflect on the body of a girl wearing a bikini. I inquire about her. Elena. She lives three quarters of the year at Florida, and spends her summers at Provincetown. I made it with her last night . . . 15 people stayed overnight. Wall to wall mattresses. I was just handed a letter Mary (Woronov) wrote to me when I was at Chicago three months ago. The letter traveled thousands of miles, passed through many hands and came to me still sealed. Got into an argument with Andy that was triggered by the accusation made that I didn't clean up the dirty dishes, when in fact I hadn't made anything for myself to eat, nor was I anywhere near the house when the mess was made, nor was I aware of the fact that there was a mess. The friends gathered tonight in the small room. Andy was acting very peculiar and seemed quite comfortable and happy, which seems peculiar.

4 September 1966.

Lou went to bed with "X". This morning I made it with Elena under the sheets in the living room, and for the second time. I don't know whether George was uptight, but everybody who was awake must have known what we were doing. Eric is living with Nico and her son Ari. Eric resembles Ari as a big brother and people who see them walking on the street with Ari on Eric's shoulders probably think that Eric is Ari's father. Ronnie made a full-color magic-marker-and-ink portrait of me for my trip book. It's the first time I ever really paid any attention to Ronnie. Maybe it's because we're both very shy of one another. And I hope it will become a genuine relationship, although I'm never really certain of myself and my attitudes when it comes to getting involved with other people. Andy went to a small gathering with Nico and Paul. Andy told me earlier that he liked my trip book very much because of the way I record events and news of the day, which, in a sense, is a taking in or a review of the day's happenings. I don't remember what I wrote in my book earlier in the day and I hope I haven't said anything that would make Andy uptight.

George gets uptight because I tell him I'll be back in half an hour but I return a half hour late.

The last show of The Exploding Plastic Inevitable Eric proves to be a visual-physical freak-out; Susan refuses to dance on the panel board in front of the projectors. During the "Heroin" number in the last show I get on the dance floor to go thru my mime motions and Eric gets on my platform and his friends come on stage and start dancing around me. I begin to feel both internal and external suffocation and really wonder if I am not just hallucinating on my own circumstance which is unknown. Susan blocks the spotlight and Alan and Roger pick up the strobes and aim them not at me but at Susan. I'm in almost total darkness. Mary is also in total darkness, except for occasional sequences where I am able to aim my own flashlight on her or project one of the hand-strobes behind me. Andy seems oblivious to the situation and to my personal feelings. I wonder if he realizes that my status as a spotlight star in The Exploding Plastic Inevitable has been reduced considerably by the intrusion of too many people and the lighting assistants who can't follow directions. I think I'll write a letter to Andy for him to read, but I'll write it in my book.

Dear Andy:

It seems I'm always writing you letters to explain myself, my feelings, what's bothering me as you find it easy to say nothing, sometimes, when you know what you're thinking you shouldn't say or it is explained without words or without vibrations.

I thought the Provincetown show got off to a rough but very good start, until you were so kind enough as to let Susan and everyone else not directly connected with the show get involved with Mary and I on stage. Also, it was unfortunate that Mary had to be dancing above me and not with me.

I want to make it clear to you that (1) I was dancing with The Velvets long before you signed them into a corporation empire, and even before you knew them; (2) that my dancing is an integral part of the music and the show as is your movies; (3) I do not represent a 'go go' dancer in the show but an interpretative-visual happening. You are slowly taking this away from me by allowing outside elements to interfere with my dance routines. Also Larry was supposed to have the spotlight on me when not projected on The Velvets. Instead, that spotlight wandered away from what was supposed to be seen happening on stage.

On more than one occasion I found my flashlight missing and then discovered that Roger was dancing with it somewhere near the end of the show. On more than one occasion I also discovered other people handling the strobes which were inconveniently placed on the stage. All this led up to Mary and me dancing in total darkness, at times. The only way this can be rectified for future shows is not to have troupe dancing but two people at a time. I am willing to take turns. From my vantage point on stage to have more than two dancers the show becomes a Mothers of Invention freak-out. I feel that you will do nothing in your almost absolute power to correct the mess you are responsible for, in which case I will if you won't.

Faithfully,
Gerard

Lou Reed and Andy Warhol on the bus to Ann Arbor, March 1966.
(Nat Finkelstein)

Everybody was going out of their minds trying to find a place to stay and looking for amphetamine. The pale bodies of The E.P.I. dressed in silver and black leather didn't jell too well with the healthy tans of the Boston Irish natives. There was also some trouble in a leather store when the proprietor discovered a number of belts and whips missing which resulted in the police interrupting that night's performance and untying Eric from a post, where he was strapped in preparation for being whipped by Mary, so they could retrieve the stolen goods. There was trouble with the landlord when the toilets in the house Andy's entourage rented stopped up and they solved the problem by chucking handfuls of shit out the window. And there was trouble again when Eric Emerson stole a priceless work of art from the Museum just to see if he could get away with it. Paul Morrissey had to act as a liaison between Eric and the Museum, restoring the painting in order to avoid having charges pressed.

CUTRONE: Everybody was feeling very cocky and they didn't like anybody. The general attitude was fuck you which was very punk but nobody knew what punk was. The Velvets hated everything. The whole idea was to take a stab at everything. Before The Velvet Underground almost without exception all groups came out and said, 'Hey, we're gonna have a good time, let's get involved!', faced the audience, said, 'This is a time of love, peace, happiness and sexual liberation and we're gonna have a great wonderful time'. The Velvets on the other hand came out and turned their backs to the audience. I remember one review said this is musical masturbation. Who do they think they are? They're jerking off on stage.

Now, many years later we found out with the revolution of punk, new wave and permanent wave this was accurate. They were that far ahead of their time. And to some extent that couldn't capture the entire nation. For the performances they wore all black. Everybody was wearing like balloon-sleeve Tom Jones shirts, necklaces, high boots. The Velvets were into amphetamine. They wore total black, white face. They were totally electric, extremely loud. They got run out of Provincetown on a rail.

● THE BALLOON FARM

● They had played Chicago with different personnel. In Provincetown new personnel seem to have caused some tension, at least in the dancing department. Tension was beginning to build overall as the terrific impetus The Velvet Underground had picked up from their collaboration with Warhol began to wane. Release of the record was delayed. They went back to pick up the threads at the Dom and found that the owners had reneged on their agreement and rented it to Al Grossman and Oliver Coquelin instead.

MORRISSEY: While we were gone Charlie Rothchild had arranged for the lease to be picked up from the owners of the Polish National Home by Mr Grossman and Mr Grossman then had the lease and after the summer opened it the same way that we had, only called it the Balloon Farm, and then Rothchild had the nerve – because we had nowhere else to go and The Velvets weren't making any money – to say, 'Would The Velvets like to open the Balloon Farm, Mr Grossman's club?' And since they had nowhere else to play, they went back to this thing called the Balloon Farm.

Sterling Morrison, Maureen Tucker, Lou Reed and John Cale at The Castle, Hollywood Hills, L.A., Spring 1966.
(Malanga Archive)

Paul Morrissey
(Malanga Archive)

The organization cried out for a hard-headed businessman who could have gotten down there in the mud with rock & roll executives and sorted out a good deal. But in those days so much was happening so fast, and everybody was so purely and intensely interested in what they were *doing*, nobody was interested in spending all their time doing business! Steve Sesnick kept importuning them to allow him to manage the group, but The Velvets were devoted to Andy Warhol and could not see, with the hindsight we have now, that the collaboration had really achieved all it had set out to.

INTERVIEWER: Do you see yourself as a creator, or more as a magnet who attracts other talents?

WARHOL: More like a pencil sharpener.

Richard Goldstein described an E.P.I. performance at the Balloon Farm in the *New York World Journal Tribune* that October:

On one huge screen, a lady who turns out to be a man is eating a ripe banana, her head encased in a snow white bonnet. On another screen a smiling man is eating peanuts – cracking the shells, gnawing the insides, spitting out the husks. And on the center screen, they have tied someone to a chair and are putting cigarettes out in his nose, winding belts around his neck and fitting a tight leather mask onto his face.

That film is called "Vinyl". Its creator, one Andrew Warhol, is sitting quietly in the balcony which overhands the dance floor. He is working the projector, pensive and quiet in his black-chino-polo-shirt-leather-jacket outfit. Mirror sunglasses make his eyes totally inaccessible. His hair is straight, bright silver.

'Hi,' he says. 'You have come to ask about the films. The one on the left, he says, is "Harlot". On the right is "Eat", with Henry Geldzahler as the peanut man. On the big screen is "Vinyl".'

He turns back to the projector, his fingers busily shuffling tins of film. He makes a pillow of his arms. He cushions his head. Onstage, poet Gerard Malanga is dancing with a swaying girl. He grabs a roll of phosphorescent tape and wraps it around his partner and himself. Handed a whip, he snaps it against the stage. As a finale, he smothers his body in yellow paint and grabs a purple spotlight, which makes him glow and deepens the shadow around his eyes and teeth. Bad trip makeup. He untangles two blinking strobe lights and swings them around his hips, sending violent, stabbing rays into the audience.

The third thing the Balloon Farm has going for it is light. Definitely light. An 'electrician' in black earmuffs works one spotlight from the stage, shifting color and design. Bulbs blink patterns onto the ceiling and the mirrored walls. Colored sparks twinkle ominously and those two portable strobe lights make the entire room sway in slow motion. It is all very much like sitting stoned in the middle of a tinseled Christmas Tree.

Which brings us to The Velvet Underground, Andy's group. Sometimes they sing, sometimes they stroke their instruments into a single one-hour number.

Andy Warhol says he is through with phosphorescent flowers and cryptic soup cans. Now it is all rock & roll. Andy may finally conquer the world through its soft teenage underbelly.

'It's ugly,' he says. 'It's a very ugly effect, when you put it all together. But it's beautiful. You know, you just look at the whole thing – The Velvets playing, and Gerard dancing, and all the film and light, and it's a beautiful thing. Very vinyl. Beautiful.'

'Beautiful. There are beautiful sounds in rock & roll. Very lazy, dreamlike noises. You can forget about the lyrics in most songs. Just take the noise and you've got our sound,' says John Cale. 'We're putting everything together – lights and film and music – and we're reducing it to its lowest common denominator. We're musical primitives.'

'Now it seems we have time to catch our breath,' says Sterling Morrison. 'We have more direction – that's where Andy comes in. We eat better, we work less, and we've found a new medium for our music. It's one thing to hustle around for odd jobs. But now we're not just another band. We're an act. When a band becomes an act, you get billing, you get days off. You don't work anymore – you're engaged.'

Nightly at the Balloon Farm, The Velvet Underground illustrates what distinguishes an act from a band. Blonde-haired Nico bellows flaxen sexiness into an electric harmonica while Andy projects her image on the split screens which surround the stage. All traces of melody depart early in the song. The music courses into staccato beats and then slows into syrupy feedback refrains. All this goes on until everyone is satisfied that the point has got across.

No one at the Balloon Farm seems anxious to comment on the relation of the drug experience to the creation of the new music. Sterling says, 'The whole thing is probably easier to understand under LSD because you lose your inhibitions. You stop thinking of this as a series of lights and movies and music and you start seeing it as one abstract whole. The whole thing is twice as heady when you can really let yourself go, but I'm not sure you have to use LSD to let yourself go.'

Lou is more frenetic. 'The whole LSD scene on campus is foreign to our sound. The universities

John Cale and Lou Reed rehearsing at The Factory.
(Stephen Shore)

are dead; the live music is coming out of people like us. And it's not because we're on the Lower East Side, and it's not because of junk. It's because we're us."

John Cale, who sits dreamily eyeing a glass of Coca Cola, pushes his hair back from his face exposing a bony nose, and says, 'You can't pin it down. It's a conglomeration of the senses. What we try to get here is a sense of total involvement. Maybe the hip scene is drugs and discotheques but that doesn't go for the music. Coming here on a trip is bound to make a fantastic difference, but we're here to stimulate a different kind of intoxication. The sounds, the visual stuff – all the bombarding of the senses – it can be very heady by itself. If you're geared to it. No one understands about Andy. It's a totally non-ego thing with him. People say we look like marionettes standing up on that stage surrounded by all those lights and Andy's movies. But it's not true. Maybe Andy has given us a sense of direction, but the sound, the words I mean, the whole scene – that's pure us.'

Now The Velvet Underground is popping eardrums and brandishing horsewhips with the expertise of pros. Their new single on Verve-Folkways is a rather restrained performance (All Tomorrow's Parties/I'll Be Your Mirror) in the vein of English groups like The Yardbirds and The Who, but is still the sound. And the boys are brimming with the glow of innovation.

'We want to try attaching two guitars and playing them as a single instrument,' says John. 'We're working on an electronic drum which would produce sub-sonic sounds. That is, you can feel it but can't hear it. We'd be able to add it to a piece of music and it'd be like underlining the beat.'

Onstage, Gerard Malanga motions wildly; they have run out of records. John drains his glass and puts a black corduroy jacket over his black turtleneck. He slides his hair over his face, covering his nose again. Lou tucks his shirt in.

'Young people know where everything is at,' he says. 'Let them sing about going steady on the radio. Let the campus types run hootenannies. But it's in holes like this – places on the West Coast without cover charges – that the real stuff is being born. The University and the radio kill everything, but around here, it's alive. The kids know that.'

On the floor, everything stops in anticipation. The electrician flips the switches and turns knobs. The stage throbs under a carpet of tangled wires. Gerard plays with a pile of limp fluorescent tape. The group walks onstage – all four of them – together, live, and the projector begins to whirr.

With a single humming chord, which seems to hang in the air, the group launches into a set. John squints against a purple spotlight. Lou shouts against a groaning amplifier. Gerard writhes languidly to one side. Sterling turns his head to sneeze. The noise, the lights, the flickering images –

happen. Everybody listens.

And from the balcony, Andy Warhol watches it all. 'Beautiful,' he says. Sterling sneezes audibly, but it all seems to fit in. 'Beautiful,' Gerard hands his partner a bullwhip. 'Just beautiful.'

It was not 'beautiful' for the band. Morrison says they found it 'repellent' and quit shortly after this account.

MORRISON: What we found 'repellent' was not the 'show', but rather the fact that we were back in what we considered to be 'our' ballroom, and even worse, were working for the very people who had taken it from us. Given a choice between working for them or nothing, we chose nothing. Like so many other decisions, flukes, or whatever in our history, one can hardly speculate about the course of events had this incident not occurred. Perhaps we would have sold the lease and become real estate tycoon/slumlords.

Morrissey says that his perception was that The Velvets just didn't want to do anything anymore. They thought they would be famous as soon as their record came out and decided to wait until that happened.

MORRISSEY: With The Velvets not wanting to play, the guy who had the downstairs-part of the Dom, Stanley, wanted to bring a white crowd to the bar and he thought the best way was if Nico would sing. Nobody from The Velvets would play guitar behind her, neither Lou or Sterling, anybody. Nico had to open. The 'gracious' Lou offered to play her guitar solos on a tape recorder and she had to sit there and push a tape recorder button and sing to a tape recorder, which was horrible, and that went on for a week or two. If Sterling filled in one night it was maybe only as a great favor and it would probably have gotten Lou mad. On the second or third week I said, 'Well, we need somebody else there beside Nico', and I hired Tim Buckley to play with her. Then it was Nico and Tim Buckley who was not known at all at the time, and he played his own guitar. Sitting in front of the bar every night was this little boy looking up at Tim Buckley. I spoke with him. His name was Jackson Browne and he said, 'I'm a fan of his. He's from Orange County. He's my hero. I came east just to see him. I follow his career.' He's 16-years old. He says, 'I write songs, I play the guitar.' I said, 'You play the guitar!?' Then I heard him play his songs and I thought his songs were great. And I said, 'You know, these songs are great. Nico should sing them but you play the guitar in the back of Nico.' He did, and then he learned the guitar parts for her other songs from The Velvets, and that was the first job he ever had and the first time his songs were performed for anybody I think. So he got up in back of the bar with Nico while Ari was running in front of the bar waiting for her to go home. And he played the guitar in back of her to get rid of this terrible tape recorder that she had been left with, which was so humiliating, and she sang those songs. Tom Wilson, who was great, thought Nico was wonderful and said he wanted to make an album with her too because she was getting a lot of publicity. And Jackson Browne played the guitar for most of the songs on that album, because he had been playing in back of her at the Dom and it was recorded with her and Jackson on the solo guitar and then Wilson went off and put all those other instruments which I think were great, behind it.

Meanwhile, as a taste of what was to mushroom out of what The E.P.I. had pioneered, Timothy Leary was conducting his Celebrations for the League of Spiritual Discovery (LSD) around the corner at the Village Theater that would later become the Fillmore East. Standing in front of films upon which he projected slides and working with various celebrity guests like Allen Ginsberg, Leary was doing his own Exploding Plastic Inevitable. In June Denis Deegan, catalyst extraordinaire, a friend of Warhol and Malanga's called from Paris with a series of concert bookings for The E.P.I. This offer was, however, never taken seriously by Andy, and the opportunity for the group to cross the Atlantic, which might have made a big difference in their future, was passed up.

Tom Wilson

● ON THE COUCH AT THE FACTORY NO.2

Lou Reed at The Factory
(Stephen Shore)

● (This tape was made by Nat Finkelstein of Lou Reed talking about his music at the Factory in the Fall of 1966.)

REED: All by myself. No one to talk to. This is very peculiar. Come over here so I can talk to you. It's very hard for me to sit here with a microphone like this. No, you just come over here so I'm talking to you, or go over there so I don't see you. One or the other.

We were playing together a long time ago, in a $30-a-month apartment and we really didn't have any money, and we used to eat oatmeal all day and all night and give blood to (indistinct) among other things, or pose for these nickel or 15c tabloids they have every week. And when I posed for them, my picture came out and it said I was a sex maniac killer that had killed 14 children and tape recorded it and played it in a barn in Kansas at midnight. And when John's picture came out in the paper, it said he had killed his lover because his lover was going to marry his sister, and he didn't want his sister to marry a fag.

Andy Warhol with the banana, Fall 1966.
(Billy Linich)

And then we decided that since we were playing all the time anyway, why not try to get paid for it, so we ended up at a terrible coffee house working six sets a night, seven nights a week, $5 a man a night, and that lasted a week-and-a-half and we were fired, because they hated our music so much.

And then we met Andy. And we're now able to play the kind of stuff we really like to play. Well we always have played the stuff we really like to play, but now we can play it and not get fired from terrible coffee houses. We've had so many ideas about things, we wanted to get lots of cheap Japanese guitars and string them and tune them all right and lots of amplifiers and they'd all be humming to different pitches and we can play against them.

Or we wanted to have 30 metronomes with contact mikes all over them, so when you walked in . . . you walk into a theater and there'd be no seats, everybody would be on the floor and Andy's silver balloons would be all over the place with his cows on the ceiling and on the walls and on the floor, and the metronomes would be going, electrified, and Mo would be playing a drum solo against it and Sterl and me and John would just be watching.

Then John had an idea about the electric eyes they have in supermarkets – when you walk through the electric eye it makes the door open. Well, if we had an electric eye that could change pitch, and was fed by solar energy, sunlight for instance, then if we played outdoors, depending on the weather conditions, and cloud formations and everything, that would determine the pitch. Music of the earth.

We want to play a recital hall because that's where rock and roll should be as opposed to serious music, by serious dead people. And that's really awful.

We've been trying to get Sterling to play the trumpet again, but he won't. He's too busy looking for a psychiatrist to get out of the army.

One of the nice things is working with Andy because he thinks the same way and let's anyone do whatever they want, which is always nice. One of the ideas he came up with, which was very beautiful, was that we should rehearse on stage, because the best music always takes place in rehearsals, so why not rehearse on stage, which was the best idea probably anyone had come up with.

But now everything's changing because we're getting more and more equipment and the ideas are just opening up so fast, so quickly, that the best thing is not to be able to play an instrument. We were thinking of taking Mo and blindfolding her and plugging her ears up, and then she'd be able to play along with us because you can never be out of rhythm. There's no such thing as being out of rhythm or being out of time. It's very nice playing. Especially with Andy's movies, 'cause our music's like Andy's movies and Andy's movies are like our music, and they just go together. For instance, Andy did a photograph of a banana for the album cover, and now I've just seen a blow-up of the banana and it's really gotten huge and enveloped all other types of significance as a banana. It's an extremely pretty sexy banana, and the album cover peels which is nice, to reveal the inside of a very sexy, groovy banana.

What we really would like is oh, if we had bagpipes or if we had a lot more violins and thousands of guitars and what we really want to do is build machines if we could get some money, we'd build machines, we never seem to have money because every time we do a show everyone says oh, this show has to be the most fantastic of all, and so we run out and get more projectors and more lights and more instruments and so the show is fantastic and we're broke, which has always been the way it is.

But it's nice making something pretty.

Some of the music we really like is records by The Eldorados or The Harpchords, all the really very nice old, old records. The El Chords, The Starlighters, "Valerie", Alicia and The Rockaways, Buster Brown, Bo Diddley.

Everyone's going crazy over the old blues people, but they're forgetting about all those groups, like The Spaniels, people like that. Records like "Smoke From Your Cigarette", and "I Need a Sunday Kind of Love", "The Wind" by The Chesters, "Later for You, Baby" by The Solitaires. All those really ferocious records that no one seems to listen to anymore are underneath everything we're playing. No one really knows that. But the records everyone's making now are just fabulous. Everything's fabulous. Everything's absolutely better than it's ever been. Because all the people are getting so beautiful. The young people are getting beautiful, and that's why very young people like music, because the music's very beautiful and if it scares people it's because the people are that way, and they're scared anyway. But our stuff's very pretty. The show is very pretty and Andy is very beautiful, because he lets it happen.

We're attacked constantly. No one ever writes anything nice about us, or even looks at it very seriously, which is fine. You get tired of being called obscene. It just seems to go on and on and on and on and on. We're going to use all the put-downs for the liner-notes on the album. Anyone who writes for a newspaper or something has to be sick. People who criticize other people. There must be a reason for it. They must have something else to do. Why don't they go do something with themselves. They think it's so easy.

Our favorite quote was 'the flowers of evil are in bloom. Someone has to stamp them out before they spread'.

What the music really has to do with is electricity. Electricity and different types of machines. One of the ideas we had was like, for instance, John would be playing one of his viola solos and we'd have two jack-cords coming out of the viola; in other words, he'd have two, three, four contact-mikes on the viola, put into two, three, four different amplifiers, and then Nico and me and Mo would

John Cale.
(Nat Finkelstein)

control each amplifier. One amplifier would be concerned with the bass and another amplifier would be concerned with volume, and another one ... or we could have a mixer, or we could have lots of mixers and what we would all be playing John is what it would amount to.

Or another version of it is if Mo, John and Sterl are playing and I play the amplifier. And we have a number that we did using that where John has a thunder machine, which is a fabulous instrument and the only kind in the entire world. It's in our apartment on West 3rd Street. Our new apartment. We're being evicted. And we were playing again today and for the second time a cop came up and threatened us, but he doesn't like the music and he told us to go into the country if we were going to play that way or be that way. He also stopped us at the door once and accused us of throwing human shit out the window. And what's worse is that we thought it was just possible.

We play in the dark so that the music's just there.

Andy had a great idea for "I'll Be Your Mirror" at the end. We would have the record fixed with a built-in crack so it would go "I'll be your mirror, I'll be your mirror, I'll be your mirror", so that it would never ever reject, it would just play and play until you came over and took the arm off.

Our music's for the pretty people, all the beautiful people. We're just starting, if we ever got any bread, to build some of the machines we'd like to build, there'd be no end to what's happening.

A lot of it just takes a little bit of money. John wanted to get car horns, go down to used car lots, or the car dump and just get car horns. Thousands and thousands of car horns and wire them, so they don't stop.

At the Fillmore Auditorium in San Francisco, we played one particularly good set. Towards the end of the set we did one of our instrumental numbers, we set all the instruments up, turned them on, had them running, so they were humming by themselves and we all played drums and as the instruments played themselves we finally left the stage and they played and played and played, and we told the other group, why don't you leave our machines on and you can play against them. But by then the manager of the theatre had gotten afraid, and because he was scared he turned all the machines off.

Anybody who made love to our music wouldn't necessarily need a partner. Andy mentioned that some of the records we're doing end up sounding so professional. No one wants it to sound professional. It's so much nicer to play into one very cheap mike. That's the way it sounds when you hear it live and that's the way it should sound on the record.

In the album we had out we wanted to have one professional record and one unprofessional record and then one backwards record. No beginning, no middle, no end. Angus's 'Crystal' tape was sent back from a record company for that reason; they said they couldn't differentiate between the beginning, the middle and the end. They missed it.

Sometimes we set our instruments up so that anyone can play them and it would be nice to manufacture a guitar that's just a book to tell people this instrument can be played, all you have to do is touch it. So that way the guitar has its particular sound. You touch it it makes its sound. People have their sound. If you touch them in the right spot they make it. Trees. Concrete, plastic. It's unfair of people to ask you to be concerned about them dropping dead in your room. You have to concentrate on your tape recordings. If you push them on high enough you can bow it like a string. And then eventually you don't need a bow.

John had a composition once which involved taking everybody out into the woods and having them follow the wind. As of late though we play indoors so we have to be the weather.

Lou Reed at The Factory, Fall 1966.
(Billy Linich)

Lou Reed at The Factory, Fall 1966.
(Billy Linich)

CRUSADING

MORRISON: We never did anything to ingratiate ourselves with the media, through lack of interest more than arrogance. I was convinced that if it was going to happen it would happen anyway. We were all really contemptuous of hype. Crusading was the word I always used. It took absolute conviction that we were doing the right thing – that was the only thing that could sustain us.

In the Fall of 1966 John and I got a place on E 10th street just east of First Avenue. Shortly thereafter, Lou got his place on E 10th just west of First Avenue, so the three of us were living about 50 yards apart. We would have lived together if we could have found a place large enough. We were hanging around together day and night.

From the end of October through the middle of December The E.P.I. played a number of dates in the Midwest, Canada and on the East Coast. The following extracts from *The Secret Diaries of Gerard Malanga* give a unique sense of life on the road with The E.P.I.

October 29, 1966.

Today Benedetta (Barzini, Malanga's love obsession at the time), Rona (Page, who starred in the Pope Ondine sequence of "Chelsea Girls") and Rene (Ricard, poet) and I are to go to Boston for an Exploding Plastic Inevitable show with The Velvet Underground and Nico and films by Andy. Also Andy has a show of his paintings in an adjoining exhibition room of the Boston Institute of Contemporary Arts. We reach Boston; we take our belongings and bags over to Gordon's (Baldwin, architectural artist) apartment. He gives us his bedroom to have for the night.

We rush over to the Contemporary Arts Institute just in time to prepare for the first show. In the meantime, the movies, including "Vinyl", are being projected and two spot-lights are aimed directly upon the revolving mirror-ball giving the entire auditorium a luminous revolving atmosphere. The movies end; The Velvets, one by one, walk onto the stage and prepare setting up and tuning their instruments. After about 15-minutes into their first number I walk on the stage and begin my interpretative dancing to the electronic sounds being projected out into the audience. Rona and Ronnie (Cutrone) join me on stage for the last long number. I interpret an entire Crucifixion scene with Rona standing behind me, arms outstretched with two flashlights in each hand, aiming their beams through my outstretched arms, at the audience.

BOSTON October 30, 1966.

We were to do a show this evening in a small town outside of Boston. The first show was in the late afternoon. Benedetta became extremely nervous and said she couldn't stay for the second show and that she had to get back to New York. I decided it would be foolish of me to stay behind with Andy and The Velvets and instead decided, along with Rene and John (Wieners, poet), to go to New York with Benedetta. We immediately left after the end of the first show. Andy was quite annoyed with me, but even more annoyed with Benedetta for acting as an unconscious influence.

MORRISON: The show took place in a converted airplane hangar in Leicester, Mass. The promoter was John Sdoucos from Boston and he had assembled an audience of young teenies to see us. I remember looking at them sadly and thinking that they were too young and innocent to be exposed to our music. I didn't think there was any reason why they should like it and I hoped they wouldn't. I needn't have worried. They didn't.

October 31, 1966.

I tell Benedetta that everyone, including Andy, The Velvets and Paul feel that I am the most replaceable in the show because of my abrupt departure last Sunday before the last show. The Velvets and Andy don't realize that I am the irreplaceable part of the show because no other dancer could interpret The Velvets' music as well as build up a concrete structure of dance around their music and the light show, and interpret their music into choreographic arrangements the way I could. No one will be dancing with me on stage. Last week The Velvets tried to dump Nico. This week they're trying to dump me. John Cale blackmailed Paul into giving him money at the airport before going to Chicago last June. He admitted his guilt jokingly one night last week in front of Paul and me when going to Paul's apartment to sleep. Faison carelessly neglected to bring the strobelights to Boston. He also held up the show. Andy didn't tell me, when I spoke to him on Sunday at approximately 1:20, that there would be a 3:00pm show that same afternoon at Leicester.

The changes that would lead to the end of this group-collaboration continued. The Velvets no longer rehearsed at the Factory, although they all continued to drop by and never really stopped.

At the beginning of November they went out on the road for a brief tour of Ohio.

November 2, 1966.
This is my last night in New York with Benedetta before leaving for my round-the-states tour of Ohio with The Exploding Plastic Inevitable.

L-R: Lou Reed, Sterling Morrison, Nico, Maureen Tucker and John Cale rehearsing at The Factory, Fall 1966.
(Stephen Shore)

November 3, 1966:
I meet The Velvets and Nico and Paul at the Factory (Andy didn't go on this tour again, because he wasn't needed.) We ride out to the airport to catch a jet to Cincinnati, our first stop on the tour.

NEW YORK-CINCINNATI:
The Velvet Underground, Nico, Paul and I are at Cincinnati. My head is about to burst from all the amphetamine I took before boarding the jet in New York.

November 4, 1966:
Last night The Velvets quit playing and wouldn't let Nico sing. John and Lou have yellow eyes and might end up in the hospital. Nico has plans to leave the group. Paul suggests it wouldn't be a bad idea if I leave the group, also. Nico doesn't know if she wants to sing with the group.

November 5, 1966:
Today Paul, Nico and I took pictures in the Columbus, Ohio bus terminal. We're on our way to Wheeling, West Virginia to do a concert for $900.00 at the University of West Virginia. On the bus from Columbus to Wheeling, Nico is sitting beside me. I look at her and remember at one time we had an intense relationship which has developed into a lifelong friendship.

November 6, 1966:
Sitting with Paul in the front part of the bus. Left Pittsburgh one hour ago. On the last leg of our tour to Cleveland with hope that we can board Flight No. 146 to New York without any hassles. Lou Reed's sister Elizabeth, who was a student, showed up at the Cleveland gig. She immediately reminded me of Suzanne Pleshette.

MORRISON: I don't remember seeing Lou's sister at this time, but met her later at one of the La Cave dates. Lou obviously liked his sister, and was very protective of her. This was a weakness that John and I could not help but exploit for our amusement. The technique by then had been well established, each of us being impervious to direct abuse from any of the others. What you had to do was get at them through people they cared about in their 'personal' lives, by rudeness, slander, or whatever. So when Lou walked into the dressing room and announced that his sister was going to drop in, and would we please try to act like humans, John and I leaped at the chance to make merry at his expense. We began with

speculation about his sister's maidenly virtue, or lack thereof, and conjured up lurid visions of her secret life as a coed. Horrified, Lou expressed strong displeasure with this conversation. John and I pressed on happily, delighted with Lou's response, each of us offering to pay the other $100 if he could seduce this unseen sister, with the amount to double if she turned out to be ugly. Lou was almost speechless, but did manage a few phrases of profound loathing as John and I laughed and laughed.

Later Lou's sister did drop in for a moment, and seemed pleasant enough.

12:45 a.m. November 7, 1966:

John, Nico, Paul and myself are on board United Flight #146 en route to Newark Airport, making one stop at Philadelphia. We are above the clouds. I see only darkness outside my window. The lights inside the cabin of the jet have not been turned off. I wish they would be, so I could get some sleep. I feel like I'm up on the amphetamine I took yesterday with the coffee I drank.

By the time they went to Hamilton, Ontario in Canada, November 12th, 1966 even an art magazine was billing them as The Velvet Underground and putting Andy Warhol's Exploding Plastic Inevitable in small letters, although Barry Lord writing for *Arts/canada* still saw The E.P.I. as a visionary Warhol work: 'His interest in the reputation of an image screened at different values of detail and intensity led naturally to the newspaper photograph, and thereby to the motion picture: the successive frames of a film are a vertical correlate of the still photo reproduced with varying screens, and a Warhol film, like the one of the Empire State Building with its lights going on and off over a period of many hours, is a logical extension of works like the Jackie Kennedy series, where the uneven screen sets up a comparable play of light values on an immediately recognizable image.

'These characteristics – significant distortion of the image, interest in the visual and psychological results of its repetition, collaboration with others, the maintenance of a single environmental effect through experienced time, and a concern with mechanically produced light effects – are evident in Warhol's latest work, The Exploding Plastic Inevitable. The inevitable is neither painting, nor sculpture, nor cinema; it cannot be called a happening, since it recurs at regular intervals on schedule. Nor is it an environment limited to one place, as McMaster University in Hamilton proved by inviting it up to open an arts festival in November.

'On a wide screen behind the stage, Vinyl, a film by Gerard Malanga, Warhol's foreman in his New York art factory, was projected from two machines: to the right, the first part of the film, in which Malanga dances, exercises, sits watching a man and a girl, and finally becomes aggressive; to the left, shown in the same time period, the second part, in which Malanga is beaten, stripped to the waist, and bound to a chair with his head encased in a black vinyl hood covered with metal studs. The same persons remain or re-appear in both halves, so that we are watching two images similar in general character, but significantly different in specific detail – a cinematic equivalent to the repeated faces of Marilyn and Liz in Warhol's screened paintings of several years ago. The loudspeakers provided sound, the film dialogue purposely distorted on one track, and on the other the recorded sound of The Velvet Underground, the group which Warhol chose to play with The Inevitable.

'Gerard Malanga, Warhol's art foreman and film-maker, is also the group's dancer. Before a constantly flickering battery of strobe lights, Malanga uses a variety of props – a Marlon Brando shirt, a variety of sashes and ropes, and spoon and gear for a 'fix' in the set piece Heroin. Sometimes he used the strobes directly, sometimes a candle – suggesting again the Warhol interest in light values. The final half-hour song created an environment in time as well as place, so that it began to seem to at least some of the McMaster audience as if life had always been this way. To others, it had been a confusing, noisy, probably frightening experience, and when the lights went up it was found that a good number had left. The ones who stayed had been a little more than an audience; like the newspaper photographs and Brillo boxes that Andy formerly used, they had become part of a Warhol art work.'

Returning from this job in Hamilton, Ontario, outside Toronto, it was discovered that Nico had purposely left her German passport, which had expired, in New York because she didn't want anyone to discover her birth-date. Consequently she had to be smuggled back into the States through a minor border checkpoint. Her vanity almost caused her to be detained in Canada.

The troupe played a pop wedding at which Andy gave the bride away to the tune of The Velvets doing "Here Comes the Bride", then moved on to their most pop-oriented show so far, The Detroit Music Festival hosted by Dick Clark at which they played on the same bill with The Yardbirds. Everybody was very up-tight. Jeff Beck was carrying a gun in his guitar case.

Empire State Building, 1965.
(Andy Warhol)

● DESPITE ALL THE AMPUTATIONS (1967-1970)
The Velvet Underground Story

RONNIE CUTRONE: You couldn't blow your cool ever. You were not allowed to be a human being even. Everything worked through guilt and paranoia.

● THE BANANA YEAR

Nico had always been a problem. She wanted to sing all the songs. What was she supposed to do when she wasn't singing? Looked at from today it seems just right – the tall, thin hauntingly beautiful blonde in a white suit standing in front of four thin guys (it took people some time to catch on that Maureen was a . . .chick) in black wearing sunglasses – but then, Nico was uptight. She didn't have anything to do. She felt uncomfortable just standing there. Why couldn't she sing more songs? Nico was always very unhappy. Everybody was uptight. Lou was always jealous of her. It all came to a head one day when he stormed into the Factory screaming, 'So she photographs great in high contrast black and white, I'm not playing with her anymore!' The record's release had been delayed. A special machine had to be made to make the original cover, on which the banana peeled. Zappa's Mothers of Invention "Freak Out" record had already been released. Nico was still playing downstairs in the small bar called Stanley's. She stood behind the bar backed by an acoustic guitar. Sterling says that he, John and Lou took turns as did Rambling Jack Elliott, Tim Hardin (who Paul called 'Tim Heroin'), Tim Buckley, and Jackson Browne, who was living with Nico on Columbus Avenue at 81st Street. They still ran the films behind her. Paul Morrissey was pushing Nico's solo career. The press continued to pay attention to the "Andy Warhol Superstar". Paul was always trying to persuade Nico to stop taking drugs. Among other personalities on the scene an earnest Leonard Cohen attended her every performance, and later made use of some of her techniques on his own recordings.

By the time *The Velvet Underground and Nico Produced by Andy Warhol* (which is how the first album is represented) was released in March, 1967, The E.P.I. was naturally dissolving.

BOCKRIS: How were you feeling when the record came out?

TUCKER: I was very excited. I ran out to the store and bought one.

BOCKRIS: Didn't they give you a copy?

TUCKER: Oh yeah, but I wanted to buy one. Finding it in stores was nice, but that didn't last long because MGM fucked up. They didn't really distribute it at all. But I was very excited, and Sterling was too, as I recall, and I'm sure John and Lou were thrilled.

MORRISON: I was never more excited about anything, and used to call up Cashbox to find out our chart position before the magazine hit the stands. I couldn't wait to know.

BOCKRIS: What were you doing in March?

TUCKER: I lived on Long Island during the group's days, so I didn't really hang out much, because they were all in the city. I don't think Sterling and Lou did that much socializing really. They might meet at Max's by chance, but they didn't hang out together that much.

MORRISON: We lived close by, and were together most of the time. We went to Max's every night that we were in town. That's where our friends were.

MORRISSEY: As soon as the record came out The Velvets didn't want to work anymore. They thought they became very famous when their album was finally released. I think they just wanted to separate from Andy, although we went on tour with them all over the country! I forget who booked that tour but God Almighty I could never forget that gruelling ordeal on the buses. We were going on buses! We got all these bookings.

Andy Warhol and Lou Reed
(Malanga Archive)

The success of "Chelsea Girls", which was now showing in a major theater in New York, had drawn Andy and Paul into the movie business. During '66 they had spent little time filming anything except "Chelsea Girls", focusing the majority of their time on The E.P.I. Now as Andy began the incessant filming that was to lead to the 24-hour movie released at the end of '67, the focus of his attention was shifting. In essence they had done everything they could with the rock and roll genre – in the space of one year isolated and frozen for inspection several groundbreaking ideas – and they could see that any further collaboration was not going to lead to anything different.

MORRISON: Antonioni wanted to use us as the band in the rock club sequence in "Blow-up", and we were more than willing. However, the expense of bringing the whole entourage to England proved too much for him. The sequence was one of the last things to be shot in the film, and he was running low on funds. So he used The Yardbirds doing a Who impersonation.

MALANGA: Are you surprised by the longevity of The Velvets now?

MORRISSEY: I am in a way, but I do think it was good music, it was a good album, it was different, it was unusual. I think most of the songs were really good. They certainly were an innovation, but you know we went on tour with them, I was a manager of the goddamn thing for almost a year or more and I remember, because they never released the album, but once the album came out I think that's when they wanted to go off and be themselves, and not have any revenue go back to Andy and me, and they didn't want to do anything. They said they didn't want to work and suddenly the whole thing was over. The album didn't take off or anything right away.

BOCKRIS: What was Andy's take on working with The Velvets?

CUTRONE: It was great for Andy because he got a totally captive audience to watch such films as "Eat" and "Sleep", whereas before the general public would see it as a curio, last twenty minutes into the film and split, or sit it out just to be cool. Now here was a way to display his films – the boring ones are great classics but they're still boring – and have an audience totally captive watching a man eat an apple in a rocking chair. That was a giant breakthrough.

BOCKRIS: Was their career largely based on intuition?

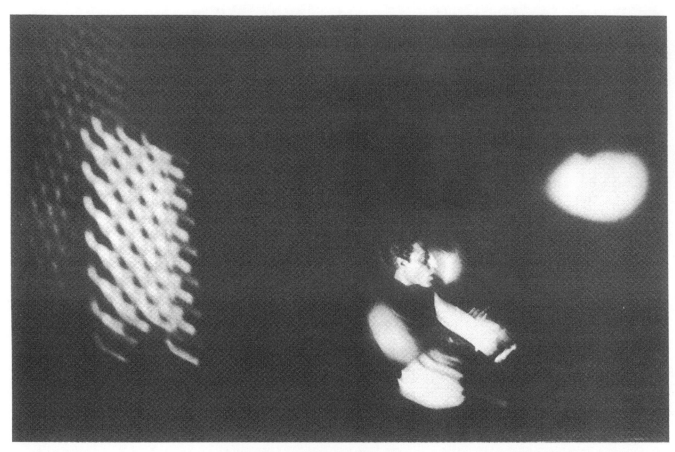

Lou Reed at Rhode Island School of Design,
Providence R.I., March 1967.
(Bill Carner)

CUTRONE: I think it was largely as unspoken as possible, because you have to remember that being cool then was really important. And you couldn't blow your cool ever. You were not allowed to be a human being even. Everything worked through guilt and paranoia and through what feels best and what looks best that night. It was pretty much surface. I mean, however deep and intense the music was. One of Andy's famous quotes from that period is, 'Your worst reviews are your best reviews.' So, from the I-will-not-budge-an-inch attitude, their bad reviews were the kind of publicity that set The Velvets apart from anybody else. From a dollars-and-cents point of view that was not too cool. That was just like, you know, 'Uh, uh, we hope we make some money here too.' So there were mixed feelings about the critical reactions. The Velvets always got put down but instantly other groups started recognizing that art sometimes goes with music and they could really cash in on captivating an audience in that particular way and giving them not only music but visuals, and then it just took off.

MALANGA: There was always a problem between Lou and John ultimately when it came to who was the leader of the group.

MORRISSEY: Well, you know, I don't think so. I think John idolized Lou. And he thought anything Lou said was wonderful and Lou knew. And when Lou was against Nico, John was a thousand times against Nico 100%. In the end Andy's connection with The Velvet Underground, like anything that happens to Andy, just made a gold-mine of good fortune for him and he became identified with rock and roll and the young generation. So, in a way, it was the best thing that ever happened to Andy to connect with a group that became that well-known. So, in a way, it was a very good thing that happened to him. But I did it hoping to make some money. Do you remember we went to a place in Detroit with Dick Clark and they gave us a check, it was a two-party check, and I never could collect the two-thousand five-hundred dollars, because it had only one signature on it? Oh, it was all so awful, that life. I always felt sorry for rock and rollers afterwards – what a horrible life they lead running around to these horrible things. But we worked with The Velvets from the beginning for pure commercial reasons.

It is one of the paradoxes of Warhol's career that he is constantly criticized for being too much of a business man to be an artist, and that his major motivation is money. After doing great innovative work in a field, he often immediately left it for others to reap the sometimes great financial benefits. This was particularly true in his film work (i.e., "My Hustler" in terms of its influence on John Schlesinger's very successful "Midnight Cowboy"). Warhol's films deserve the highest praise for doing the ultimate in art – making people see life differently, as it really is. His work during 1966 in rock, where he literally created the light show and developed the whole multimedia dimension that was gobbled up by every conceivable rock entrepreneur, is still hardly credited in the plethora of rock histories that have been published.

The Velvets had made a great record, and were at the vortex of the most creative scene in New York when it came out, but they were not feeling as great as we might imagine. MGM was trying to do something new with its Verve label by bringing out some freaky records, but everybody got uptight when it was noticed that The Mothers of Invention's *Freak Out* album was getting all the publicity. MGM either didn't understand The Velvets, or were censoring their subject matter and sound. It's also true, however, that Zappa had a rock and roll manager Herb Cohen, who was experienced at working with music industry executives, whereas Warhol and Morrissey were not. The group sorely needed some business muscle in the music industry which is where they were getting ignored. While The E.P.I. had a good electrican who knew how to work a fuse-box, a good roadie, good projectionists, good dancers, good photographers, great musicians and fabulous art directors, The Velvet Underground didn't have anyone who really just wanted to be a good business person for them, which is probably the major factor in the faltering momentum of The E.P.I./Velvet Underground that became apparent. But then again, even if they had been able to get the gritty business together, they'd really done what they set out to do.

In the face of this total lack of support from their record label The E.P.I. once again joined forces and played Rhode Island School of Design. April 11th they returned to the scene of their first real triumph, the University of Michigan in Ann Arbor, where they played for the Architecture School. At a party after the show a young man called Jim Osterburg, a/k/a Iggy Pop, caught his first glimpse of The Velvets, Andy and Nico who was playing with them again.

Edie Sedgwick in "Beauty No. 2" by Andy Warhol at Rhode Island School of Design, Providence, R.I., March 1967.
(Ronn Spencer)

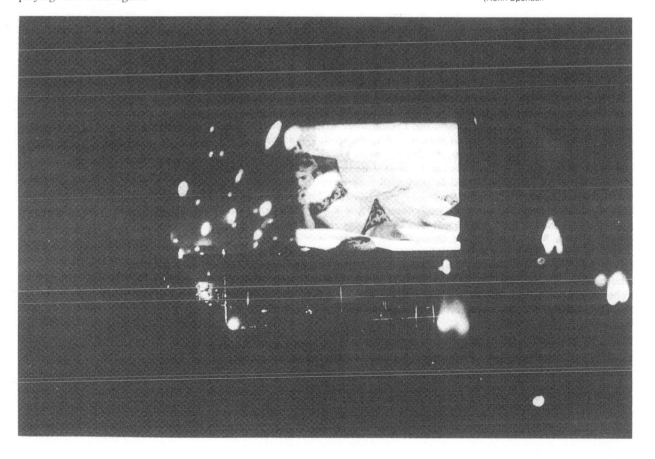

    In April, the son of the Dom's Polish owner approached Andy with an idea for a new club in New York. Originally a Czechoslovakian health and social club in the East 70s, it was called the Gymnasium. The idea was to leave all the gym equipment for the guests to play on. The E.P.I. played there and tried to resuscitate the atmosphere they had created the previous April at the Dom, but they couldn't get an exclusive lease on the place and the location was poor.

CHRIS STEIN: Everything picked up when "Sgt Pepper" came out in 1967. I used to play out in Brooklyn with my friends' bands. It was just an ongoing thing, it wasn't career oriented, it was just communication. Everybody was always on the periphery of the art scene and I had this friend who was a cute little boy with super long blonde hair who was a gofor for Andy at the Factory. One night he said, "Listen, I can get you guys a gig opening for The Velvet Underground at the Gymnasium". I had never seen The Velvet Underground but we had the Banana album and everybody knew who they were, so we said, 'Oh fantastic!' The night of the gig we got on the subway with our instruments and we were totally hippied out. We had balloons and a couple of girlfriends and everybody was dressed in beads and feathers. It was like a be-in on the subway floating towards Manhattan. We were ready to go, although we had previously only played in the living room or the basement.

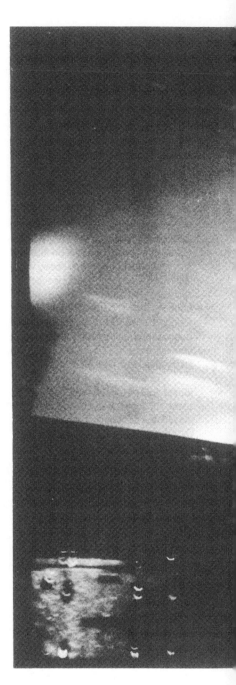

    It was pretty late at night by the time we got out of the subway in Manhattan and headed toward the Gymnasium. Walking down the block with our guitars we actually saw some people coming down the street and they said, 'Oh, are you guys the band, because we've been waiting there all night and we couldn't take it anymore, we left because they never showed up.' So we said, 'Yeah, we're the band.' We went inside and there was hardly anyone there. Somebody said Andy was supposed to be there, but he was off in the shadows with his entourage, we never saw him. We hung around for a little while and they played records, then we headed up for the stage. It was a big echoey place, we had absolutely no conception of playing a place like this whatsoever, but Maureen Tucker said we could use their equipment. So we plugged into their amps and the amps were all cranked up superloud. All Maureen had was a bass drum and a snare drum, but they were both turned on their side so the drummer was completely thrown off, but she said, 'Well, it's okay, you can put them right side up,' and somehow they produced a bass pedal from somewhere. Then we tried to play, but we were totally floored because we couldn't play in this huge resounding echo. It was a giant gymnasium with basketball hoops and everything was echoing so we couldn't really handle that, but we hacked our way through our little blues songs and people sort of watched us at first and then some of them tried to dance. The only song I remember doing was "You Can't Judge A Book By Its Cover". We must have done a few more, but I remember sitting down after a while because the whole thing had gotten me pretty discouraged. Then somebody came over and said, 'Oh Andy likes you, he thinks you're great'. We must have played five or six songs then we just gave up. By that time the rest of The Velvets had arrived. After a while they started to play and they were like awesomely powerful. I had never expected to experience anything like that before. They just completely filled up the whole room with their sound. They were really into this huge fucking volume, and it was completely awesome. I was really disappointed that they didn't have Nico, because we thought she was the lead singer, but I distinctly remember the violin and their doing "Venus In Furs" because a couple of people in dark outfits got up and started doing a slow dance with a chain in between them. They did practically all the stuff from the Banana album. There were maybe thirty people there. It was very late, but it was a memorable experience. It was the dominant confident power of the whole thing that stayed with me.**

BOCKRIS: Is it true that John Cale's father is deaf and his mother is mute?

BETSEY JOHNSON: No! His father's got a coal-miner's sense of humor. They don't talk in Wales, they sing. He was very very funny and their whole thing was watching Tom and Jerry. They had no cars on the street in Cumminford. We were there the Christmas of '67. We lived together a year before we got married.

BOCKRIS: When did you first become aware of The Velvet Underground?

JOHNSON: When they asked me to do clothes. That must have been the linkage.

Lou Reed, Sterling Morrison and John Cale
at Rhode Island School of Design,
Providence, R.I., March 1967.
(Bill Carner)

That's when I fell in love with John. Lou and I don't and never did sync. It's in the stars, because underneath John is an old-fashioned romantic who wants to come home and have the wife with apron, kiss and hello, scratch his back and get his slippers and pipe. After going to Wales I really understood what he was all about. The first real time I talked with The Velvets was on a work-collaboration. I figured that's when we really had something to say to each other. Lou wanted grey suede. For Sterling and Maureen I did dark green and maroony velvets with all the little nail-head studs. But John wanted his hands to be on fire while he played. And he wanted to wear a mask. I think he wore masks a couple of times. I never did masks for him but I think he had them in black. I remember them a lot in Philadelphia and Boston. I thought that they were great. I mean, they were our band. I fell in love with John and we started living together when we were both in the Hotel Chelsea. Janis Joplin was there. Later I got a loft on La Guardia Place, and we were there for a while, and then we just decided to get married. The awful thing was *The Ladies' Home Journal*, the Magazine of Togetherness, was very much interested in us freaks then. I must have established some kind of something for

John Cale at Providence, Rhode Island
(Malanga Archive)

myself at Paraphernalia, the press was really great. *Ladies' Home Journal* found out we were getting married and was going to pay for this huge bash. They just wanted to be there and photograph the freaky little rock & roll scene wedding ceremony and party even though we did it at City Hall. It was all set up and we had all the wedding invitations printed and they were all set to go to the mail box and the day that they were supposed to go in the mail John was turning bright yellow! He went to the hospital and I said, "Well, dear, when shall I mail these out? I'll wait for you to get your blood test". He didn't even leave the hospital. He went straight into quarantine with hepatitis and a non-existent liver. He was in the hospital for four months. Then the doctors took a sample and he walked out with a perfect liver. They could not believe it! They were afraid he was going to kick over, he was so saffron. *Ladies' Home Journal* was so outraged that they wanted me to go on with the whole wedding, go to City Hall, no John –and then they said 'Well later we'll take a picture of John and strip him in!' Lou was not very happy John was getting married period, to me period. Because it was like two guys wanting to be stars. They were the perfect match, but they were the perfect mismatch in that their true-deep-down directional head for music was very different and I think John really respected Lou's more commercial kind of ability. That was when the group was together because Lou was just . . . it was like the girl breaking up the group . . .

BOCKRIS: What sort of financial state were they in at this point?

JOHNSON: Well . . . I don't remember chipping in. I loved John. I loved his work. I loved the group's craziness. I had a place. I was making money. He didn't have to worry about rent or food.

BOCKRIS: It's hard to know from this perspective to what extent The Velvets recognized their talent and lived the lifestyle to the full.

JOHNSON: They never did. In the sixties none of us did.

BOCKRIS: It was always very uncertain?

JOHNSON: The Velvets were totally insecure all the time I think. I worried that John was going to be alive every day, even though I didn't want to know at all about what he was doing to himself. It was an on-the-edge kind of time every day. That was the great side of it.

BOCKRIS: Was this vulnerability like, in a sense, a very strong paranoia or just sheer fragility of the creative being on the edge the whole time?

JOHNSON: All of it. I never took a drug in the '60s. I wanted to smoke grass but John could never smoke grass, so I never got introduced.

BOCKRIS: Why not?

JOHNSON: He'd get paranoid craziness. So I didn't even go near. I thought he was real special because of that, that craziness to me was incredibly interesting. But especially after I moved away, too. He was really the kind that would be afraid to go out into the street – from paranoia or whatever makes you that way. I don't think any of us were too secure outside of our little realm. I always felt very out of it because I was in a commercial business with a price-tag. I felt, they're the creative people, I'm the commercial kind of thing. I had that kind of schedule to keep to.

BOCKRIS: Did you get the sense that The Velvet Underground was John's whole life?

JOHNSON: Yeah! But then I remember Terry Riley and his peanut butter "Eat Me Out!", being around a lot, and LaMonte Young. Nico under the sink! Nico used to come over and live under my big stainless steel sink. And the whole loft was just music. We had a little bed in the corner.

BOCKRIS: Did you see John's personality breaking in two, in the sense that on the one hand he was a very creative personality balancing on the edge, on the other hand he had a very old-fashioned romantic sensibility?

JOHNSON: Yeah . . . and on the other hand he always wanted that hit-45 or hit Single. He's the same way now.

FINKELSTEIN: I could never figure out whether John Cale wanted to be Elvis Presley, the Frankenstein monster, or young Chopin.

Nico.
(Billy Linich)

● "THE VELVET UNDERGROUND AND NICO"

CALE: We were trying to do a Phil Spector thing with as few instruments as possible. On some tracks it worked. "Venus in Furs" is the best, and "All Tomorrow's Parties" and "Sunday Morning". The band never again had as good a producer as Tom Wilson. He did those songs, plus "Heroin" and "Waiting for the Man". They were done in L.A. at Cameo-Parkway. Andy Warhol (credited prominently as producer) didn't do anything; the rest were done by a business-man who came up with $1500 for us to go into a broken-down studio and record the thing. I wasn't writing songs until Lou and I did "Little Sister" for Nico's "Chelsea Girls" LP. Whenever Lou and I worked together, I'd play piano and he would flip whatever version he had around it. I didn't contribute lyrics to any of his songs; he contributed to some of mine. We collaborated slightly on "Sunday Morning", "Black Angel's Death Song" and, later, "Lady Godiva's Operation". Most of it would be written, but a small part would be unresolved and Lou would resolve it.

● **Side One:**

● **"Sunday Morning"** was originally composed by Lou Reed and John Cale sitting at a piano together in a friend's apartment at 6 a.m. one Sunday morning after being out all night (according to Lynne Tillman who was going out with Cale at the time).

● **"Waiting For the Man"** is about scoring heroin in Harlem.

● **"Femme Fatale"** was written for Nico, with Andy's encouragement by Lou, partially in collaboration with Sterling Morrison.

REED: We wrote "Femme Fatale" about somebody who was one, and has since been committed to an institution for being one. And will one day open up a school to train others.

● **"Venus in Furs"**,

REED: The prosaic truth is that I'd just read a book with this title by Leopold Sacher-Masoch and I thought it would make a great song title so I had to write a song to go with it. But it's not necessarily what I'm into.

MORRISON: We do love songs of every description. "Venus in Furs" is just a different kind of love song (Malanga knelt on stage and kissed Mary Woronov's black leather boots during this song). Everybody was saying this is the vision of all-time evil and I always said, 'Well, we're not going to lie. It's pretty. "Venus in Furs" is a beautiful song. It was the closest we ever came in my mind to being exactly what I thought we could be. Always on the other songs I'm hearing what I'm hearing, but I'm also hearing what I wish I were hearing.

● **"Run Run Run"** is about Union Square, a notorious drug park, between 14th and 17th Streets in downtown Manhattan.

● **"All Tomorrow's Parties"**, Andy Warhol's all-time favorite Velvets' song was also written by Lou for Nico.

● **Side Two:**

● **"Heroin"**,

MORRISON: "Heroin" is a beautiful song too, possibly Reed's greatest and a truthful one. It's easy to rationalize about a song you like, but it should be pointed out that when Reed sings he's only glamorizing heroin for people who want to die. The real damage, particularly in New York, has been done through the cult of personality. Rock fans have taken heroin thinking Lou took heroin, forgetting that the character in the song wasn't necessarily Lou Reed.

REED: I'm not advocating anything. It all happened quite simply at the start. It's just that we had "Heroin", "Waiting for My Man", and "Venus in Furs" all on the first album, and that just about set the tone. It's like we also had "Sunday Morning" which was so pretty and "I'll Be Your Mirror", but everyone psyched into the other stuff.

● **"There She Goes Again"** is a tough song about a tough chick.

● **"I'll Be Your Mirror":** Lou must have been in love with Nico when he wrote this beautiful, tender love song.

Sterling Morrison
(Nat Finkelstein)

● **"The Black Angel's Death Song"** was a precursor in a number of different veins.

MORRISON: A good friend of ours who saw many shows (and even played bass in one at the Dom) Helen Byrne ran up to me after the release of the album and exclaimed, "The Black Angel's Death Song – it's got chords!" Apparently she hadn't noticed in the live performances. "Of course, it's got chords!", I replied. "It's a song, isn't it?"

● **"European Son":** Dedicated to Delmore Schwartz (who hated rock lyrics intensely, which is why the piece employed the fewest words on the album) simply because they wanted to dedicate something to him. John Cale ran a chair into some metal plates which scatter and sound like broken glass on this track.

MORRISON: "European Son" is very tame now. It happens to be melodic and if anyone actually listens to it, "European Son" turns out to be comprehensible in the light of all that has come since – not just our work but everyone's. It's that just for the time it was done it's amazing. We figured that on our first album it was a novel idea just to have long tracks. People just weren't doing that – regardless of what the content of the track was – everyone's album-cuts had to be 2:30 or 2:45. Then here's "European Son" which ran nearly eight minutes. All the songs on the first album are longish compared to the standards of the time.

'Their themes were perversity, desperation and death,' reads an RCA press-release for Lou Reed's *Rock & Roll Diary* (1978) describing The Velvet Underground: 'Instead of celebrating psychedelic trips they showed us the devastating power, horror and false transcendence of heroin addiction; they dared to intimate that sado-masochism might have more to do with their – and our – reality than universal love. Musically as well as verbally they insisted that

possibility, far from being limitless, was continually being stifled and foreclosed. At a time when hippie rock musicians were infatuated with the spontaneous jam, The Velvets' music was cerebral, stylized. They maintained a poignant ironic tension between the tight, formal structure of the songs and their bursts of raw noise between their high artfulness and their street-level content, between fatalism and rebellion.

'Though The Velvets overall sound owed nearly as much to John Cale, Sterling Morrison and Maureen Tucker, it was Reed who defined the band's sensibility, embodied its contradictions. He was a romantic alienated bohemian and anti-romantic pop ironist, a middle-class Jewish kid from Brooklyn who came on like a street-wise punk in tight jeans and shades, a classical piano student turned rock and roller, Bob Dylan cum Nelson Algren cum Jean Genet. He talked his songs in an expressive semi-mumble that made you think of James Dean without the naivete. Not that Lou did not display his own kind of innocence. His songs hinted, when you least expected it, that underneath the meanness and paranoia, the affectless brutality that smothered pain, there was after all the possibility of love. His depictions of urban hell contained occasional glimpses of redemption. Still, the inhabitants of Reed's universe experienced love mainly through its absence; the glimpses were not only rare but as likely as not to be illusory.

'*The Velvet Underground and Nico* came out the same year The Beatles released *Sergeant Pepper*. It offered an extended tour of the urban underworld that included the now classic "Waiting for My Man" and "Heroin". The latter saga of a man on his way to spiritual death, fighting and embracing it at once, is the most profoundly moving and disturbing drug song ever written.'

Fair enough in the "sensibility embodied by contradictions" department which is its main point, but the sound was an equal collaboration and anyone wanting to really appreciate the sound captured on their first album should imagine Cale, Morrison, Tucker and Reed in the studio together all banging away and pulling as hard as they can in their different directions creating out of dissension a tension that lives today, while Warhol encouraged them with his confidence and support. As Danny Fields now says, 'What Andy did was very generously reproduce the sound of The Velvets for them, making sure they got it down the way it sounded to him when he first fell in love with it'.

While it cannot produce the effect of the combination of films, lights and dancing interacting with a live performance that was The E.P.I., *The Velvet Underground and Nico* produced by Andy Warhol is an extraordinarily, classic work arising out of their collaboration. 'I was worried,' Andy says, 'that it would all come out sounding too professional. But with The Velvets, I should have known I didn't have to worry – one of the things that was so great about them was they always sounded raw and crude. Raw and crude was the way I liked our movies to look, and there's a similarity between the sound in that album and the texture of "Chelsea Girls", which came out at the same time.' The record did not, however, receive the same amount of front-page coverage his film "Chelsea Girls" was getting. In fact, the album was banned on the radio in New York because of its content, unacceptable sound, and length of tracks.

MORRISON: Even advertising for the album was refused by the fledgling FM rock radio trip in NYC. AM advertising was likewise out of the question. Perhaps a restraint of trade suit was in order, but we just grit our teeth. WBAI (Bob Fass) was the only one who played the album; he would air a few cuts a night for a long time. Then we had a falling out over a bail-fund benefit at Thomkins Park, and even he wouldn't play it. The silence was complete thereafter on the homefront.

CUTRONE: With songs like "Heroin" you're certainly not going to get any radio play in 1967. The Beatles were singing about broken relationships and 'all you need is love'. "Sympathy for the Devil" was the heaviest The Rolling Stones ever got. And then you get a group coming out and saying, 'When I'm rushing on my run/I feel just like Jesus' son' you're not going to get any radio play – it's as simple as that.

It was ironic that the music was banned in New York. They were the only band who spoke for the city, delineating so accurately the love-hate relationship it inspired. New York was an equivalent for The Velvet Underground of what Paris was for Baudelaire. In each case the city provided an existential justification for their creations. However, after the album was banned they refused to play New York with the intent of punishing the city by their absence. After the spring of 1967 The Velvet Underground didn't play New York City again until they returned to Mickey Ruskin's Max's Kansas City in the summer of 1970.

BOCKRIS: Did you feel the reaction was flat considering what a striking record it was?

TUCKER: It was rather flat, and I think the problem was it hadn't been advertised very much, and it hadn't been distributed properly.

BOCKRIS: Why did MGM sign you up, do such an expensive production job on the package, and then cool off so completely to the product?

TUCKER: I don't know what the hell their problem was. I think someone had said let's go psychedelic. So they signed us and The Mothers, then they went after the Boston groups. But I think they just didn't know what the hell to do with us.

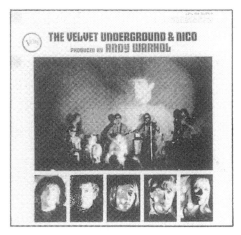

Despite the attempts of Tom Wilson to render "Sunday Morning", a hit single (in a longer, poppier version released before the album), it too flopped and the album peaked in the *Cashbox* charts at 103.

Cashbox December 17, 1966 "Newcomer Picks" Sunday Morning/Femme Fatale "The Velvet Underground and Nico have been zooming the length and breadth of the land making a name for themselves and now follow the personal stuff with a potential filled deck. The top side, "Sunday Morning", is a haunting, lyrical emotion-stirring chant. Listen very closely. Eerie, unusual number back here."

To add to their problems Eric Emerson, whose face was on the back cover in a still from "Chelsea Girls" upsidedown just above Lou's face, refused to sign a release for MGM unless they paid him and further delays in the distribution were caused as Eric had to be airbrushed off and the cover had to be reprinted.

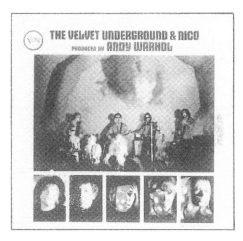

MORRISON: The whole Eric business was a tragic fiasco for us, and proves what idiots there were at MGM. Photos by Billy (Linich), Stephen Shore, Nat and others were used in an 'art' montage in a show that took place in an art museum (Chrysler). This montage was photographed by Hugo, who sold it to us, who consigned it to MGM. Who even knows who took the original photo of Eric, but MGM was far removed from any liability. They responded by pulling the album off the shelves immediately, and kept it off the shelves for a couple of months while they fooled around with stickers over Eric's picture, and then finally the airbrush. The album thus vanished from the charts almost immediately in June, 1967, just when it was about to enter the 'Top 100'. It never returned to the charts. We never had a 'Top 100' album. As for Eric, he never got any money as far as I know. I don't think that anyone even bothered to complain about the destructive audacity of his action. He was, shall we say, too far out.

Some originals did reach the public. A copy of the original cover with Eric's face and the banana unpeeled, is worth $25 to $30 today.

Considering MGM's inability, or lack of willingness, to handle the product, one has to wonder why they released it in such an expensive package. The only explanation would be an attempt to emphasize the Warhol connection, which a rare advertisement they used certainly does, in the hope that it would sell more copies. Most magazines even banned the ad on account of the record's content. There were few reviews, and no radio spots. It's not hard to imagine how The Velvets, who were fully aware of the relevance and significance of their music, must have felt to have their product treated so negligently by MGM while the very West Coast bands they despised – Jefferson Airplane, Mothers, Grateful Dead – were beginning to receive national promotion.

The album is still selling today. It is doubtful that it will ever stop selling as long as people listen to records. There are unfortunately no Velvet Underground videos although there are four films (apart from Warhol's) that are known to exist, though shown rarely, if at all: Rosalind Stevenson filmed some simple footage of them in her apartment in 1965. Jonas Mekas filmed the Psychiatrists' Convention, the first show they played with Andy Warhol's choreography, January 8, 1966 at Delmonico's Hotel in New York. A team filmed at the Balloon Farm, October 1966, and Ron Nemeth filmed at Poor Richard's in Chicago, June 1966.

Apart from standing out over time and being recognized as an influence on countless other musicians, "The Velvet Underground and Nico" fulfilled the ambitions with which the band had approached the concept of playing together, creating a symphonic rock format in which they would never have to repeat themselves.

● EVERYBODY BECOMES PART OF THE E.P.I. /EXIT NICO

● **CUTRONE: The last time we played as The E.P.I. (without Nico, who had returned to Ibiza) was in May 1967 at the Steve Paul's Scene where Tiny Tim used to hang out and Jim Morrison played. Before this people came to watch The E.P.I. dance and play, they were entertained, and got a show. But when we played at the Scene I remember Gerard, Mary and I were dancing and the audience came on stage with us and totally took over. Mary and I looked at each other and had this look on our faces. It was half desperation-half relief that finally everybody was part of it. I looked at her as if to say, 'Okay, Mary, looks like this is it'. And she looked at me like, 'Yeah, this is it'. Everybody became part of The E.P.I. It was a bit sad, because we couldn't keep our glory on stage, but we were happy because what The E.P.I. intended to do had worked – everybody was liberated to be as sick as we were acting! From that standpoint it was interesting socially that it happened that way. All of a sudden there were no dancers, there was no show; the music had just taken everybody at that point. That was the last time I danced, and I think the last time Mary and Gerard danced. I mean maybe they tried futilely after that, but it didn't work.**

After the failed attempt to find a home at the Gymnasium, and the couple of performances already mentioned, The Velvets didn't play much around the release of their album, confounding the accepted laws of the situation and doing the exact opposite of what was expected. It seems a tremendous loss that they played to so few audiences and didn't record their shows.

MORRISON: The unanimous opinion was that we were ten times better live than on records. We never played a song the same way twice – never wanted to, maybe never could. And Lou changed lyrics all the time. One of his great talents is that he can spontaneously generate lyrics on stage – just like the old blues singers, Lou can go on forever rhyming.

Their decision not to promote the record may also have been partially due to the changes everybody was going through. In May Andy, Paul, Gerard and Eric Emerson went to Cannes to show "Chelsea Girls". They were out of town for a month. Steve Sesnick asked The Velvets if they'd play at the Boston Tea Party (on the weekend of May 26-27) which, unbeknownst to everybody, he owned. It was a ballroom with high ceilings and a very high stage that could easily accommodate a couple of thousand people and boasted a very large dance floor. The Velvets, who were glad to be offered a forum at the time, accepted.

They informed Nico of the upcoming date and she was faced with a dilemma. She still had some time to go on her latest Dom engagement and she needed the money. On the other hand what would her not going to Boston with The Velvets portend? Nico considered the problem and decided to stay in New York. The Velvets took this in their stride and moved on without her, but then Nico changed her mind and turned up at the Tea Party on the second night, timing her entrance to perfectly coincide with the beginning of their last song. When they refused to let her come up on stage with them, Nico was miffed and returned to New York, causing a series of uptight vibrations to pass through the organization that had been known as *The Exploding Plastic Inevitable*.

MORRISON: It was all very informal. We stopped working for a while. We used to do that periodically – just refused to do anything. Nico needed money so she went out on her own. She was working downstairs at the Dom (Stanley's) and we said 'Sure, do anything you want', and so she was doing that. We'd take turns backing her up. I'd do it for one week, then John Cale, Lou, Ramblin' Jack Elliott, Jackson Browne – everyone was showing up as Nico's accompanist. When we decided to start work again we told her about it and she said, 'Oh, I have three more weeks here'. So we told her to decide what she wanted to do and she decided that perhaps she should go on her own and be a big star, and we said okay.

CUTRONE: You have to remember that there were at least five extremely strong egos involved in this group. There were drugs. And consequently there were egos. Everybody wanted to be the star. And you can't have everybody being the star. Lou kept a very low profile. John did. Nico's ego was way out of proportion. I mean, so was mine, so was everybody else's that I ever came into contact with from that era. One common cause couldn't support all those egos. It had to fracture, it hadda break.

L-R: Gerard Malanga, Andy Warhol, Sterling Morrison, Mary Woronov, Maureen Tucker, Lou Reed and John Cale. At The Factory.
(Nat Finkelstein)

BOCKRIS: So when you went up to the Boston Tea Party did Andy go?

MORRISON: No, he didn't.

BOCKRIS: So at that point you were playing on your own without E.P.I.?

MORRISON: Right. We couldn't put on The E.P.I. thing because the room was too small. Eventually Nico showed up, on the second night. We declined to have her play with us. She came in late. I think we were on the last song. There was always a problem of what to do with Nico when there was a song that wasn't one of her songs. She wasn't playing an instrument. She wanted to sing all the songs. It was really awkward about what to do. It wasn't that we wanted to get her out of the group . . .

Nico in "Screen Tests", 1966.

BOCKRIS: Did Lou have a very strong ego at the time? Was he vying for leadership of the group?

NICO: Lou likes to manipulate women, you know, like program them. He wanted to do that with me.

JIM CONDON: He wanted to manipulate you when you were with The Velvets?

NICO: He told me so. Like, computerize me.

CONDON: Would you say that he was the leader of the group?

NICO: He always will be . . .

REED: Nico's the kind of person that you meet, and you're not quite the same afterwards. She has an amazing mind. She isn't the type of person who stays very long in any one country. Nico's fantastic. She always understood immediately what I was after with a song.

FINKELSTEIN: I felt that there was an underlying current of competitive hostility between John and Lou.

BOCKRIS: Was that a constructive creative tension?

FINKELSTEIN: Artistically, certainly – on a personality basis though, unless there were super egos involved, which there were, it would have destroyed everybody.

BOCKRIS: Did you think The Velvets were very important music-wise?

FINKELSTEIN: From the first time I saw them I said, 'Wow! Wow! Wow! They're going to kick these guys out on their ass for the next ten years!' Everybody hated them. That whole macho East Village group really hated The Velvets – just put-down after put-down – the hatred had nothing to do with their music; a lot of it had to do with the gay image. One of the reasons I got tossed out of that whole Lower East Side group was the fact that I was working with The Velvets. Also Lou and John were really good musicians, whereas Ed Sanders and Tuli Kupferberg wouldn't have known music if it'd bit them on the ass.

BOCKRIS: Were they confident at the time?

FINKELSTEIN: Lou was very confident.

BOCKRIS: Would he react to criticism?

FINKELSTEIN: He was about as fragile as a piece of stainless steel. As far as Lou was concerned, you got the idea that no matter what, this guy was going to survive, this guy was going to make it. You also felt he was following a historical trail that other people in his situation followed.

BOCKRIS: Was he more outstanding than John?

FINKELSTEIN: In the sense that he was much more open than John. Lou never stopped learning, Lou never stopped developing.

CUTRONE: I have the feeling that Lou always felt he was the leader of the group, and didn't have to prove it. I think John contributed to the group immensely. You couldn't duplicate the group without John, even without Mo and her garbage cans, you just couldn't. They were willing to experiment in a time when everybody was getting very studio-produced. The Beatles had stopped touring and they were the only group that I know of who were out there trying new things and making mistakes that actually sounded great – all that feedback was hit-and-miss. There was no way you could really plan feedback, but it was working in the music and everybody was contributing to the basic sound.

BOCKRIS: How did Nico come to not be with the group anymore?

CUTRONE: In those days I don't think anybody ever had the balls or the honesty to say I think you're through. Maybe that did happen and I'm not aware of the politics, but everything was run by guilt or by elimination then. Like somebody was designated to say to somebody else, 'We can't use you tonight,' leave it at that and let the paranoia rear its ugly head, make the person feel all shitty inside and inferior. I have a feeling that that's what happened. Breaks are never that clean-cut. Think in terms of romance. People see their Xs for years after. If there's strong bitterness you avoid each other, or you talk behind each others' backs, and if there's not extreme bitterness then it just goes on. Instinctively you know when it's over. That's the point I'm trying to make. Like at the last gig at the

Scene, instinctively we knew that was the end. I think The Velvets as a music group knew that they had other things to do. And Andy, of course, had other things to do. Andy's not primarily a rock & roll producer – he does many different things – and The Velvets were primarily a rock & roll group.

REED: When we worked together, we were very close. It was just people working to get onto something. The thing is that Andy works very hard. One of the things you can learn from being at the Factory is if you want to do whatever you do, then you should work very, very hard. If you don't work very hard all the time, well then nothing will happen. And Andy works as hard as anybody I know. He used to say things to me that were involved around our working. Whenever he'd ask me how many songs I'd written that day, whatever the number was Andy would say, 'You should do more'. And the thing is that I had to learn certain things the hard way. But one of the things I learned was work is the whole story. Work is literally everything. Work should be taking place 24-hours a day. He just works very hard. I mean, The Velvet Underground really loves him, in any way or any level you want to take it in. Working with him was really fantastic. We worked until the show couldn't exist anymore because it was just so expensive. They took our club. We tried to open the Gymnasium, but again there was some problem. No one knew the business. People just constantly think he's strange, he's this or that. They don't understand they're talking about a very, very good person. A very good, honest person who's enormously talented. Therefore, those who know him really love him.

CUTRONE: Both Lou and Andy, as I recall, thought it would be the healthiest way if the band wasn't associated with a pop artist, and if Andy wasn't associated strictly with music. Because by then light shows had become such a cliche that it was over for us. I had to do my art, and Mary was studying to be an actress, and Gerard was writing poetry and making films and so the three of us just continued with our own work. The band became more of a rock band without us, because the impact was over, the shock was over.

MILSTEIN: A quote from Lou Reed: "I fired Warhol. He said to me 'Aren't you tired of playing museums?' I thought about it and fired him. I was just trying to do what Andy suggested." Is that more or less the truth of the matter?

WARHOL: It wasn't that dramatic.

CUTRONE: Lou was just trying to take it out of an art context and Andy said, 'Fine. That's perfect.'

MILSTEIN: So was that more or less the end of your formal relationship with the group?

WARHOL: I guess so.

MILSTEIN: They became a band in their own right apart from all the theatrics of The E.P.I.?

CUTRONE: Not just a band, a very special band . . . In other words, we really sort of innovated something in that year-and-a-half. After that it was like beating a dead horse and people became accustomed to it. It became boring to us. And Lou wanted to make it in the record industry. As it was, we weren't getting airplay due to the nature of the songs.

MORRISON: By the summer of 1967 John and I had left 10th Street. The tenant underneath us was some old Austrian who had suffered under the Nazis; he kept calling the police to complain about noise, but we really never made any. Finally, he took us to court and told the judge that we 'marched around in jackboots'. The judge looked at us hatefully, and then at this wretched mental defective, and dismissed us with a stern warning. Within a month we were back before the same judge for the same reason. This time I planned to defend us eloquently (we said nothing at the first trial), but as we entered the courtroom John said menacingly 'Now don't say a word! Not one fucking word!' So I remained silent. The judge delivered an impassioned harangue, the gist of which was that the two of us would go to jail immediately if he ever laid eyes on us again. And so we left 10th Street and lived here and there with other people (Paul Morrissey put us up for a while), settling down for the summer on West 3rd Street, along with Lou.

MALANGA: Another thing is I'm curious about the direction in which your

John Cale and Nico at The Factory.
(Billy Linich)

relationship with Lou was going. I know you kept in touch with him and he used to come by late at night just to see you at the Factory.

BILLY LINICH: We would see each other or we would go to a hangout. I remember there was an afterhours place a couple of blocks away on University Place we would go to sometimes. It was just as buddies. We had always struck it off from the beginning. We were empathetic toward each other, we had a common sense, and we sort of appreciated each other or respected each other. I'm going to Dutchess County Community College now and there are kids up here – I'm old enough to be their father – who have Lou Reed on the back of their leather jackets and I swear to God scraped on the men's room wall this past year was "Nico and The Velvet Underground". Can you imagine?

The benefit they did for Merce Cunningham on the same bill as John Cage, whose music was orchestrated by Viola, Gong, Radio and Door Slam plus the windshield wipers and engine-turnover of three cars at architect Philip Johnson's Glass House in Connecticut in July 1967 was the swan song to the whole sensation. It was outdoors in the afternoon. Lou, John, Sterling and Mo played without lights or films. Gerard danced alone. Steve Sesnick had been continually importuning The Velvets to accept him as their manager, and on the way back to New York after the gig they discussed the matter in some detail.

LINICH: Coming back from Philip Johnson's they were trying to decide whether or not Steve should be their manager. I sensed they were in need of a professional arm, so to speak, to deal with the music and record industry. That they were actually not suited, or didn't want, to do that themselves – they wanted to make music. They really needed a professional who was capable of doing that. As far as Steve goes, I know he was a lot of mouth. I didn't think he had connections or anything like that. However, there was no one else bidding for the job so I recommended that they take a positive stance and just do it. There was no other option and they would just have stagnated otherwise.

BOCKRIS: Were you involved in the conversations about Steve Sesnick managing you?

TUCKER: Yeah, I remember being in the car driving back from Johnson's. As I recall it was a limousine.

BOCKRIS: Steve was not in the car?

TUCKER: No.

BOCKRIS: On what basis was that decision made

TUCKER: We all just felt that he was more our style. There were a couple of other guys lurking and they wanted to manage us, but they were just too businessey and I think we thought we wouldn't relate to them too well. And Sesnick was much more our type of person. And he was very enthusiastic. The other guys were too, but they were business-types, they weren't hippies. Two gentlemen in suits. I don't know if they heard us play somewhere . . . or read about us; but they came to Philip Johnson's to listen to us and talk to us, too.

BOCKRIS: Billy Linich was in the car with The Velvets driving back from the Philip Johnson gig in the summer of '67, which is the time they apparently had a long conversation about agreeing to go with your proposal to manage them . . .

SESNICK: I see . . .

BOCKRIS: I don't know if you're aware of that . . .

SESNICK: Billy liked me very much as I remember.

BOCKRIS: Billy was apparently the one who suggested they should go with you.

SESNICK: I believe that's accurate, yes.

BOCKRIS: He told us that and Maureen was in the car and remembered it quite well, too. So for the sake of historical accuracy is it correct that you formally became their manager in the summer of 1967?

SESNICK: Yes, I would say yeah.

BOCKRIS: This must have been an extreme change for you to suddenly achieve this goal that you have been wanting to achieve for some time. From what Maureen told me it was very much of a full-time job.

SESNICK: It certainly was!

Wandering around Philip Johnson's field in Greenwich, Connecticut.
(Stephen Shore)

sure   O—. . . .dance—the top of the fly dance . . . Lou   P—. . . a week before.Not Last week, the week before. Lou an . . . . . an extra check   O—I know I'm not allowed to go to the bathroom, but . . . D—Gerard, aren't you coming up?   G—Yeah, I'll be-I'll be back O—Do you suppose that . . . Hey, Paul, uh . . . uh, Lou? Who else? Who else would have it? Who else would you do?   Lou—He was here now

O—If somebody comes in . . . . . WE'VE ran into another Armenian wedding, thank you   L—Oh, was it going on AGAin?   O—It certainly is, and they don't know—they don't know Warhol at all, they said no I don't know what it is—I think it's one of the Ed Sullivan shows L—Ya gonna eat anything?   O—Yeah, but he left plenty of . . . in the oven. He looked so glittery I couldn't believe it   P—Do you have a pen?   O—I have one   P—I don't need tha now   O—Heah—help yourself to mah jacket . . .Oh, wow   Lou, howanya   Whatsa matter with—uh.Aaaow, she's gotta pen back there. I thought she had a pen back there. That dress is so . . . yabbadabba . . . It sounds like you're taking off material and going out of your thing. I CANt get nooo . . . (satisf-). What're you doing this evening, Lou? What're you doing this evening. Hey, Maddy. Lou, what're you doing this evening, what're you doing?   L—(mumble)   O—You're not going theAH? To the-uh to the Ah Gymnasium? are you.   O—Since about 11—I don't know-uh what time it is now, so I wouldn't. Two hours of tape so far or wha? Or an hour?   D—An hour   O—Just about an hour   D—Is Jackson coming here?   L—What happened in . . . (indistinguishable)   O—A lot. A lot—you should have come   P—Uh   O—A lot—I was waiting for you, and then all of a sudden . . . I realized that you weren't there, an, uhhh, woaow—whddifhe had come? An I said: whew (whistle) It was a little too much. Look, maybe you could get up—I been sitting here for a while. Unless you've been sitting here for hours an hours. Oh, well, nevah mind nevah mind. I thought maybe Lou's here. Huh . . . Oxydol's rese-uh electrifying; he really did   L—Who showed up? O—Uh . . . the RIGHT people   L—Rudine?   O—An everything . . .   L—(indistinct)   O—Whaaddya mean? Yer book? And-uh . . . uh uh ooh—I had it. And-uh whatchamacall-uh And all of a sudden I went out-uh. . . . (fades out)   P—At the Gymnasium with the Velvet Underground which they didn't get paid for   O—And I was going to the gymnasium whether I like it or not, so Rudine went, And-uh with an amphetamine mixture, and she gave me the proper amount, but-uh behind my tongue-uh, back there, and it got me up—Boy, did it ever get me up. wheeh (whistle) Now-uh/ah, now . . . have we gotten a thousand a day yet, noo   P—A few weegs ago-uh . . . last week   O—It was-uh . . .

it was-uh. It was-a . . .the night that the shit hit the fan and-uh cleared the place. It was a very important night, ya know, and-uh. In as much as the people who missed it missed it; the p-people who didn't miss it were rrrriGHT there. heh heh. Not that that means anything—its a clever . . .

L—Crux and Nee Co. and everybody were around here-uh . . . uh Nico . . . uh . . . Before   O—Nobody heard the bell . . . Nobody heard the bell   L—Oh, is that what it was . . .   O—It was ma/a/aD after a while, I'm sure. No one heard the telephone, an I unnerstan it had been ringing all morning. We didn't hear one phone call. Alan, you know that all you do in-uh. . . . (fade) . . . is take some sleep   God, you were-uh. I mean, thatsa   DISTORTION: about five simultaneous conversations

Oaow, what's tonight at the Gymnasium? The people who do gymnastics were havin like a year-end final. (ha)   Ah. When the curtain opened, and you saw them all in their-uh ah-electric blue shshsh-s-s/sweat shirts. 1967's champions. They were rather-uh . . . oh, Jesus, they were awful—the place looked like a BAH-arn, it was lit so strangely   What did they have that a . . .   They had Like-ah crepe paper, and-uh The SONG OF BERNADETTE . . . I . . . nihnah . . . they didn't even HAVE songs . . . I'm beginning an abcess on the side of my arm . . . It's delightful: I mean, I gave it to myself so-uh-ooo level. Anyway, wha happened   We went to this thing called Pennisiffic-uhsociation . . . and elevated after our exposure   Oh: it must be daown Park, divided by four. It's so-uh scary, you walk in, and it's marvelous . . . (Ixsam's own particular variety of distortion)   O—IT CAN STAND UP . . . No, it can, ih can, you can POINT it   UNIDENTIFIED PERSON— Rodey was saying that he likes her using the earphones with it. He said that he thought she should use it throughout the entire show   P— Broadcast THAT part? are you sure??   O—Barbara . . . truly Barbara . . . uh, laaah   L—Did we tell you about the song Ondine's gonna do on the . . .

Oh, really?? On the next album?
Look what went on?
It's on the upstairs jukebox
Isn't it divine??
It's such a . . .
It always was
The Vlevets song
The Velvets are so good . . .
It's so poor
It doesn't matter maybe you hafta be bridges. You're so beautiful . . .
    Loud grunts from adjoining tables

From "a, A Novel" by Andy Warhol.

BOCKRIS: Did you move to New York at that point?

SESNICK: Later. But there was quite a bit that went on prior to that decision being finalized. There were months of negotiations with various people acting as messengers between Lou and myself and the group, so there was quite a bit of time that was spent that spring and summer before it was settled.

BOCKRIS: What was the nature of these negotiations?

SESNICK: Those are the things I don't want to talk about.

FIELDS: It was so weird for them to go from whom they had been with, which was us, to Steve Sesnick. It's like your daughter marrying someone from the wrong race. He wasn't so bad after all. He was devoted to them. He just wasn't our kind of person. He kept them together for a period of time.

BOCKRIS: When you were managing them were you still trying to make some arrangements with Brian Epstein to do things together?

SESNICK: Publishing.

BOCKRIS: He was trying to buy the publishing rights to their music?

SESNICK: That's correct. It had nothing to do with management.

BOCKRIS: He was not approaching them on the basis of trying to manage them?

SESNICK: No.

BOCKRIS: Is it true that he proposed to arrange a European tour for them?

SESNICK: Not to my knowledge. I had no negotiations or discussion with him about that.

BOCKRIS: When did Brian Epstein come into the picture?

TUCKER: When Sesnick was first managing us. Sesnick met him through Lester Persky.

BOCKRIS: But if Sesnick was managing you, why would he introduce you to Brian Epstein, who was apparently offering to manage you himself?

TUCKER: I suppose there was some deal they could have struck. Maybe he had it in mind to get us on Capitol.

FIELDS: I had given Brian the Banana album once and one night I was with Lou at Max's and Brian came in briefly. He said he was on his way uptown. I went outside to his limousine with him and then I said, 'Wait a minute, I have an idea'. And ran back in and said to Lou, 'This is your big chance to talk to Brian Epstein, come uptown'. He got in the car but there was like total silence because they were both too proud to say anything to each other. We're on our way to Ondine (the disco). Finally Brian leaned over and said, 'Danny recommended this album to me and I took it to Mexico with my lover. It was the only album we had there. We rented a phonograph, but we couldn't get any more albums, so we listened to it day and night on the beach in Acapulco. Consequently my memory of my whole week in paradise was your album.' They dropped us at Ondine's and then Lou had to take a taxi back to Max's because he was really in the middle of a conversation. I dragged him out and nothing happened. Brian Epstein didn't want to manage The Velvets. He didn't want anything. He was just looking around. He was trying to build an empire and trying to figure out what to do next. He must have been a little bored with his enormous reputation. I'm sure he wanted to do something new. He was intrigued and he loved the music. I'm sure he got captivated periodically with what was brought to his attention. As far as I know it ended there and then.

MORRISON: Brian was looking for a group, though, and eventually settled on the Cyrkle (Red Rubber Ball, etc). He did want us, and we had numerous dealings through Nat Weiss on this and the other matters mentioned (publishing; tour). Why Sesnick chooses to deny the tour plan is best known to him.

One cannot help but wonder what would have happened if they'd signed with Brian Epstein. Would The Velvets have become big stars? Would Epstein have lived to see the punks he loved take over? Unfortunately, we'll never know. However, it is interesting to note that The Velvets considered themselves to be working at least upon the same level as The Beatles.

REED: I remember him best for a story that may or may not have been true. In his mansion Brian Epstein kept Spanish servants, none of whom could speak English. Let that be a lesson to us all in discretion.

Danny Williams, who had left The E.P.I., in July of 1966, after the Chicago shows, died under mysterious circumstances that summer. Shortly after his return to his parents' home on Cape Cod he had driven to the shore, undressed, left his clothes in a neat pile by the car, and swum out until, according to some, he drowned. Sterling Morrison questions whether it was suicide, pointing out that Danny was a good swimmer and he may have hit his head on a rock or something, but shortly thereafter a brown paper parcel containing two brass doorknobs arrived at the Factory addressed to Andy Warhol by Danny's parents. Apparently, in a suicide note, Williams had left instructions that the doorknobs be sent to Andy who he thought would appreciate them. Nobody at the Factory could figure out what this meant. Lou has his own theory about Danny Williams' death.

REED: Tony Conrad, who had by now become a film-maker, did a thing called "Flicker". Now "Flicker" was using the same basic idea, playing around with strobes, that we used with The E.P.I. The guy who was doing the lights in our show, Danny Williams, committed suicide eventually. But he got into the same idea, which was combinations of strobe lights. If you didn't do it randomly – people still think that "Metal Machine" is random, which it isn't – people could literally get bowled over. Tony showed "Flicker", which was exposed frames and unexposed frames, at the old Cinematheque, and the first night he showed it two kids had a heart attack. The next day they had to have a disclaimer. People thought they were kidding, but bam! There was an epileptic fit. It worked. Danny Williams would sit for hours up at the Factory using himself as a test-subject for seven strobe lights we were using when we were doing The Exploding Plastic Inevitable. You can imagine! That's why John and I used to wear sunglasses when

Paul McCartney and George Harrison with Brian Epstein
(Dezo Hoffmann)

we played. We didn't want to see it. We knew. Danny was so far gone he killed himself.

In July 1967 Al Grossman sold his lease on the Balloon Farm to Jerry Brandt for a lot of money. Brandt turned it into more money when he opened the Electric Circus, a plush new multimedia club that emphasized just how much rock & roll had changed since The E.P.I. had played its first show on the same site slightly more than a year before.

Although they continued to live in New York, Boston became the Velvet Underground's number two stronghold as soon as they started playing at the Tea Party.

FIELDS: They were phenomenally popular in Boston. I think that everybody in New York loved them, but they really could make a living in Boston. It was just circumstances that prevented them from making a living in New York.

REED: Boston was the whole thing as far as we were concerned. It was the first time we played in public and didn't have all those things thrown at us: the leather freaks, the druggies, the this or the that. It was the first time somebody just listened to the music, which blew our minds collectively...

BOCKRIS: The Boston Tea Party would mark a turning point?

SESNICK: Well, there was a lot that went on in between. There was a lot of, for the lack of any better word, negotiations going on between what was happening with them in New York and with Andy I guess. I was a part-owner of the Boston Tea Party which was famous and very successful at that point and then through various ways Lou and I got together.

BOCKRIS: When you say you owned the Boston Tea Party and it's not known, do you mean it wasn't known then or the fact has never been released?

SESNICK: It's not known till today.

BOCKRIS: Did Lou know that you owned it?

SESNICK: Sure. I was a partner, I wasn't sole owner, but I was the person I guess who ran it. I did all the booking.

BOCKRIS: What was your perception of their relationship with Andy during this period. I gather you felt they really needed a real manager, and he wasn't acting in that capacity...

SESNICK: Oh, that goes without saying, because any group does. Andy needed his own management – he's an artist. He has a different method of projecting what he feels he does, and they needed what they needed. It was really not a very complicated thing.

BOCKRIS: But did you feel he was beneficial to them to a certain point?

SESNICK: Oh immensely, immensely. I wouldn't have gone to Andy originally if I didn't feel he was helpful.

BOCKRIS: Am I right in thinking that you were closer to Lou than other members of the group?

SESNICK: Pretty much.

MORRISON: The second round of talks with Brian Epstein was about Three Prong Music, our publishing company. He wanted it to merge with Nemperor, The Beatles publishing company. We fretted and fretted over this and decided that if Epstein thought the stuff was so great, maybe we should hang onto it. We couldn't see any advantages to being part of Nemperor – who was ever going to record our stuff? So that was the end of that.

"Chelsea Girls" was being premiered in San Francisco in late August 1967 and everyone was keen to go on this trip, but for the first time Andy chose not to take Gerard Malanga. When Gerard found out he wasn't going he got very uptight and decided to accept an invitation to go to the Bergamo International Film Festival in Italy and show his film "In Search of the Miraculous" about three generations of the Barzini family. However, when Malanga told Warhol of his plans, Andy got uptight because he had counted on Gerard to run the Factory while he was in California. Consequently, Andy changed his mind about taking Gerard to San Francisco, but Malanga told him that it was too late. Knowing that Gerard only had a one way ticket and no money to get back Andy replied that if he needed a return ticket to let him know and he would send one.

While Andy was out on the West Coast with "Chelsea Girls" and Gerard was in Bergamo, Nico was at the Monterey Pop Festival with Brian Jones. In New York The

Mary Woronov and Gerard Malanga pose for a "Venus In Furs" publicity shot in the window of The Dom.
(John Palmer)

Velvets went into Mayfair Sound the second week in September to record *White Light/White Heat.*

MORRISON: The so-called 'Summer of Love' was a lovely summer in New York City, for in addition to the usual eastward migration of the vapid chic set (comprising socialites, Arabs, and whatnot) to the Hamptons, another and even more welcome exodus took place – westward, to San Francisco. Inspired by media hype, and encouraged by shamelessly deceitful songs on the radio (Airplane, Mama's and Papa's, Eric Burdon), teenage ninnies flocked from Middle-America out to the coast; hot on their heels came a predatory mob from N.Y.C. Roughly speaking, every creep, every degenerate, every hustler, booster, and rip-off artist, every wasted weirdo packed up his or her clap, crabs, and cons and headed off to the Promised Land. This sleazy legion – like Harvey Korman's goon squad in "Blazing Saddles" – then descended upon the hapless hippies (and their dupes) in San Francisco. And the rest, as the saying goes, is history.

But behind them in Manhattan, all was suddenly quiet, clean, and beautiful – like the world of Noah after the Flood. If you hadn't seen a particular lowlife for a while, there was no need to inquire about his or her whereabouts: you knew where they all were, and had a pretty good idea of what they were up to.

And so at the height of the "Summer of Love" we stayed in NYC and recorded "White Light/White Heat", an orgasm of our own.

REED: We wanted to go as high and as hard as we could (Reed had a Gretsch Country Gentleman guitar, which had been fitted with preamps and speed/tremolo controls so that it could virtually play itself, producing 16 notes for each one he played).

JONATHAN RICHMAN: Sterling helped Lou work on The Country Gentleman by giving him a pickup off his own Stratocaster to put on it. That's brotherhood. I saw Lou play with: a Fender solid body 12 string guitar, a Gibson semi-hollow body, a Gibson stereo semi-hollow body, an Epiphone semi-hollow body (towards the end at Max's Kansas City) – pretty much stock I'd say. The Gretsch Country Gentleman had four pickups (they usually have 2), built in pre-amp, built in tremolo unit, added Gretsch pickup, added Stratocaster Fender pickup for more treble. Those guys used Vox amps and Vox fuzz boxes for the first two albums. On stuff like "Sister Ray" and "The Gift", the fuzz is important. Vox fuzz boxes are distinct from other fuzz sounds. Lou used to use the built-in mid-range boost peculiar to Vox amplifiers a lot. Their sound changed when the group switched to Acoustic brand amps in '69 then again when they switched to Sunn brand in '70. The Voxes had a darker sound with more mid-range tone. Much more. And it was easier to get feedback out of 'em. Like on "Heroin", "European Son" etc. Some of that feedback was John Cale on his electric viola playing through the Vox amps. One thing more. That Gretsch was converted to stereo enabling him to get low bass and hi-treble at the same time.

BOCKRIS: Was it true that "White Light/White Heat" was recorded in one day?

MORRISON: No, but almost. Gary Kellgren was the engineer. He was completely competent. The technical deficiencies on the album are attributable to us. We would not accommodate what we were trying to do to the limitations of the studio. We kept on saying we don't want to hear any problems.

BOCKRIS: It says on the record Tom Wilson was Executive Producer. Was he actually in the studio working with you?

MORRISON: He was in there, but no producer could over-ride our taste. We'd do a whole lot of takes.

BOCKRIS: How were the working conditions in the studio when they recorded "White Light/White Heat"?

SESNICK: That's a long complicated question. They were quick. To sum it all up it did go very fast. I think it was done in three days of recording. They were very rapid. They were well prepared when they went in. And their method of recording was such that it could be done very quickly and they believed in that particular manner at that time and it just went real fast.

BOCKRIS: Would it be accurate to say that Lou was particularly proficient in working fast in the studio or is that putting too much emphasis on his contribution?

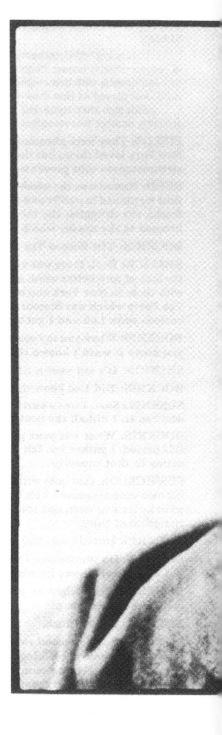

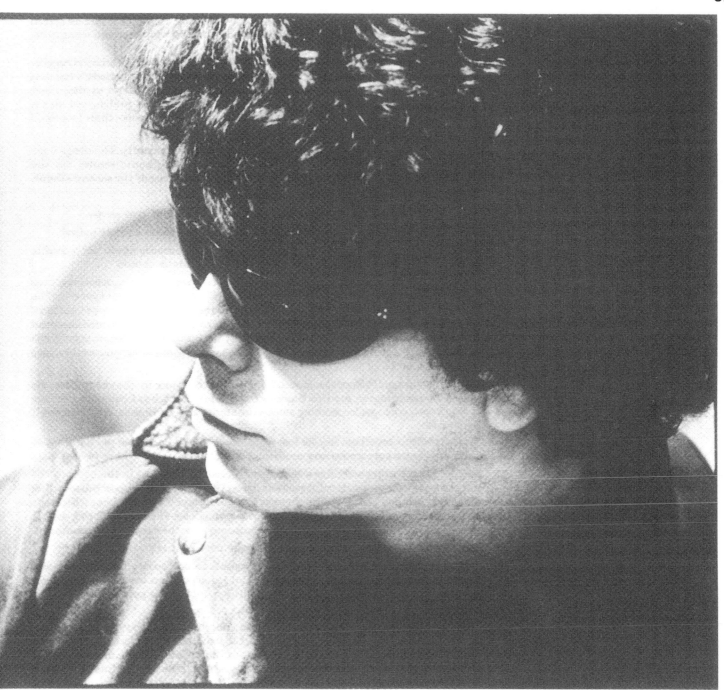

Lou Reed.
(Nat Finkelstein)

SESNICK: I would say that Lou was beyond proficient. He was a master at understanding the time and reasons for things.

BOCKRIS: At the time of recording that album were he and John Cale working well together or was the tension that caused the split between them already obvious?

SESNICK: It was not obvious at that time. They worked together fairly well because of the speed with which things were done. Had they had more time who knows what would have happened? But no, there was no problem at all. They were rehearsing quite a bit too. We arranged for various rehearsals and particular dates were set up to do certain things to augment our recording.

MORRISON: There would be a big brawl over which take to use. Of course everybody would opt for the takes where they sounded best. It was a tremendous hassle, so on "Sister Ray" which we knew was going to be a major effort we stared at each other and said, "This is going to be one take. So whatever you want to do, you better do it now."

And that explains what is going on in the mix. There is a musical struggle – everyone's trying to do what he wants to do every second, and nobody's backing off. I think it's great the way the organ comes in. Cale starts to try and play a solo. He's totally buried and there's a sort of surge and then he's pulling out all the stops until he just rises out of the pack. He was able to get louder than Lou and I were. The drums are almost totally drowned out.

CALE: The second album was like hanging by your fingernails. The songs were hypes. We always played loud in order to get the symphonic sound, but the loudness was supposed to bring clarity, and that wasn't true of the second album.

BOCKRIS: How long did it take to record?

TUCKER: Approximately seven sessions over a period of two weeks.

BOCKRIS: How were the group to work with in the studio at that point?

TUCKER: From my end it wasn't uptight. A few arguments about 'let's do this and let's not', but nothing major – relaxed and straight ahead.

MORRISON: If you were a producer trying to tell us what to do, that wasn't too good. What we needed in a producer was really an educator. Everyone in The Velvet Underground was strong-willed, but Mo took a quiet role in our conflicts. She always said there was no reasoning with any of us, that we were all crazy, and there was no sense in arguing. I think basically the band had three uncontrollable personalities, and if you throw drugs into the confusion then you really have problems.

REED: Maureen Tucker's so beautiful. she has to be one of the most fantastic people I've ever met in my life. She's so impossibly great, but I can never believe it, you know, when we're walking round the studio and I run into Mo, I just can't believe it.

MORRISON: I love Lou, but he has what must be a fragmented personality, so you're never too sure under any conditions what you're going to have to deal with.

REED: I think everybody has a number of personalities, just in themselves. It's not just people having different personalities. I mean you wake up in the morning and say, "wonder which one of them is around today?" You find out which one and send him out. Fifteen minutes later someone else shows up. That's why if there's no one left to talk to you can listen to a couple of them talking in your head.

BOCKRIS: What are the effects of a steady dose of meth-amphetamine?

CALE: It changes the muscle structure in your face, so you can't smile anymore. Your face gets limp and sags. You smile and it looks like a weird, Frankenstein grimace. So people can't tell if Lou's joking or not. He's got a great sense of humor.

MORRISON: Will he be boyishly charming, naive – Lou is very charming when he wants to be. Or will he be vicious – and if he is, then you have to figure out what's stoking the fire. What drug is he on, or what mad diet? He had all sorts of strange dietary theories. He'd eat nothing, like live on wheat husks. He was always trying to move mentally and spiritually to some place where no one had ever gotten before.

BOCKRIS: How did you rehearse?

MORRISON: We never changed our method from back on Ludlow Street. We would practise the beginning and the end of a song. As we never played it the same way twice it didn't matter if we practised the middle. If there was anything weird about it then we went over that. But the songs we practised most – the truly polished pieces – we never recorded. We knew we could do them, so there was no more interest. We wanted to see if we could make something else work. Our best stuff, about 80% of it, was either radically reworked in the studio or written there.

CALE: There's a lot of improvisation on "White Light/White Heat". Most of the recording was done straight through; "Sister Ray" was one piece. "I Heard Her Call My Name" and "Here She Comes Now" evolved in the studio. We never performed them live. "The Gift" was a story Lou had written a long time ago

Maureen Tucker and John Cale backstage
(Nat Finkelstein)

when he was at Syracuse University. It was my idea to do it as a spoken-word thing. We had this piece called "Booker T" that was just an instrumental, so instead of wasting it we decided to combine them. The cover is a very dark picture of a biker's arm with a tattoo on it – a skull and cross-bones.

BOCKRIS: Did the four of you have a strong connection about the sound you wanted?

MORRISON: Yeah, but we also put each other on the spot. Like you can come up and say 'I'd like to try this'. And then someone would say, 'Okay, fine, try it', but you only got about two tries. And then after that that's the end of it. We had had a problem with "Heroin" between the one we did initially and the one that we did out in L.A. There had been a lot of quick shuffling. So, when we got to "Sister Ray" we solved the problem by deciding there was only going to be one take. Naturally everyone prefers the take where they sound the best. That put an end to that bullshit. So, if you have anything to do you better do it right this second, otherwise we don't want to hear about it. I do believe that was an accurate representation. One take that would eliminate all arguments. I quit the group for a couple of days because I thought they chose the wrong mix for "I Hear Her Call My Name", one of our best songs that was completely ruined in the studio. Overall I think the album is a technical failure. We didn't want to lay down separate tracks, we wanted to do it studio live with a simultaneous voice, but the problem was that the current state of studio art wouldn't let us do it. There was fantastic leakage because everyone was playing so loud and we had so much electronic junk with us in the studio – all these fuzzers and compressors. Gary Kellgran, the engineer, who is ultra-competent, told us repeatedly, 'You can't do it – all the needles are on red'. And we reacted as we always reacted: 'Look, we don't know what goes on in there and we don't want to hear about it. Just do the best you can.' And so the album is all fuzzy; there's all that white noise.

In the Fall of 1967 I moved in with Martha Dargan and her brother Tom on East 2nd Street. John moved in with Betsey at the Chelsea somewhere around this time, and Lou was here and there, mostly on Perry Street, and later at the loft on Seventh Avenue and 31st Street. Maureen was living on Fifth Avenue and 9th Street.

Andy Warhol contributed the cover concept, a photograph of a tattoo on Billy Linich's upper arm, but otherwise had nothing to do with the record. The group consisted of the original Velvets without Nico, who was already working on her first solo album (for MGM/Verve) "Chelsea Girls", and to which, to indicate the continuing spirit of collaboration and support that existed between all these people, both Lou and John contributed songs and played on some of the tracks. Cale received his first solo song-writing credit on "Chelsea Girls" which also contains a song credited to Lou Reed and Sterling Morrison, another first.

In October Brian Epstein made his third approach, offering to set up an international tour of Europe, and The Velvets said that would be fine. However, just as they were about to sign the contracts, he died, effectively closing down that channel. This was particularly unfortunate, because going to Europe was one thing that might have had a very positive effect upon the group. It's likely they would have been more appreciated there than they were in the States, as is evident from Gerard Malanga's experiences in Italy at the time. According to this letter Lou wrote Gerard in Italy at the end of 1967 groups were asking for permission to record Velvets' songs.

December 23, 1967

Dear Gerard – hope this finds you well. Have sent you a check for $167.00, your share of last year's show at the Trip, for which we finally got paid. Know you need it so I sent it by registered special delivery and you should have it by now. Also did write your friends (Equipe 84) to say, yes, record "Heroin". I think that's great and it's nice of you to think of us. You know we used a beautiful picture of Mario Anniballi's for the back of our new album "White Light/White Heat" which is coming out in January. The cover is a black on black picture of a motorcyclist tatoo (sic) by Billy. Beautiful. ALL BLACK! I have a loft, you know. You now have my address so write direct to me rather than through Roz who has kept me well informed. It is Xmas soon but in New York it is warm, 58 degrees, nice walking. Ondine, Mary and Rene are in a great play, "Conquest of the Universe" and it's too much and I can't describe it, which gives you a hint. Andy did his 25 hour movie and it was ENORMOUS and beyond. Hope all holidays are delightful as the New Year is inevitable: Do write – Lou.

NICO exclusively on MGM/VERVE RECORDS

● 1968-THE BLACK YEAR

● **MORRISON: I don't see 1968 as a black year at all, except that we ended it without Cale (an event that blackened it as much as possible, to be sure). I considered it our best year – our touring was successful, and our playing was excellent. Perhaps the possibility of real success suddenly became so tangible that we pursued it into megalomania and ruin. Our struggles to succeed on our own terms, once directed outwards at audiences, record execs, radio stations and what not, perhaps turned inward towards the group, with unfortunate consequences. We decided that the major market was here. Success was succeeding here, not in England, Germany, or Scandinavia. It had to happen here first. We were frequently exhorted to go over to Europe for a bit. Perhaps we should have.**

How did The Velvets feel on January 30th of 1968 when their second album "White Light/White Heat" was released? Cocky and confident say some; paranoid, vulnerable and fragile say others. John Cale was the sort of guy who was afraid to go out on the street. Lou could be bitter, cynical, sarcastic at times. They were the perfect match and the perfect mismatch. They held an adverse attitude toward everything. John and Sterling are both on record as saying the second album was a hype, a technical failure.

The Velvet Underground were highly appreciated by a very small coterie of alert, intelligent people. For this group, who hung around the Chelsea Hotel and Max's, they were 'our band'. They knew what they were doing was really good but they were dismayed by the lack of support from the record label. They were frustrated by their inability to reach larger audiences, and even had some trouble getting jobs in the aftermath of their emergence from The E.P.I. as a four-piece unit. The majority of The E.P.I. shows had been booked after all on the strength of Warhol's name. Tom Wilson interviewed Lou and John on Boston radio in February of '68 and asked Lou what his plans were.

REED: We wanted to ultimately work on a tape that would take up every minute of every hour of every day of the entire year! I didn't bother to figure out how many hours that is. It would just be one extremely long tape and it would fit into your wall and it would be personalized because what would happen is that you would come to us – The Velvet Underground – and say I want a tape from you and we'd say, 'Here'. Then you'd take that and we'd take you by the hand over to Gary (Kellgren, engineer) at the recording studio and Gary would stare at them a lot

Sterling Morrison on the road. Fall 1968.
(Sterling Morrison Archive)

until he figured he knew them and then he would reflect their personality and then they'd take the tape back and they'd install it in the wall and it would be like theirs and it would go on all day like one of Andy's movies, like "Empire" could be on the other wall, like the music going on all the time. Like John said the other day the albums that should come out would have a coloring book and toys. People are starting to do that but they haven't really gotten into it. They're messing around with covers trying to be hip and doing things but they haven't really started what you could have. But it would go on all the time.

WILSON: You can tell a man by the records he plays.

REED: We'd supply arm-bands and labels. We'd re-classify...

WILSON: Fantastic: It's frightening and yet enormous and it seems logical in terms of things that are going on now.

Steve Sesnick in the lap of luxury, Beverly Wilshire Hotel, May 1968. (Sterling Morrison Archive)

CUTRONE: I loved "White Light/White Heat". Again it was this great understatement. The cover was a darkened photograph of Billy Linich's tattoo that you had to scrutinize to see the image. It was so cool that people weren't ready. It was just too cool, it was the coolest thing in the world at that moment. Nobody knew what white light was. People thought it was acid. And white heat? Nobody understood that it was an amphetamine rush that made your toes hot and made your eyes go blind and see just clear white heat. I think the words, the imagery, the subtlety of the album cover confused a lot of people. Again, The Rolling Stones were making 3-D album covers, The Beatles had beautiful little pictures of them looking cute, and then this dark album comes out with a very subdued picture of a tattoo. It doesn't fit in anywhere, so that was strange.

BOCKRIS: What was The Velvets' reaction to the reception of "White Light/White Heat"?

CUTRONE: Everybody's egos were so strong that they already assumed they were the greatest. In terms of money I'm sure it hurt. I mean it would be great to be successful in terms of money, but musically there was no compromise. It was "go on, believe in this, do this", and as it turned out twelve years later they proved to be absolutely on target. Now the sales on that album, if it's even available, are probably phenomenal. I don't run into too many people these days who don't know about The Velvet Underground, even just from word of mouth. It's a pity that some of their records are unavailable because they're much better than a lot of the stuff that we hear now.

BOCKRIS: Did you feel "White Light/White Heat" was a great record when it came out and people were really going to like it?

TUCKER: I was very happy with it. I thought it was a real good record. We were all disappointed once more by MGM. It was never in the stores, the same bullshit. In certain towns like Boston it did well and everybody loved it. A lot of people who could get their hands on it really liked it. But our record audience was limited to people who saw us live. Because we were never on the radio. MGM just didn't do anything to promote us. I mean the fans that we made then were really crazed. And they still are. I'm stunned by what people still think of us.

BOCKRIS: How did you feel about things at the beginning of '68?

TUCKER: I was always very positive about the group. I really did believe that we had something special, not in a Beatles way, in a more important way. I really did think we were damn good.

BOCKRIS: And presumably the rest of the group felt that too?

TUCKER: They enjoyed what they were doing. I don't know if maybe – being males – they didn't allow themselves to think, 'Holy Shit, we're great!'

BOCKRIS: Were you performing much when the record came out?

TUCKER: I couldn't swear that in the month surrounding the release of the record we were playing, but Sesnick kept us pretty busy. We went to California a couple of times, and to Canada, St. Louis and Texas.

BOCKRIS: How was Sesnick to work with?

TUCKER: I enjoyed him. I always had fun with him, liked him a lot. He was terribly enthusiastic and incredibly positive.

BOCKRIS: You felt your relations with him were pretty straightforward?

TUCKER: I did at the time. I'm really not sure quite what to think now. I knew he always had our interest at heart and he worked damn hard. I think one reason it just didn't work, was that he just had too high of a dream, seeing us as the next Beatles and having people screaming in the streets. Having that big of a dream, he turned down a lot of things, thinking this isn't the right time to do that.

BOCKRIS: How were relations in the group?

TUCKER: Real good.

BOCKRIS: Wasn't the developing split between John and Lou causing a lot of tension?

TUCKER: At certain times there'd be a lot of tension between them, but I got along just great with everybody so I never felt, 'Oh boy, this sucks. I think I'll quit'.

BOCKRIS: Was Steve Sesnick like a fifth member of the group?

TUCKER: Yes, he was.

BOCKRIS: By the beginning of 1968 were you living in New York?

SESNICK: Yes.

BOCKRIS: Did you all feel very positive about this new beginning?

SESNICK: Yes, we felt very positive, we did, very much so, we thought the record was great. We certainly were shocked when radio stations didn't think it was so great. But we were used to that. We never had airplay then – it just didn't happen – so we didn't care about it.

BOCKRIS: I presumed that you must have felt very positive at the beginning of '68, yet '68 was a pretty bleak year in many ways.

SESNICK: Oh, not really, I don't think so, I went to a party that year with Lou – it was fun.

BOCKRIS: How did people react to the second album?

MORRISON: They were stunned.

Lou Reed with Stephen Shore
(Nat Finkelstein)

● "WHITE LIGHT/WHITE HEAT"

What exactly did they serve up on *White Light/White Heat*, the only album recorded in their original formation without the presence of any other singers or influences other than their engineer Gary Kellgren and producer Tom Wilson?

● **Side One:**

● **"White Light/White Heat":** A raucous, humorous, celebration of amphetamine. Wayne McGuire, writing in *Crawdaddy*, said: 'The track "White Light/White Heat" best illustrates my contention that John Cale is the heaviest bass player in the country today. Most bass players play two-dimensional notes, but John plays three-dimensional granite slabs which reveal an absolute mastery of his instruments and a penetrating awareness of the most minute details of his music.'

● **"The Gift":** Author Lou Reed, never puts a foot wrong throughout the piece, possibly inspired by Shirley Jackson's short story "The Lottery", which is perfectly related by a deadpan John Cale in his best 'BBC voice'.

WILSON: Let me hip you to the stereo version of this record. When you're at home you take that balance-control, you flip it over to one side and you get the information that's on one groove-wall of your record and that's the short story by itself without the music. Of course, if you just reverse your balance-control or your channel-selector you'll get some very groovy music to hang out with, somebody you'll like. And if you're a mad fiend like we are, you'll listen to them altogether. That's where we're at. We got stereo prefrontal lobes.

● **"Lady Godiva's Operation":** A Burroughsian rendition of the Lady Godiva legend.

● **"Here She Comes Now"** is a rather pretty 4-line dissertation on the possibility that a girl might come.

● **Side Two:**

● **"I Heard Her Call My Name"** is an intense declaration of love for a girl who has been dead for some time.

McGUIRE: This track contains one of the most pregnant and highly charged moments I've ever heard in music: a split-second pause of silence after the second 'my mind's split open' foreshadowing the following feedback explosion.

CALE: Lou's an excellent guitar player. He's nuts. It has more to do with the spirit of what he's doing than playing.

REED: When Jimi Hendrix came over the most striking thing beside his truly incredible guitar virtuosity was his savage, if playful, rape of his instrument. It would squeal and whine going off into a crescendo of leaps and yells that only chance could program. (See, we are extensions of Mr Cage, it's all so modern and primitive at the same time, how simultaneous). Anyone who does that night after night must go mad. It was the frenzy of self, for frustration can only be acted out in violent ways, never mime. If any part of it becomes sham, then vital energies are used to mimic the worst aspects of self and both mind and body are soon exhausted.

● **"Sister Ray"** was written on a train coming back from a bad gig in Connecticut.

REED: The only way to go through something is to go right into the middle, the only way to do it is to not kid around. Storm coming – you go right through the center and you may come out alright. Most people don't even know there's a center. All the people I've known who were fabulous have either died, or flipped, or gone to India. Either that or they've concentrated on one focal point which is what I'm doing. "Sister Ray" was done as a joke – no, not as a joke, but it has eight characters in it and this guy gets killed and nobody does anything. The situation is a bunch of drag queens taking some sailors home with them, shooting up on smack and having this orgy when the police appear. When it came to putting the music to it, it had to be spontaneous. The jam came about right there in the studio. We didn't use any splices or anything. I had been listening to a lot of Cecil Taylor and Ornette Coleman, and wanted to get something like that with a rock & roll feeling. When we did "Sister Ray", we turned up to ten flat out, leakage all over the place. That's it. They asked us what we were going to do. We said 'We're going to start'. They said 'Who's playing bass?' We said 'There is no bass'. They

THE VELVET UNDERGROUND exclusively on MGM/VERVE RECORDS R-1938

asked us when it ends. We didn't know. When it ends, that's when it ends. It did a lot to the music of the Seventies. We were doing the whole heavy metal trip back then. I mean if "Sister Ray" is not an example of heavy metal, then nothing is. But we discarded it because we got tired of it. Maureen was perfect on that song. She works for a computer company now, and you can tell from us that she was born to the job. All we wanted was someone who could play on a telephone book.

"'Sister Ray" shows that recorded pop is at last making decisive steps in a direction with far-reaching implications for the creative development not only of pop itself but of 'serious' music too,' wrote Tim Souster in *The Listener* July 4, 1968 (the album had a May release in the UK). The long laudatory review focusing almost entirely on this single track ends, 'A final note of congratulations to the producer Tom Wilson for having got onto a record a very creditable replica of a pop group's live sound. I have never before heard the aura of high frequencies and distortion which binds the sound together into a single phenomenon coming out of a gramophone record.'

Summing up the whole album and The Velvets progress in his *Crawdaddy* article, Wayne McGuire writes: 'Why is John Cale the heaviest bass player in the country today? Because his nervous system is an aristocrat among nervous systems, because of the deep dark electricity he is able to convey through his bass and viola. And why is Maureen Tucker the perfect drummer for the V.U.? Because of her spirituality and nervous system. No other drummer in the world could play the archetypal 1234 with such perfection, with a weight that verges on religious ritual (not necessarily a Black Mass). And it is that ritualistic quality which is a mainstay of the Underground's powerful stylistic unity, a stylistic element which is immediately recognizable from the initial bar as the driving pulse of a machine-like organism (just listen to one bar of "The Gift"). In essence, she's playing Elvin Jones to Lou Reed's Coltrane or Sonny Murray to Reed's Albert Ayler. Lou Reed is fast becoming an incisive lyricist, creating a folk mythology of New York City and our generation which rings deep and true through the pap of fumbling unfocused artificial surrealistic imagery and facile pseudo-mystical-morality lessons produced by most new groups.'

The critics were not completely deaf, but MGM continued to be dumb and did nothing to market their valuable product, so despite a few reviews, the excellent album received sparse airplay and sold less copies than its predecessor peaking in the *Billboard* Charts at 200.

Billboard Album Review, February 24, 1968, *White Light/White Heat*: Dealers who cater to the underground market will find this disk a hot seller, for The Velvet Underground (minus Nico) feature intriguing lyrics penned by two of the group, Lou Reed and Sterling Morrison. Though the words tend to be drowned out by the pulsating instrumentation, those not minding to cuddle up to the speakers will joy to narrative songs such as "The Gift", the story of a boy and a girl.

WILSON: After I see the things that people are willing to buy and do, I sometimes think that a 13-year old girl who buys a rock & roll record may be exercising just as intelligent a choice as her parents are when they do important things.

REED: I agree. I know she's doing something important.

● EXIT CALE

● 1968 seems to have been a year of amputations. It was a year in which everybody's position changed or was changed. The Velvets set to tour the U.S., making $600 one week, $2500 the next. It was the only way they could make money and they liked to play, but the pressures of life on the road did little to assuage the developing tension between Reed and Cale, who are said to have come to blows on occasions during this period.

BOCKRIS: Were you on the road for months at a time playing one-nighters?

TUCKER: No, we were never into that. The longest we were ever away was two months and that was hell. If we went out to the Coast we couldn't afford to fly back and forth so we'd stay out there for six weeks and play up and down the coast a little bit. Being on the road is mostly real boring. The only real good thing is playing. We didn't really do full tours, though. We played five or six times on the West Coast, and we'd play Chicago and Texas and a few places, but it wasn't like long tours playing every night.

BOCKRIS: So during this period did you have a road manager?

TUCKER: Yeah, we had Hans Onsager. He was with us from when Dave Faison left through to the end.

MORRISON: Faison left late in 1966 because he needed more money. He later did well in sound systems and various rock music ventures on the West Coast. Next came Phil Schier in 1967. He was Lou's room-mate for a while at Syracuse and played bass with him at times. He was a Formula I race driver, and general car freak. When he left late in 1967 or so, it was to open up a recording studio in LA, which became successful. Hans Onsager was our equipment manager from then on. His father won the Nobel Prize in Physics in 1968 while at Yale. Hans is a New England Yankee, well brought up, and fun to be around.

John Cale and Betsey Johnson married in New York in April 1968. The band was in Los Angeles, playing and recording when the news of the Andy Warhol shooting reached them on June 4th.

BOCKRIS: Do you remember where you were and what your reaction was to Andy Warhol being shot?

Sterling Morrison, Nico and Lou Reed with John Cale and Betsey Johnson on their wedding day.
(Betsey Johnson Archive)

15c

Vol. XV, No. 34 • New York, N. Y. • Thursday, June 6, 1968

ANDY WARHOL

Voice: Fred W. McDarrah

Andy Warhol

The Shot that Shattered
The Velvet Underground

by Howard Smith

It was an ordinary afternoon at The Factory, the huge, new loft on the north side of Union Square which is the center of the Warhol scene. Sun came in the windows and gleamed off the mirror-topped desks. Paul Morrissey, Warhol's executive producer, and Fred Hughes, an assistant, sat around talking with Mario Amaya, a visiting art magazine editor from London.

Suddenly the elevator doors opened and Andy Warhol walked into the loft with Valerie Solanis, a sometime writer and super-woman-power advocate who had appeared in his film, "I, a Man." She had come by The Factory earlier in the afternoon looking for him outside in front of the building for three hours. They walked over to talk with Morrissey, Hughes, and Amaya. It was typical Factory small talk. Hughes recalled. "You still writing dirty books, Valerie?" he asked.

Hughes wandered off, and Morrissey took off to the bathroom. Then the telephone rang, and

VALERIE SOLANIS

Voice: Fred W. McDarrah

Warhol went to answer it. While he spoke with Viva, the reigning superstar, Valerie Solanis pulled a .32 automatic out of the pocket of her trench coat. Warhol turned and saw the gun. "Valerie," he yelled, "Don't do it! No! No!" She fired three shots, and Warhol fell to the floor.

Then she turned on Amaya, Continued on page 34

SESNICK: I was with Lou. We were going down in an elevator in the Beverly Wilshire Hotel. In that particular hotel they put the morning papers on the floor of the elevator. We were both extremely shocked and startled when we looked down and saw the headlines. Bobby Kennedy was shot a few days later. I remember the two incidents came at the same time. We were both extremely upset. It also struck us as very scarey because apparently Lou knew who the girl was who did it. So we were upset for Andy and I was upset and concerned for Lou – that something like that might happen to him some day. As a manager who watches over those things, it was a very serious shock.

In the aftermath of the shooting, as all those who loved him waited to see if Andy would survive, a blackness descended. The image became more seriously negative. The party was really over. It was a hard, depressing time for everyone. Lou and John were constantly at odds. Nothing seemed as pure and noble as it had. The silver tarnished. July 19-21st they were at the Avalon Ballroom in San Francisco. Even the original rock & roll animal was beginning to feel the grind.

REED: Who can you talk to on the road? Long-haired dirty drug people wherever you look. The boy passes over a bag of green powder and passes out. Don't take that, it has horse tranquilizer in it. Oh, I shot up to your song. I got busted to your song. Oh, please bless me and touch me and make it all go away. I loved to you.

CALE: I was thinking one time about creating weather by using music. In brain surgery they use ultrasonics for cutting away tissue. They do that by a heating process. I think of high frequencies creating heat in matter. Low frequencies are made up of pulses and movements of columns of air – an example of an extremely low frequency would be a hurricane or a whirlwind. In France a professor has studied a death-ray machine which propels very low sounds. He has this organ-pit which is several hundred feet long and when they tested it out they killed a lot of people in the factory. A lot of people became sick. The machine made everything vibrate. The music I'd been writing six-years ago was a set of instructions for the wind and listening to it – all the vibrations of sound. Some of the things I've been finding out about electronics seem to suggest that it's possible to produce sound to alter the temperature, make the air warmer or cooler, according to which combination of pitches you use. I'd like to have a tape that would create a 75-degree temperature. Over a period of days you could play a tape that would regulate the heat around you. The kind of heat that would give off would be in some cases like summer or autumn.

It's a pity Cale couldn't have created music that would have altered the way he and Reed reacted to one another.

LYNNE TILLMAN: The relationship between John and Lou was symbiotic in a certain way. They were very close. They loved each other, but they also hated each other. It was competitive musically. John knew Lou got much more attention because he was the singer in the group, but then John cut a more flamboyant figure. He was being dressed by Betsey Johnson. Lou used to call him the "Welsh Bob Dylan".

BOCKRIS: What about his relationship with Lou?

JOHNSON: I don't remember any specific crack. He just wasn't with them. It seemed real logical to me. I just really supported him and thought he ought to do his own music. It was really his music and then Lou's music. It seemed like they went as far as they could go in a way being The Velvet Underground. There was no kind of growth for them. Now they're heroes for what they did, but then, to keep a group together for what? – a record contract, social acknowledgement, acceptance? Not people like that. John's split was personal, but it was kind of more John just realizing he had to do his own stuff.

BOCKRIS: What was the atmosphere of these gigs? How were they together?

JOHNSON: I wasn't very comfortable. Probably because I wasn't taking drugs but I was very attracted to people taking drugs, or just attracted to anything that I hadn't been around when I grew up. Going to a gig I remember not saying much, feeling what I said was not very important. I remember hanging around with Susan Pile. I remember them being very quiet. They weren't the buddy-buddy gang. Mo was a woman of a few succinct, wonderful words. I really liked her. And Sterling was very, very sweet. They were never like their image except for Lou

Lou Reed backstage at The Boston Teaparty at John Cale's last gig, September 28, 1967. (The Modern Printer)

A sombre John Cale contemplates his future, backstage at The Boston Teaparty during his last gig with The Velvet Underground, September 28, 1967. (The Modern Printer)

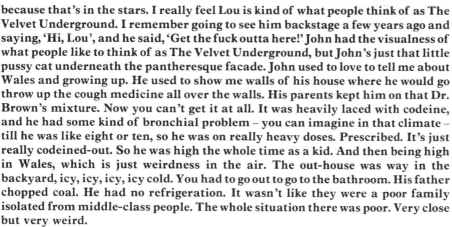

because that's in the stars. I really feel Lou is kind of what people think of as The Velvet Underground. I remember going to see him backstage a few years ago and saying, 'Hi, Lou', and he said, 'Get the fuck outta here!' John had the visualness of what people like to think of as The Velvet Underground, but John's just that little pussy cat underneath the pantheresque facade. John used to love to tell me about Wales and growing up. He used to show me walls of his house where he would go throw up the cough medicine all over the walls. His parents kept him on that Dr. Brown's mixture. Now you can't get it at all. It was heavily laced with codeine, and he had some kind of bronchial problem – you can imagine in that climate – till he was like eight or ten, so he was on really heavy doses. Prescribed. It's just really codeined-out. So he was high the whole time as a kid. And then being high in Wales, which is just weirdness in the air. The out-house was way in the backyard, icy, icy, icy, icy cold. You had to go out to go to the bathroom. His father chopped coal. He had no refrigeration. It wasn't like they were a poor family isolated from middle-class people. The whole situation there was poor. Very close but very weird.

BOCKRIS: John said it took him a long time to regain his vitality after he left the group.

JOHNSON: No collaboration.

MORRISON: John and I were very happy with "Sister Ray"–type music. Although I'm teaching English now, I don't really care about lyrics in music. I like energy and emotion, yelling and grunting. Snarls and hisses like in "The Black Angel's Death Song" – that's Cale hissing. Lou placed heavy emphasis on lyrics, while Cale and I were more interested in blasting the house down.

In August Lou called and asked me to meet him at the Riviera Cafe in the West Village. When I got there Maureen was also present. Lou had called a meeting to announce John was out of the band.

I said, 'You mean out for today, or for this week?' And Lou said, 'No, he's out'. I said that we were the band, that it was graven on the tablets. So then a long and bitter argument ensued, with much banging on tables, and finally Lou said,

John Cale
(Nat Finkelstein)

'You don't go for it? Alright, the band is dissolved'. Now I could say that it was more important to keep the band together than to worry about Cale, but that wasn't really what decided me. I just wanted to keep on doing it. So finally I weighed my self-interest against Cale's interests and sold him out.

BOCKRIS: Do you remember the meeting Lou called at the Riviera to announce that Cale was out of the group?

TUCKER: I wasn't that shocked because the tensions were there and John was obviously not too happy, but I was real sad, and worried that we wouldn't proceed. Sterling was rather furious as I recall. I guess he felt that it wasn't really fair for one person to say this guy's out.

BOCKRIS: Was Lou presenting it as if he had fired John?

TUCKER: Yeah, and his idea was, 'Do you wanna go with him or do you wanna stay with me?' I felt disappointed, but I guess I knew it was coming. I knew it was what had to happen because of the personality problem. I myself never understood what the problem was between them. I think maybe John wanted to have more of a hand in writing the songs. Maybe going in a different direction. But it just became too much tension. For Lou I guess, and John. There was a bad period right around when John left. Like I said, I lived out on the Island so I wasn't around it every day. But when we were together you could really sense it.

WARHOL: Why did he break up with John? They had a fight?

CUTRONE: That I don't know.

WARHOL: You know.

CUTRONE: It was ego.

CALE: We were very distraught at the time. There was pressure building up – God knows from where – and we were all getting very frustrated.

BOCKRIS: Did he feel betrayed and fucked over by Lou?

JOHNSON: I just remember a real edge with Lou all the time. Ego-jealousy. Lou was definitely the star. Any guy that is out there singing is the star. It was hard for John because he was back-up star. He had so much charisma. He had the balance of The Velvet Underground charisma. Lou without John, it wouldn't have had the edge. John gave it that romantic . . . I mean the sound of The Velvet Underground was John. The words and the music were Lou but it was those weird nails on the blackboard sounds and the holding of the notes and that LaMonte Young/Terry Riley preface to The Velvet Underground – that cold edgey Wales edge and John just visually was the person I always looked at. I don't know if John knew that . . . John knew it enough that he was jealous. I just didn't feel so great about Lou either.

BOCKRIS: What was it about Lou that put you off.

JOHNSON: Just that we didn't click. I was definitely not with the in-crowd. I was John's wife. I wasn't jumping in with the drugs. I had a place there because I was John's wife and I was doing something.

BOCKRIS: What was happening with their records? They're great great records and they must have realized how great they were.

JOHNSON: I don't remember ever talking business to John, ever feeling that it was interesting enough to talk about.

BOCKRIS: What was Warhol's reputation at the time?

JOHNSON: He was the one that made it happen because he was a Sixties success story. The clothing, the music, was all under the label of art. I don't remember any wonderful laid-back feeling of success. When you're doing something that interesting, to get good coverage, it's never successful financially for you. It's only when you don't get coverage that you know you're really doing well. I just remember more struggle than craziness, and funny stuff. How could John ever talk to me about music? I knew the frustrations within the group. I was going through the same frustrations. I don't think he felt good about Steve Sesnick. I don't think inside the group they thought of Lou as being leader of the group. I know personally it was hard for John because he really felt that Lou was the leader of the group. But they were so good together that I think that's why it was so hard for John to break . . . it was a survival thing.

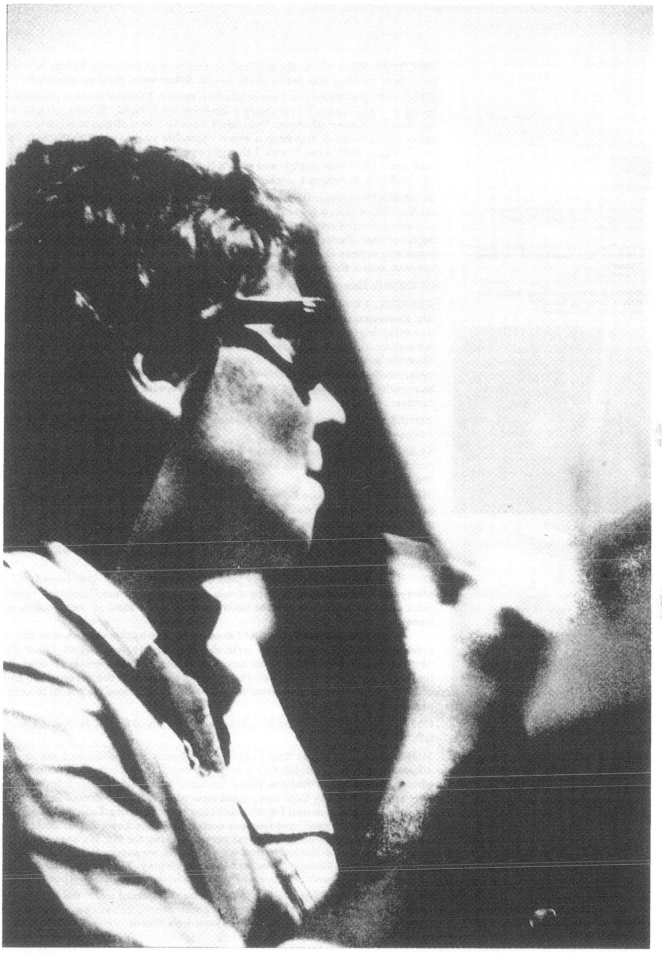

Maureen Tucker.
(Billy Linich)

Maureen Tucker and Sterling Morrison
backstage at The Boston Teaparty.
(The Modern Printer)

Steve Sesnick sucking on a bottle of booze
with Doug Yule, backstage at The Boston
Teaparty.
(The Modern Printer)

Sterling Morrison and Doug Yule at The
Boston Teaparty, Fall 1968.
(Sterling Morrison Archive)

BOCKRIS: What about the musical atmosphere at the time. In '66, '67 and '68 they were making this really great music. What were they up against?

JOHNSON: Jim Morrison. I never liked his music. The Stones were underground enough. They weren't everybody's favorite rock band. It was alright to be whatever you were all about. You didn't have to join a clique to be able to make sense being there. It was such a weird vegetable soup. I used to think it was so much bigger than what it was. I thought everybody wore silver and mini-skirts and now when I look back it was such a tiny group of people. We were all getting screwed and we weren't working in any kind of establishment.

MORRISON: I agree. It seemed that it was happening all over to everybody, but really it wasn't. In a sense it never happened at all. At this moment school girls are being hassled anew by school administrators over the wearing of mini-skirts. Sad, but true. Perhaps the Sixties will have to repeat themselves every 10 or 15 years just to keep driving home the same lessons. I used to think everything was obvious, now I think that nothing is.

BOCKRIS: How did everyone feel about Cale leaving the group in September?

SESNICK: I think it was a relief for everybody concerned. I think Lou wrote a line about that in "Pale Blue Eyes". It went 'down for you is up'. I don't know if he was referring to my ways or not, but nothing much ever bothered me. Down for me was up. I couldn't care less what anybody thought. I liked what I was doing, I liked the people I was with, and other people's views didn't matter much. So we never really got down and Lou was very impressed that I could take that much, but you're not taking that much when you're with people you like. It doesn't matter.

BOCKRIS: So I gather your involvement with The Velvets was pleasant and enjoyable?

SESNICK: I never lost a night's rest. Except with John. That was a very critical incident. And we felt badly about it, but there was nothing that could be done to stop it.

MORRISON: I told Lou I'd swallow it, but I didn't really like it. John was playing great at the time. He was always exciting to work with. If you listen to his bass part on "Waiting for the Man" it's illogical – inverted almost. He had really good ideas on bass. Or take a song like "What Goes On": if you'd heard us play that in the summer of '68 with Cale on organ you would have known what it was all about.

I'd have to say Lou bumped John because of jealousy. One friend said Lou always told him he wanted to be a solo star, Lou never confided that to us, but John and I always knew that he really wanted some kind of recognition apart from the band.

There are a lot of songs that I should have co-authorship on, and the same holds true for John Cale. The publishing company was called Three Prong because there were three of us involved. I'm the last person to deny Lou's immense contribution and he's the best song-writer of the three of us. But he wanted all the credit, he wanted it more than we did and he got it, to keep the peace.

CALE: Lou and I eventually found the group too small for the both of us, and so I left.

MORRISON: The thing that I didn't like about what I did was I sat back and allowed myself to watch John Cale leave the band. Essentially the problems came when John left. The band was never the same for me after John left. He was not easy to replace. Doug Yule was a good bass player, but we moved more towards unanimity of opinion and I don't think that's a good thing. I always thought that what made us real good were tensions and oppositions. I saw Velvet Underground music as crusading and it was a real personal thing for me. We were not going to compromise and in the sense that we never did, we succeeded. We actually did have an audience though we never did have airplay. The second hurdle was we had to have a commercial success and there's no way to do that without changing.

REED: I only hope that one day John will be recognized as . . . the Beethoven or something of his day. He knows so much about music, he's such a great musician. He's completely mad – but that's because he's Welsh.

BOCKRIS: Was John fired or did John quit?

SESNICK: That's a real long story and I don't want to get into it.

John Cale played his final gig with The Velvet Underground at the Boston Tea Party September 27-28 according to Jonathan Richman, a big fan of The Velvets who was backstage. Doug Yule, who had previously been in the Boston-based Glass Menagerie, came into the band kind of naturally having been friendly with them for some time. He was living at 63 River Street off Central Square in Cambridge and Sterling had stayed at his apartment when they played at the Tea Party.

MORRISON: The River Street place belonged to David Daly bon-vivant, student of Oriental religions, chef at the Orson Welles Restaurant. I liked to stay there and at Ed Hood's whenever I was in Boston, which was often. Doug used to stay there too, sometimes, so I knew him a little. I actually thought that Hans brought him into the band, because Hans had been the financial backer of the Glass Menagerie. I recall being asked about him, and I said that he plays well. He does.

Doug Yule came down to New York on the Wednesday after Cale's departure and met the band at Max's. They jammed on songs till Friday and played their first date at La Cave, on Euclid Avenue in Cleveland on October 2nd. By October 18-20 they were out in San Francisco playing the Avalon Ballroom again.

In November they continued to record the third album at TT&G Studios (now called Sunset Highland Sound) on Sunset Boulevard in LA.

BOCKRIS:Doug was brought into the group shortly after John quit.

TUCKER: Sesnick had sung his praises saying he was a good player and enthusiastic and young and pretty. It was fine with me. My concern was that we didn't really know him. And I was worried about a personality problem with him. Not because I knew him, but because we didn't know him. We had such a nice relationship all of us, and I know how tenuous those things can be, so I was thinking 'oh shit, here's someone new I wonder what he's going to be like. Maybe he can play the bass well, but is he nice?'.

BOCKRIS: What was your initial perception?

TUCKER: I liked him. I was a little concerned because I went to Louie's loft on 28th and Seventh by Penn Station to help rehearse one evening. Doug had just worked out a bass-part to "Jesus" and when I came in Louie said, 'Listen to this, it's great, it's great,' and I thought, oh God, don't swell this kid's head before he even gets out in the street. I'm not quite sure why that hit me so vividly.

BOCKRIS: I have the sense that Lou had a pretty symbiotic or was it perhaps a clone-like relationship with Doug Yule.

TUCKER: For a while. I think he was just glad to have somebody in the group that he didn't have to worry about. He liked Doug enough, he was okay and pleasant to be around, but I don't think he ever thought, 'Wow I really like this guy!' To tell you the truth, I'm sure Lou found Doug fairly boring. Except on stage, to be honest.

REED: I was working with Doug's innocence . . . I'm sure he never understood a word of what he was singing. He doesn't know what it's about. I mean, I thought it was so cute . . . I adore people who are like that, they're so cute y'know.

BOCKRIS: How different was it to be playing with Doug?

TUCKER: I enjoyed playing with Doug. He was a good musician. And good on stage, because he was a bouncy, smiley little thing. I missed having Cale being crazy on his viola. This is going to sound absurd, but I don't think it hurt the music that much. I don't think it changed it to weaker music, it just changed it.

BOCKRIS: I understand that Doug Yule joined the band within a week of John's quitting. Is that correct?

SESNICK: We were pressed. We were supposed to go on tour.

BOCKRIS: Were you responsible for bringing Doug into the group?

SESNICK: No. I thought Sterling was responsible. I don't really know. I'd never seen him before in my life. I don't know if Sterling was friendly with him, but we were in need of somebody quick and it just came up.

BOCKRIS: Talking about the third album, one thing many people comment on

Lou Reed backstage at The Boston Teaparty.
(The Modern Printer)

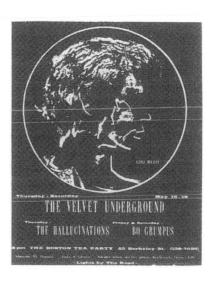

Sterling Morrison.
(Sterling Morrison Archive)

is how radically different a record it is. I asked Maureen if Steve Sesnick was a fifth member of the group, and she said, 'Yes, absolutely'.

SESNICK: That was very nice of her.

BOCKRIS: Were you involved in shaping that third record?

SESNICK: I think I was trying to find out more about Catholicism.

BOCKRIS: Who in the group was a Catholic?

SESNICK: Me! And Maureen. I guess Sterling was too, but not practising. Maureen was, and did go to Church, and I was very mystified by how I had gotten away from going to church as I grew older. I didn't really know why until I finally figured out why and that record helped me understand things that I already knew and was doing.

BOCKRIS: Why did Lou choose to have Doug sing vocals on the third album?

TUCKER: Well, Doug had a sweet little voice and he could sing certain ones better than Lou.

MORRISON: The main reason for Doug doing the vocals is that Lou's voice wasn't up to it when we were in the studio. Lou has never had a durable voice, which is one of the reasons why we tried not to play too often – a long series of one-nighters would be out of the question. Lou had used up his voice at the Whiskey, where we played during the time we were making the album. Since we wanted to get the album finished and since Doug could sing, he got the nod. The same thing happened with "Loaded". Lou's voice was wasted by the nights spent playing at Max's. It shows on the vocals he does, and some he couldn't do at all. Listen again to the Banana album, and note how good Lou's vocals are. He was well rested because the Trip had been closed down and we had nowhere else to play. We should have been so lucky while making our other records.

BOCKRIS: Was the third record recorded in LA?

TUCKER: Right. We had recorded in TT&G Studios for the first album. I guess we liked it and we got it all arranged so we could record there, and lay around in the sun.

BOCKRIS: How was the atmosphere recording that album as opposed to the previous?

TUCKER: A little less tension.

BOCKRIS: Sterling says his approach was pretty much of acquiescence.

TUCKER: Sterling's a pain in the ass!

MORRISON: All I mean by 'acquiescence' is that I didn't argue hotly about this or that feature in the album. My contribution was as much as ever, probably more even, but I just didn't try to get my own way all the time. Perhaps the Cale business left me all argued out, or perhaps I just didn't feel that strongly about the material one way or the other.

TUCKER: I guess that's around the time Sterling was beginning to get disgusted with Lou, pissed off, whatever the word is, why I don't know. It had a lot to do with them being males I'm sure. I know that sounds tacky, but I've thought a lot about this, and I think it has a lot to do with it, ego problems and all. I mean if Lou said to me, 'Mo, try some cymbals on this one, I want to hear what it sounds like', fine, that didn't bother me. But for Lou to say, 'Sterl, try this', didn't sit quite so well. I think that had a little to do with it. Actually I can't honestly say that I recall Lou ever saying, try this or do that, to me. I just fooled around until it sounded like I liked it, and as long as everybody else liked what I was doing, fine.

BOCKRIS: You never had any problems with Lou?

TUCKER: No, not at all. We got along very well. I just found it totally acceptable if Lou was being crazy, or being a pain in the ass, to say 'oh well' and forget it, whereas Sterling couldn't do that.

December 12-14 they played the Boston Tea Party on the same bill as the MC5. One of their guitarists remembers the incident.

WAYNE KRAMER: There was a radical gang of thugs with pseudo-political ideas called the East Village Motherfuckers. They were the East Village equivalent of the White Panther Party – people who thought the Black Panthers were bad because they had guns and were ready to fight it out, so their attitude was 'we're bad, we've got guns and we're ready to fight it out'. A guy named Ben Wish had got into a beef with some soldiers in Boston, stabbed one of them and gotten arrested. The Motherfuckers had come into town to try and raise money for Ben's defense and the revolution, or something like that. And because of our phony political ideology that we were all sharing they came to our gig and we all started throwing around this militant rhetoric. Some of the Motherfuckers got up on stage after our set and started haranguing the kids suggesting they burn down the place because it wasn't large enough to hold their energies, and take to the streets.

The Velvets came out on stage and Lou addressed the audience: 'I'd just like to make one thing clear. We have nothing to do with what went on earlier and in fact we consider it very stupid. This is our favorite place to play in the whole country and we would hate to see anyone even try to destroy it.'

Wayne Kramer

KRAMER: I remember listening to The Velvets. I remember the rhythm because I didn't really notice in the beginning that it was a girl drummer. That was fairly rare in those days. And I remember I thought she had a good sense of time. I thought the music was relatively minimalist. It was just one or two chords and then a kind of straight ahead chanting. I don't remember them as being terribly exciting to me as a rock & roller because I didn't really hear rock & roll so much as a weird blend of these guys who sort of sounded like folk players with electric guitars and a heavy beat. I must admit I wasn't really up on Lou or the lyrical thing other than "I'm Waiting For My Man" and "Heroin".

BOCKRIS: There wasn't any sense of camaraderie between what you were doing and what they were doing?

KRAMER: Not consciously, no. In fact, we had a whole different approach to music. We might have had 600 or 700 in there. It was the first time we had ever played Boston and we were getting a push, because we had just signed with Elektra.

BOCKRIS: So you were hotter than The Velvet Underground in terms of publicity?

KRAMER: Yeah, yeah, yeah. I remember that the dressing room was up above at the other end of the room from the stage so you could look down from there and see the stage and I watched them for a while. That's why I didn't know it was a girl playing drums because it was a distance away.

BOCKRIS: The Velvet Underground didn't have a revolutionary rep at all at this time?

KRAMER: No, I think they had more of a rep with people who were into art, a cultish kind of thing. We had a group of 15-20 of The Motherfuckers there and they're all rabble-rousing and they're all MC5 fans and then we had just the kids that had heard our record and come out to see us. There seemed to be two different kinds of energy 'cos everything The Velvets did was more sinister and blue green, whereas our thing was just blast blast blast, real loud. We had these huge stacks of Marshal amps and they probably had little gear that they brought from New York. I seem to remember they went over real well and they had their fans, but it was two completely different things. We were trying to be a show band and we had these spangly clothes and sequins, and The Velvets were very plain-looking, with their New York dungarees.

MALANGA: Is there any comparison between The Velvet Underground and the MC5?

MORRISON: I have always liked the MC5 musically. I didn't like their being associated with narrow political causes. I consider music to be more important than politics, and much more important than pissant politicians like John Sinclair. I thought they were surrounded by and exploited by leeches.

● 1969-THE GREY YEAR

BOCKRIS: As you moved into '69, did you and the group feel that things were on the up and up?

SESNICK: Definitely. We had at this point made contact with Ahmet Ertegun. I'd been in touch with him all along. We sent letters back and forth, there'd been phone conversations. We were getting ready for our move to another level entirely. Things were progressing beautifully.

MORRISON: Lou had a place over in the East 60s then. He was paying an outrageous amount of money for it so I thought I'd go over and see what this palace looked like. Well, you know how those high-rise apartments are – they're real barren. And his was totally unfurnished, nothing except some kind of pallet that he had pushed up against one corner. And a tape recorder, and some old tapes and I guess a notebook, and an acoustic guitar. There was nothing in the fridge except a half-empty container of papaya juice. I mean nothing, not even vitamins. It was just the picture of isolation and despair.

FIELDS: After the glamor died down it was Lou Reed and a back-up band. It was like any other rock group on the road.

1969 reveals The Velvet Underground in a whole new light. Their third album, *The Velvet Underground*, was released in March. The package itself is mysterious. The front cover, a photograph taken late one night at the Factory by Billy Linich, with whom Reed maintained a close friendship, shows Lou smiling with a copy of a fashion magazine in his hands. The magazine's name *Harper's Bazaar*, has been airbrushed out. Yule and Tucker sit to the left, pointedly looking at Lou, while Morrison sits in the foreground to the right, looking down into the right-hand bottom corner of the photograph and definitively away from Reed.

TUCKER: As I recall, Lou had just said something about the cover of the magazine and we were listening to him, that's why Doug and I are looking directly at him.

The back cover lists the songs, with no writers credits for the first time, and the name of the engineer, the aforementioned Val Valentin. The sole remaining credit goes to Billy Linich (listed as Billy Name) for photos and convolutions.

REED: He's part of the Factory. He does all our covers. He's a divinity in action on earth. He does pictures that are unspeakably beautiful. Just pure space. For the people who have one foot on Earth and another foot on Venus, they would like that kind of picture because it's out-and-out space.

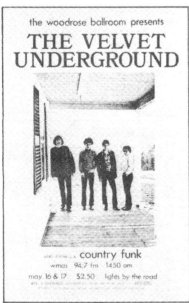

The convolutions on the back cover were a sitting-from-the-knees-up-eye-drooping-cigarette-in-hand photograph of Reed which has been cut in half and turned upsidedown with one half juxtaposed to the other. No wonder some writers began to see The Velvet Underground as Lou Reed's backing band. Yet the packaging of the album also suggests, as does the advertising copy, that they are a band who did things together. According to Yule it was Sesnick's idea that the less said about something the easier it is to change it. Everything was as discreet as possible, i.e., on song-credits he'd ask if anyone helped with a song, if so they got co-credit, even if they only did a little bit. This way everyone was kept vaguely in the dark. There is nothing vague, however, about the record itself.

BOCKRIS: MGM switched you from Verve onto MGM for this record.

SESNICK: Correct. That was my doing. Why we did that was very complicated, and eventually led to getting us to Columbia or Atlantic. It was a movement out of the company.

BOCKRIS: So you were already moving in that direction?

SESNICK: Oh hell, we were getting bigger and bigger and they were getting more chaotic with the loss of presidents. I was dealing with a different president every month. They went through presidents constantly, which was good for us at the time because I could call an enormous number of shots and get us the bookings and the support that we needed without having to draw up new contracts. So we were on our way pretty much at that point. Either they were going to really do it for us, and they'd be the company that we would be with, or we would be with another company.

BOCKRIS: Were they actually giving you more support than they had on the

first two records?

SESNICK: In reality, yes, they were. They were picking up advertising, hotels and limousines. I managed to get a lot of coverage from MGM because we weren't making much money, we had no money, and if we had had to cover everything we'd have been in serious debt. We'd have been finished, so I had to really work around that.

Sterling Morrison, Lou Reed and Doug Yule at The Boston Teaparty, 1969.
(Ron Campisi)

Jane Fonda and Candy Darling.

● **"THE VELVET UNDERGROUND"**

The Velvet Underground was markedly different in both its sound and mood. The music was almost folk-like in its simplicity. It is also a realization of Reed's view of a rock record as a unified whole.

REED: This song would follow this song because this has to do with this and this has to do with that, and this will answer that and then you've got this character who matches this character or offsets this character. The third album was really the quintessence of that idea, because it started out with "Candy Says" where this girl asks all these questions. And then the next song is "What Goes On" where this guy says, 'Wow, you're asking me all these questions, you're driving me crazy, you're making me feel like I'm upsidedown'. And the third thing they've decided that they're talking about is love, so he's going to give her an example of "Some Kinds of Love" and he talks about all kinds of love being the same as long as it's love, and that's what he says to her over and over and gives different examples of it. He's trying to reach her and she's like saying, 'I don't understand,' you know, but that's stated at the beginning. Then he gets into "Pale Blue Eyes", where he talks about another kind of love which is like adultery. Then you get to "Jesus", which brings in a whole different kind of love, which is like religious love. Then they start thinking, 'Wow, I'm beginning to see the light'. At the end of "Beginning to see the Light" it says 'how does it feel to be loved' which means the person doesn't know, and it also says a number of other strange things, such as, 'here we go again, I thought that you were my friend', you know, which is such a sad thing, especially if you're going through it with a person twice, I mean that means it happened more than once. Then he says, 'Wow, I'm set free, everything's fine!' Then he says 'That's the story; see "That's The Story of My Life".' No difference between the words good and bad, wrong and right are dead, no categories, everything is just fine. So what happens, he runs into "The Murder Mystery". All this unintelligible stuff. You know, but the intent was really noble. I just meant finally after seeing the light, explaining everything and getting things right, and finally saying now I got it right. BAM, what happens. A whole new series of problems, y'know new level, new problems. "Afterhours" was like a sum-up, like it was kind of the cap, the frosting on the cake as far as I was concerned. I mean it's a terribly sad song and I didn't sing it because I figured people wouldn't believe me if I sang it. But I knew Maureen, for instance, had a very innocent voice.

● **Side One:**

● **"Candy Says"** is a song about the late transvestite Candy Darling who would appear in Reed's classic "Walk on the Wild Side".

● **"Some Kinda Love"** is one of the songs with which Lou Reed makes rock lyrics function as literature.

● **"Pale Blue Eyes"**.

MORRISON: Cale's departure allowed Lou Reed's sensitive, meaningful side to hold sway. Why do you think "Pale Blue Eyes" happened on the third album, with Cale out of there? That's a song about Lou's old girlfriend in Syracuse. I said, 'Lou, if I wrote a song like that I wouldn't make you play it'. My position on that album was one of acquiescence.

● **"Jesus":** (figure it out for yourself.)

● **Side Two:**

● **"Beginning to See the Light":** Reed discovers, once again, some kind of reaffirmation in the distinction of being loved.

● **"I'm Set Free":** Reed's statement is undercut by his assertion that he has been set free only to find a new illusion.

● **"That's the Story of My Life":** Even though he accepts Billy Linich's dictum that the words *wrong* and *right* are dead, the difference between right and wrong is the story of his life.

● **"The Murder Mystery":** No attempt at explication. Eight-minutes and 35-seconds. A mystery to all for all time (the lyrics were published in the winter 1972 issue of *The Paris Review* #53, as a poem).

● "Afterhours" is a celebration of afterhours clubs.

MORRISON: We did the third album deliberately as anti-production. It sounds like it was done in a closet – it's flat, and that's the way we wanted it. The songs are all very quiet and it's kind of insane. I like the album.

RADIO INTERVIEWER (1969): Any plans for the future?

REED: Not really. Just to play around. We really enjoy playing. I think it's fantastic that we can play this stuff in public and that people like it. It turns me on that it turns them on. We don't have any point to prove or any axe to grind. It's just nice that people show up and that we can play for them. We have fun.

BOCKRIS: Was the reaction to the third record markedly different than the reaction to the second?

SESNICK: Not that I can remember. The mystique of the group was such that no matter what they did it was accepted. We had set that in motion from the outset. We organized the management and the playing, we knew exactly what we were doing, and we got the response and reaction that we felt were positive without having things on charts or airplay. We had to measure ourselves completely differently to most acts, and look at our progress in a different way. As long as we were continually being recorded and were in demand around the country we were making progress.

Lou Reed, Maureen Tucker, Sterling
Morrison and Doug Yule at The Boston
Teaparty, 1969.
(Ron Campisi)

BOCKRIS: The third album is a very different record. Was the reaction any different?

TUCKER: Ah, Jesus, I never saw any reviews. I was pleased with the direction we were going and with the new calmness in the group, and thinking about a good future, hoping people would smarten up and some record company would take us on and do us justice.

Record World June 28, 1969
'Underground by virtue of their name, the Velvet Underground sound as if they're about to break through to a large audience. The fourman group have a passel of intriguing thoughts to give out with. Good work.'

Cashbox June 28, 1969
'The Velvet Underground takes a journey through musical psychedelia, low-keyed in the main, but a trip that should be interesting to a good number of listeners. The Velvet Underground composed, arranged and conducted all selections on the album. Vocally and instrumentally, the group creates an evocative, sensuous sound, and the LP could pick up considerable sales.'

BOCKRIS: MGM had switched you from Verve to their larger label. Were they treating you better?

TUCKER: Not that I knew of.

BOCKRIS: It would seem to be the album with which they could have made the attempt to present you in a more commercial way.

TUCKER: Yeah, but still they just didn't bother putting anything behind it.

BOCKRIS: Well, why were they putting your records out at this point, then?

TUCKER: I don't know. I used to think they just signed us to keep us away from other people. Which is stupid, but. . .

BOCKRIS: Were you still living out on Long Island with your parents?

TUCKER: Yeah. I had had an apartment in the city for a little while, and then I moved back because I had no money.

BOCKRIS: What was the financial situation?

TUCKER: Grim.

BOCKRIS: Were you living on $200 a month?

TUCKER: Probably less. I used to go, when I'd be home, and get a temporary job for a week, to make some money. I didn't need money as much as Sterling, Lou and Doug, because they had their apartments and I lived at home rent free, so that didn't really bother me. If they got more than me, they needed it. We never got any royalty checks, that's for damn sure. Maybe one or two little ones that I can recall.

BOCKRIS: But when you went into the studio to make an album would you get some kind of minimal advance?

TUCKER: Advance!, oh Gee, I don't think we ever got any kind of an advance.

BOCKRIS: Well, wait a minute, you must have made some money.

TUCKER: We made some but it went pretty fast. I didn't see shit. We bought new equipment now and then too and we had to use it to travel because MGM didn't pay for any of that, then we had living expenses. It wasn't a hell of a lot. We went out playing because that's where we made money.

BOCKRIS: Was Sesnick in there strongly pushing this album?

TUCKER: Oh, yeah. He was right up there in the gung ho area.

BOCKRIS: It would seem that here was a product easy to push and you would think it would make some impact, but actually it seems like nothing happened when this record came out.

TUCKER: Yeah, as far as I can remember, they just didn't distribute it. I remember specifically we played in St. Louis long enough after the third album came out that it should have been in the stores, especially if we were going to play there. We had never played there before and expected thirty people to show up and we really packed the place. It was one of those open ballrooms and a couple of thousand people showed up. The guy who owned the club was ecstatic. He said,

Maureen Tucker with her mallets at The
Boston Teaparty, 1969.
(Ron Campisi)

'Oh shit, I've never had a night like this bla bla,' and the next day we went out poking around and we couldn't find our record anywhere, and one guy who owned a record store, who had come backstage to talk to us, said, 'Gee, you know, I can't get your record. I called,' and shit like that.

BOCKRIS: That's a horrible horrible story.

TUCKER: I don't understand it, I just don't get it. And now Polydor's releasing them like crazy.

BOCKRIS: What sort of relations, if any, did you have with MGM?

TUCKER: I didn't bother with anyone there, of course. Steve used to go down there every day. He'd lay around and make phone calls from their phones.

BOCKRIS: So Steve was really full-time pushing for you and going to the office, but he obviously wasn't very successful.

TUCKER: No, he wasn't, and I don't know the reason. I don't know if it was like I said before, because his schemes were too grandiose, or if they just didn't want to have anything to do with him.

M.C. Kostek, writing in *What Goes On* (No.1) remembers the first time he ever saw The Velvet Underground in March 1969. He was sixteen: 'This next song's called "Heroin".' The thin figure dressed in black on stage looks nervously around. 'It's not, uh, for or against it. It's just about it.' The two South Deerfield, Mass, cops at the side entrances are momentarily distracted from their evening's boredom (the only relief provided by teen drunks and gate-sneakers). Now this weird-o with black leather jacket and sunglasses is talking to them about heroin.

'This song's been banned in San Francisco. Hope you like it.' That small guy in the shades and leather turned out to be Lou Reed, and he didn't say much all night. Half of what he did say was about this or that song being banned (such as that one up there for *White Light/White Heat*) or maimed. The whole bizarre situation has been highlighted by some *dumb* local band opening with *lame-o* versions of "You Keep Me Hangin' On" (V. Fudge style), and then these strange figures walked through the crowd to the stage, to unleash this . . . roar. So imagine you're a kid, and you're at your second concert ever, and you're sitting in 1969 with whatever there is of the small farming town area hippie slick of kids. These people with nasty clothes get on stage and BANNNGGO! Such noise! This guy who sings funny is waving a guitar, another's haunched over the keyboards unearthing some mighty *odd* sounds, another's hunched over the bass, and the drummer, who looks like a woman, is playing with big mallets (the kind that kick the bass drum on regular kits), the better to bang her bass drum, turned on its side as a snare, with.

From the first screech, I'm transfixed. The songs, about waiting, love, call my name, all fly by in a vicious torrent. During the break, we dare each other to go chat with them. It's tempting, but they're too forbidding, and we try to relax.

A few buzzheads dance near the front of the stage, but the rest of the few hundred hipsters sit immobile on the floor, trying to deal with this howl. It gets late, and the 'leader' says they're going to do this story-song. He kicks out this riff, and while things before were intense, they are now erupting, they slowly build, and begin to fly. The singer's yelling something about 'she's sucking on my ding dong', and they kick into a harder, faster wail. The singer's hand is a blur, stroking and making this twelve-string shudder and scream, the bass player's got another guitar and is ripping up on that, the organist is leaning, slapping the keys. And the drummer – not only has she stood all night, but she's pounded steadily with those big mallets all the while, raising one up over her head for the big BAMP-BAMP-BAMP. Steady. I'm not quite sure how long this went on. It seemed a half-hour – but time, space, driver's-ed meant nothing. I was gone. No drink or drugs, I was flattened by the raw power. It rocked – but it was so twisted. Pete Townshend says rock and roll is when you stand up and forget where you are – OK, these strange people were playing the loudest crudest music I'd ever heard. They were making lots of 'mistakes', but they were obviously much more interested in getting up there and ripping it out. The roar increased, then built until I could hardly stand it.'

Sterling Morrison, Minneapolis, October 12, 1969.
(Sterling Morrison Archive)

● "1969 VELVET UNDERGROUND LIVE"

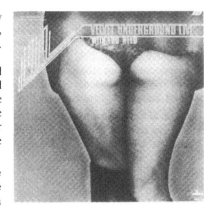

Which brings us to *1969 Velvet Underground Live,* considered by many to be among the very best live rock albums. For the next six months they were playing regularly every weekend, coming home during the week, or else touring the south, west, California, Oregon, Canada. They sometimes stayed on the road for weeks at a time.

When they weren't on the road they were rehearsing and recording. They played small clubs, like the one owned by a rich kid who just asked bands he liked to play there called The End of Cole Avenue in Dallas where some of the tapes that make up the album were recorded, or the Matrix in San Francisco from which other tapes are taken. They also made tapes at the Vulcan Gas Company in Austin, Texas, but these were lost when the club owner committed suicide. They were covering their expenses, paying the rent and making a little pocket money, but nobody in the band was getting anything like rich.

MORRISON: We never cared that much about touring. We did it once in a while by invitation, but we never solicited one. Why play Toledo, Ohio, where no one knows you and where people are not likely to be the least bit receptive? Deep down you do want to be accepted by the audience I don't care how much you steel yourself with drugs or whatever. The record companies were always bewildered by our attitude. They were dealing with something they'd never seen before – if you weren't interested in making money there was no way they could even talk to you. The one big mistake we made was not playing Europe, where we might have found a more receptive audience. But actually the Texas audience sounded pretty enthusiastic.

REED: Good evening. We're The Velvet Underground. Glad you could all make it. This is our last night here, I'm glad to see that you all showed up. Um, do you people have a curfew or anything like that? Does it matter what time you go home tonight? I mean, do you have school tomorrow?

AUDIENCE MEMBER: No!

REED: Nobody here has school tomorrow?

AUDIENCE MEMBER: Yeah!

REED: Yeah, see. 'Cos we could do either one long set or we could do two sets, you know, whatever makes it easier for you.

AUDIENCE MEMBER: One long one!

REED: One long one? Okay. Okay, then this is going to go on for a while so we should get used to each other. Settle back. Pull up your cushions. Whatever else you have with you that makes life palatable in Texas. . .

It is the consensus of opinion that these recordings reveal the band at one of the peaks of their power. On a good night they were always ten times better live than in the studio. *1969 Velvet Underground Live* is also an especially important document for fans as it not only really captures them live on the road, but also delivers "Sweet Jane" the way Reed originally composed it. He says the recording on this album was done the day he wrote the song. Morrison remembers it was originally written in Lou's New York loft and later pulled out of his bag of tricks and worked up for the performance. According to Reed the 'official' version on Loaded was edited after he left the band in 1970. Ditto "New Age". The record also

Maureen Tucker at University of Maryland in Baltimore, 1969.
(Sterling Morrison Archive)

Sterling Morrison and Doug Yule at University of Maryland, Baltimore, 1969.
(Sterling Morrison Archive)

contains never before or since released Velvet Underground productions like "Lisa Says", "We're Gonna Have A Real Good Time Together" and "Ocean", which later appeared on Lou Reed solo albums. On top of that you get "Over You", "Sweet Bonnie Brown" and "It's Just Too Much", (which it is). This double album lasts for 104-minutes 35-seconds and costs the same as a single album. After leaving the band, Lou Reed made a point of taking care of his audience. From 1972 – 1980 he toured the world constantly playing a lot of Velvet Underground songs along with new compositions. As a result of his polarising the music the record companies found it in their interest to re-issue the Velvet Underground material. *1969 Velvet Underground Live* features Lou Reed on rhythm guitar.

REED: If God showed up tomorrow and said Do you want to be President? No. Do you want to be in politics? No. Do you want to be a lawyer? No. What do you want? I want to be a rhythm guitar player.

● SHUCKED,HYPED,SCREWED

● **BOCKRIS: In '69 you actually engineered the separation from MGM. Was it a complicated series of negotiations?**

SESNICK: They were ready to let us go if we wanted to, because of our demands and lack of record sales, in that confusion that they had over their direction. At this point they brought in some fellow from California who had some choral group and was suddenly head of MGM. He's Lieutenant Governor of California now – Mike Curb. We were about as far away from being able to discuss anything with him as east meets west, so the attorney I had was able to work it out with him amicably, and also with Ahmet. Negotiations with Ahmet were far more complicated. That's where the time was being spent.

BOCKRIS: It's been written that there was a period when they didn't have a label. Is that true?

SESNICK: I think we went from MGM to Atlantic almost in a day. We were into the studio pretty quick.

BOCKRIS: At this crucial time of change in your career, did you still feel Sesnick was doing the right thing for you?

TUCKER: Sterling had been bitching about Sesnick for a while.

BOCKRIS: On what basis?

TUCKER: That he was not giving us money, not doing anything for us, and not telling us where the money's going. Sterling would storm up to Sesnick's apartment on East 62nd Street and demand to see the books.

BOCKRIS: So was he one of those typical managers who was living high off the hog while the rest of you had no money at all?

TUCKER: Not totally. I mean, he had a nice apartment, but no furniture.

BOCKRIS: But the rest of you had no money so where was he getting his money from?

TUCKER: That's what we were trying to find out. And it got to the point to where everytime I saw Sterling he'd be ranting and raving – 'that son of a bitch bla bla'. So, I said, 'Sterl, let's cut the shit and you and I both together go to Sesnick, or to the other two in the group, and say 'Come on, what the hell's going on? We really want to know, bla bla bla', but he would never do it.

BOCKRIS: So at this point even you were beginning to feel a little uncertain about where Steve Sesnick was coming from?

TUCKER: Yeah. I never felt that he wasn't trying.

BOCKRIS: But he wasn't pulling it off successfully for you, so you had to wonder what was going on.

TUCKER: Yeah, yeah. That started coming around there.

BOCKRIS: Was there a time when Lou stopped singing "Heroin"?

TUCKER: Late '69. We didn't just stop singing it, we just didn't do it every time.

BOCKRIS: At the end of '69, you went through a period of being without a label. How was the group feeling?

TUCKER: We were feeling possibly pretty low. I can remember being in Seattle, Vancouver, Portland, Chicago and having like $2 a day to eat on. We weren't feeling low, like oh we're never going to make it, not ready to give up, by any means, but feeling like what the fuck is this? I guess what pissed me off most was, if we had released the albums and MGM had pushed them and played them on the radio and no one liked it, it would be one thing, but whenever we played live we always, always did real well – people swooning in the aisles and things – so I knew, shit, if the record was out there it would sell, and that's what was discouraging to me – to be at the mercy of these people who just didn't have any sense.

Lou Reed, Maureen Tucker, Sterling Morrison and Doug Yule in Los Angeles recording "The Velvet Underground".
(Sanford Schor)

BOCKRIS: Having put out three great records and had them all mistreated, what did you think was happening?

TUCKER: I think my feeling was that they just didn't realize what they had. We were not a group who would be written up in magazines every week and things like that, where you could say 'Look! Look!' you had to come out and see us. And I guess they just never did. I remember once in LA two under-assistant west coast promo men from MGM came out to meet us at the airport and they just went crazy, they loved us. They knew about us, of course, through the albums and the company and they were very polite and cordial and all, but shit they came to see us play that night, they really went crazy! These two, they were funny. Their plan was to go back to their office and start beating some sense into these people. I don't know if they just didn't have the power. I just can't imagine how MGM could have been so stupid.

MORRISON: Everybody'd been beaten. We'd all lost on every possible level. In '65 and '66, even in '68, you could feel that something was about to happen. By now it'd happened . . . and the merchandisers had gotten rich. We were all shucked, hyped, screwed.

● THE AMPUTEES

● CALE: I got a lot out of The Velvet Underground, but it took me a long time to regain my vitality. I was glad to being something new. It gave me a chance to breathe and exercise some new ideas. Producing Nico's albums eased things up a bit. I enjoyed arranging and producing – I really didn't believe I could do it until then.

REED: It's interesting that as three so-called entities we could do one thing and apart we could all go in different directions. Together we did something that none of us could do alone, and then when you separated us we did things that we would do on our own but with the added knowledge of what we did before. I'm infinitely broader in concept and awareness because of knowing John and Nico.

Everybody was capable of doing something and at the time it was just combined. It had an intriguing result – at least it intrigued all of us and a couple of other people along the way.

People said we were esoteric, and maybe we were. But we didn't mean to be, it just worked out that way. Now that a lot of things are removed I know what I know but I also know what I want to do. Some of the esoteric things are totally gone because the people who are responsible for them are gone and couldn't conceivably be replaced – so there would be no point in pursuing it.

Cale had produced Nico's *Marble Index* and The Stooges first album, and also gotten divorced from Betsey Johnson.

JOHNSON: I remember one morning I just started crying, 'John, I can't stand it anymore!' I remember in that loftbed at night crying, hiding. Basically I was the day-time, he was the night-time. I was just kind of suffering up there in that loftbed every night with the music and the intensity of his time-schedule against mine was really rough and the whole situation was rough for us to have a relationship in. And then I could never really know what was really right or wrong or confused or clear or unclear and I didn't ever want to know what was going on but I imagined more than what really was. So, I just felt that I was so scared to leave him because I was afraid that he wouldn't be alright. It was easier for me to just work. At that time, too, I quit Paraphernalia. I was getting fed up with Paraphernalia about a year before. So, I was thinking of quitting something. He was thinking of quitting something. I remember in San Francisco we used to be on the phone a lot. He was just incredibly lonely and depressed and trying to get it together. It was between '69 and '70.

BOCKRIS: So you and John separated in 1969. Did you get divorced or did you just separate?

JOHNSON: It was awful. Then, in New York, it took two years to get separated which would then turn into divorce.

BOCKRIS: You were supporting someone whom you felt was doing really valid work.

JOHNSON: I used to hear a lot of the real work on tapes at home. I just loved that stuff. There just wasn't all that much support for John in his experimental work.

In 1969 Andy Warhol started *Interview* magazine, edited by Gerard Malanga. His movie "Fuck" (also known as "Blue Movie") was seized and declared obscene in New York and Richard Avedon photographed his gunshot scars for *Vogue*.

Doug Yule Maureen Tucker, Lou Reed and Sterling Morrison

● 1970-THE WHITE YEAR

● At the beginning of 1970, as a result of a complex series of negotiations on which Sesnick had been concentrating for some time, the band signed a recording contract with Atlantic, Ahmet Ertegun President.

FIELDS: I was working at Atlantic when The Velvets signed, but I was not responsible for signing them. Ahmet had liked them and a deal had been made. I don't think a great deal was expected from it. It was Ahmet's good taste and almost the kind of thing a President of a record label is entitled to do if he feels something should be recorded. I think that was his attitude. It certainly wasn't a forthcoming blockbuster like a Rolling Stones album.

BOCKRIS: Was Ertegun taking The Velvets on at Atlantic because he thought they were making good music? Or was he seeing it as a commercial property?

SESNICK: I think both. He expressed to us that he felt he had just signed the most prestigious act in the world. And a coming commercial success. He likened it to the early Buffalo Springfield, with that kind of capacity and capability.

BOCKRIS: When did you stop working temporarily with the group in 1970 as a result of being pregnant?

TUCKER: March or April.

BOCKRIS: Were you playing around in January, February, and March?

TUCKER: Yeah, as I recall, we were running around pretty much, like I said, out on the coast there, and in Chicago, and down in Texas.

Max's Kansas City
(Chris Shawn, photo courtesy Mickey Ruskin)

BOCKRIS: When was the famous "Lost Album" recorded?

MORRISON: Early 1970 at the Record Plant in New York City. Gary Kellgren was again the engineer.

BOCKRIS: Was it done to get out of the MGM contract?

TUCKER: The idea was to record it to shut them up. I believe at the time Sesnick was already negotiating with Atlantic.

BOCKRIS: I don't understand what was going on because this new record wasn't a piece of shit, so what was going on in terms of trying to get away from MGM?

TUCKER: We didn't say we'll just go in and lay down anything and screw 'em, but with the sense that it probably wouldn't be released by them. I think I figured it would just get picked up by the next record company, not realizing that MGM would own it. But when we switched labels, MGM wouldn't give up the tapes. They were paying for the recording studio time. So, as far as I know we couldn't put our hands on it, because I'm sure if we could have we would have released it right away on Atlantic. It was never released.

MORRISON: I have some dubs of it. That's the stuff Lou drew on when he went solo. Nearly everything on his first album was just a reworking of stuff he'd already done.

TUCKER: We did "Stephanie Says", "Lonesome Cowboys" (written for Warhol's movie of the same name), "Foggy Notion", "I'm Sticking With You", "My Best Friend", "Sad Song", "Andy's Chest", and "Ocean". I'm really pissed that never came out. It's a great album.

BOCKRIS: Was the separation from MGM traumatic or positive?

TUCKER: It wasn't traumatic. We would have done anything to get away from them.

BOCKRIS: But you had a four album commitment. So you were glad to get out without having to do a fourth album?

TUCKER: Yeah, I guess that's another point about recording the lost album without really releasing it on MGM. We weren't that interested in giving them another one to just let die.

In the middle of June, The Velvets began to play their legendary stint at Max's Kansas City on Park Avenue South in New York City, five days a week, Wednesday to Sunday, for ten weeks. It was the first time they played in Manhattan since their attempt to resuscitate The E.P.I. at the Gymnasium in April 1967. Maureen Tucker was unable to be with them at the Max's shows since she was pregnant which made it impossible for her to reach the drums while standing. Doug Yule's brother, Billy, who was still in high school, sat in on drums. To indicate the kind of financial situation they were in, Billy Yule was offered $60 for the complete ten weeks, although he ended up making about $25 a week because they paid for his daily round trip fare from Long Island plus food. Max's was a notorious restaurant where artists and rock & roll people hung out. Its backroom was legendary and many of the characters in Velvets songs were regulars. Owner Mickey Ruskin considered it Casting Central for Andy Warhol.

TERRY SOUTHERN: If you wanted to describe the back room of Max's in a, God forbid, negative way, you'd use words like 'desperation' or 'hysteria' – that sort of thing. Going the positive route, of course, you'd talk about 'sensitive', 'intense' or just plain 'hilarious'. It was like a carnivorous arena. There was always this buzz along the rialto: 'Andy's coming! Andy's coming!' All on this weird level of maybe he'll make this ultimate film or painting of me!

The Velvets were the first band to ever play there. It seemed to be a particularly appropriate homecoming. At the same time they went back into the studio to make a fourth album. Ahmet Ertegun believed they could break out of their underground if they'd stop writing songs about drugs which couldn't receive airplay, and concentrate on simple rock & roll, at which, he recognised, they excelled.

On the surface everything looked alright. Tom Mancuso reviewing a Max's performance described Lou Reed arriving at the club one evening; Before the first set begins, around eleven thirty, Lou Reed carries in his guitar, checks its tuning, takes off his nylon windbreaker, and then talks to people. He wears tennis shoes and the way he walks, even the way he talks, has an athletic composure, a reserved confidence. Lou Reed has

Maureen Tucker.
(Nat Finkelstein)

"always wanted to play in a rock & roll band". He does, and he describes what he does as "like meeting people". If someone sings one of his songs, "it's like humming your name". Another way in which he describes what he enjoys about music compares it to sports: "It's the *playing* that's nice". Modest ambitions, pleasures, and metaphors are unexpected from a rock & roll star. "I'm not a star", he says.

BOCKRIS: Was it your idea to set up the residency at Max's Kansas City?

SESNICK:It was my idea years before we did it.

BOCKRIS: Did you try to persuade them to play New York?

SESNICK: It wasn't a question of persuading them, it was just the way it was gonna be. Lou pretty much let me do whatever I felt.

BOCKRIS: Was it a coincidence they recorded "Loaded" at the same time they played at Max's?

SESNICK: No. No. There were many, many reasons for it. They weren't managed by pot luck. Quite a bit of thinking went into it.

BOCKRIS: I got the impression that everything was planned in great depth. Did

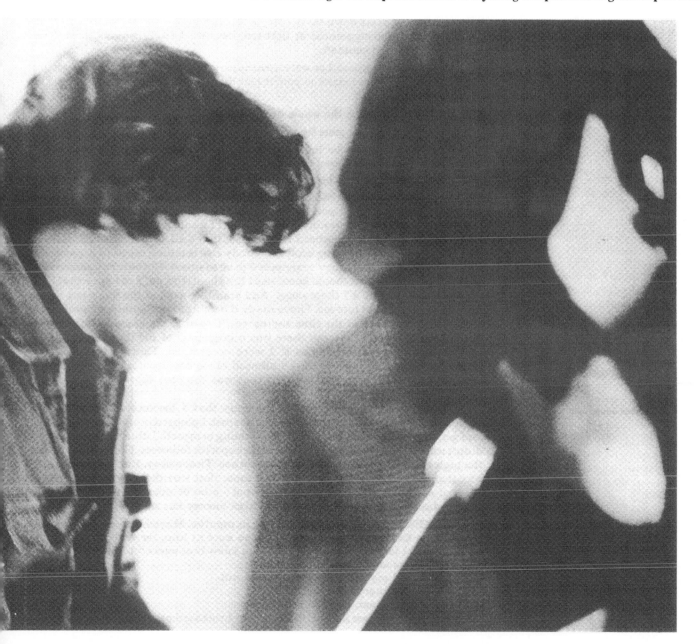

Sterling Morrison and Doug Yule at The Second Fret, Philadelphia, December 31, 1969.
(Sterling Morrison Archive)

Sterling Morrison on the road, 1969.
(Doug Yule)

things change a lot during that period?

SESNICK: That period I really don't want to talk about.

BOCKRIS: So when they were playing at Max's from the middle of June till the end of August, where were you?

TUCKER: At my parents' house out on Long Island. I stayed at Sterl's apartment for a little while. I went in to see them play a few times, and talked to them on the phone.

BOCKRIS: And your perception was you were taking a short break and you'd be back in there playing?

TUCKER: Yeah.

BOCKRIS: Did you have any sense that Lou was about to quit the group?

TUCKER: No, I didn't.

BOCKRIS: How were your relations with him at this point?

TUCKER: Fine.

BOCKRIS: You didn't play on any of the "Loaded" sessions?

TUCKER: No. I came down there to try and I couldn't reach the drums I was so fat. I was really disappointed at that too, because I really wanted to play on "Ocean" and I just couldn't.

According to Morrison, Lou was extremely paranoid, due to averaging 6 hours sleep a week, and wanted Steve Sesnick to protect him from numerous people from his past he didn't want to see.

BOCKRIS: What about the whole drug situation?

TUCKER: Oh that was gone by then.

BOCKRIS: So it would be incorrect to say, as some people have, that Lou's quitting the group was based on his being bummed out on drugs?

TUCKER: No, no, he was long done with that shit.

REED: I hated playing at Max's. Because I couldn't do the songs I wanted to do and I was under a lot of pressure to do things I didn't want to and it finally reached a crescendo. I never in my life thought I would not do what I believed in and there I was, not doing what I believed in, that's all, and it made me sick. It dawned on me that I'm doing what somebody else is telling me to do supposedly for my own good because they're supposed to be so smart. But only one person can write it and that person should know what it's about. I'm not a machine that gets up there and parrots off these songs. And standing around the bar – you don't have to get high to get into me. I have made it a point not to be oblique. And I was giving out interviews at the time saying yes, I wanted the group to be a dance band, I wanted to do that, but there was a large part of me that wanted to do something else. I was talking as if I were programed. That part of me that wanted to do something else wasn't allowed to express itself, in fact was being cancelled out. And it turned out that that was the part that made up ninety percent of Lou.

There was that comment by that guy that I became unplugged from objective reality. Well, that's not what happened. I plugged into objective reality, and got very sick at what I saw, what I was doing to myself. I didn't belong there. I didn't want to be a mass pop national hit group with followers. I knew we could do the high energy rock and everybody can dance. That's okay. But the last night I was there, when Brigid Polk made her tape, that was the only night I really enjoyed myself. I did all the songs I wanted – a lot of them were ballads. High energy does not necessarily mean fast; high energy has to do with heart.

MORRISON: I had hardly spoken to Lou in months. Maybe I never forgave him for wanting Cale out of the band. I was so mad at him, for real or imaginary offences and I just didn't want to talk. You know that poem "A Poison Tree" by Blake?

> I was angry with my friend:
> I told my wrath, my wrath did end.
> I was angry with my foe:
> I told it not, my wrath did grow.

Like that. So in his last days with the group I was zero psychological assistance to Lou.

Sterling was taking two courses at City College to earn his B.A. (he had left there in 1966 without graduating) and spent most of his time reading Victorian novels in the dressing room.

MORRISON: I had quit smoking, quit taking drugs, and spent my days playing basketball and doing schoolwork. At night I would pedal over to Max's from my place on Christopher Street, play (with some enthusiasm, I think), have a cheeseburger and two ales after the show, lock my guitar up on the third floor next to the safe, and pedal home again. An orderly life.

Doug Yule and Sterling Morrison at The Second Fret, Philadelphia, December 31, 1969.
(Sterling Morrison Archive)

The combined pressure of making the record while performing every day would have taken its toll on any group. The Velvets put themselves under a lot of pressure to produce hits and things and were not relaxed in the studio. Maureen's serene presence was missed. Sterling played on every track except "I Found A Reason", but his commitments to school and playing Max's didn't leave him much time and he chose not to hang around until 6am while Lou and Doug discussed all sorts of possible combinations of ideas they could employ on the record. After laying down his basic tracks Morrison would split. He simply wasn't as involved as he had previously been in the shape of the record. Everyone was ragged out from the arduous schedule.

Ironically the press began to respond to them really positively as they began this final series of amputations. 'The Velvet Underground plays a hard rock that is powerful and tight as a raised fist; so unified and together that it just rolls itself into a knot and throbs', said the *New York Times*. In the face of all this, Lou kept trying to deliver. 'Everybody's trying to do it in their own way and we just play some rock & roll and people dance and get some rocks off to it. Fabulous! That's enough, that's enough.' Meanwhile he was becoming more withdrawn in the face of Doug Yule's barrage of suggestions for improving the band's commercial potential and their big – maybe final – chance to consolidate with a hit album. Morrison did notice that Reed was acting strangely. One thing he didn't realise was that Steve Sesnick had been pressuring Reed to act more like a rock star on stage – which went against his natural shyness as a performer.

MORRISON: We were always anti-performers, and Lou was leaping around and making all those gestures he does now. I didn't realize it until Lou told me that later on. But Sesnick had often exhorted us all to be more dynamic on stage; I guess he had been working on Lou in particular.

We were in a bind, though, and so were a lot of other bands. The problem was caused by the gradual disappearance of the old rock 'ballrooms', starting around 1969 or so. The old Boston Tea Party, The Avalon, and similar rooms all over began closing up, and these rooms we had always considered to be best for us – holding 1500 people or thereabouts. We were left with two choices – small clubs, which in fact were too small for us and couldn't pay enough, or huge coliseums, which we couldn't fill on our own. With the latter came the real problem, for on those huge stages you would be completely lost unless something theatrical were added to the music; it was no longer enough just to stand there and play the songs. The response of other bands is apparent – the pyrotechnics used by The Who and Kiss, and the truckloads of laser lights and other gimcracks carried around by Wings. Ironically, the wisest course for us in 1970 was probably to revive The E.P.I., only 'bigger and better', load it into a few 18-wheelers, and set out once again across the Hudson! Had that notion occurred to us (which it didn't), I don't think that we could have afforded to do it, or that any money would have been left over afterwards if we had. Just another 'what if . . .', I'm afraid.

Sterling Morrison on the road, 1969.
(Doug Yule)

Lou was relying totally on Sesnick, but Sesnick felt Lou was too hard to handle and finally told him, 'I don't care if you live or die.' Lou couldn't face this. It was like a hard divorce, to be very suddenly slapped in the face by someone you trusted. One night I'm sitting in a booth upstairs at Max's eating a cheeseburger, and Lou comes up and says, "Sterling, I'd like you to meet my parents". I was astonished. Lou always had an extremely troubled relationship with his parents. They hated the fact that Lou was playing music and hanging around with undesirables. I was always afraid of Lou's parents. There was this constant threat of them seizing Lou and having him thrown into the nuthouse. That was always over our heads. Every time Lou got hepatitis his parents were waiting to seize him and lock him up. So I was thinking, 'What in the world can this portend?' and then I went back to the dressing room and kept going on "Vanity Fair".

● "LIVE AT MAX'S"

On August 23rd 1970, Brigid Polk, a long time friend, fan, and also a close associate of Andy Warhol, with whom she was conducting a series of tape recording ventures, and Gerard Malanga, went to see The Velvets play. Brigid, who was recording everything in those days, recorded the concert on her Sony TC120 cassette recorder and these tapes were later released by Atlantic, the first bootleg ever accepted by a record company.

REED: I've always arranged it so bootlegs could come out, The Max's live set, now that's another album I really love. If you want to know what Max's was really like – and now you can't – it's there, for real, because Brigid was just sitting there with her little Sony recorder. It's in mono, you can't hear us, but you can hear just enough. We're out of tune, per usual, but it's Sunday night, and all the regulars are there, and Jim Carroll's trying to get Tuinols, and they're talking about the war. We were the house band. There it is.

Brigid Polk
(Gerard Malanga)

Memories and impressions of the Max's residency tend to be extremely mixed. Mickey Ruskin says it was a non-event and few people came. Debbie Harry, who was a Max's waitress at the time and aware of the band's significance, says this is untrue, and people were very excited by it. Richard Meltzer writes: 'No other band could possibly have opened up Max's for live music and no other ambiance could possibly have served so well in reintroducing this by now legendary group to the city of its origin (they'd been stuck playing places like Boston and San Diego). Fine. Swell. Everything was metaphorically perfect from every side of the fence. But more important is the whole thing actually *worked* (whole summer of 'em playing real good almost every night), one of those rare times when anything that rock-predictable was actually worth all the bother.' Danny Fields, on the other hand, says, "The gig at Max's wasn't so momentous. It only became that when Lou left the group during that gig. You suddenly realized you were never going to see them again. I thought it was terrific."

We can at least hear the music recorded that night ourselves and make up our own minds about what it might have been like. Lou was facing an audience he had played a part in creating and yet he himself felt cheated and betrayed. He says that he enjoyed this night but the ambivalence is evident in the tone of his introduction.

REED: Good evening. We're called The Velvet Underground. You're allowed to dance in case you don't know. And uh ... that's about it. This is called I'm Waiting for My Man, a tender folk song from the early Fifties about love between a man and a subway. I'm sure you'll all enjoy it.

He then does some rather loose and non-committal renditions of Waiting for My Man, Sweet Jane, Lonesome Cowboy Bill, Beginning To See the Light, I'll Be Your Mirror, Pale Blue Eyes, without saying much. Then, sounding fragile and not a little sad and weary:

REED: This is a song about ... oh when you've done something so sad and you wake up the next day and remember it. Not to sound grim or anything, but just once in a while you have one of those days. I seem to have them nearly ... This is a song called Sunday Morning.

AUDIENCE MEMBER: Sunday Morning!

REED: Wow! It's really fun to be able to play these for you ... I really don't get a chance.

FIELDS: The ambiance at Max's during The Velvets gig was one of intimacy. As it turned out as soon as the gig was over the next day they broke up and you realised that was it, because you knew Lou wasn't coming back. It was serious and the remainder of the group continued without him and that's when Donald Lyons called them The Velveteen Underground. Suddenly there was no one left. For us it was always Lou Reed. But I think that must have been the general feeling as well because he was the one. It didn't end when Andy or Nico or John left. It ended when he left.

I was responsible for "Live at Max's". That very week they broke up, we realised Brigid had the last recorded performance of The Velvet Underground because it was clear that Lou wasn't coming back. I persuaded Brigid that we take the cassette to Atlantic since they still sort of had them on the label – this was after they'd recorded "Loaded" – and this would be their second record and a

cheap way for Atlantic to fulfil its contractual obligations. And they could buy this master and all rights to it for I think $10,000. I split it with her and then she started to be mad at me because she thought she had given me too big a cut.

Lou Reed in "Screen Tests", 1966.

● EXIT REED

● MORRISON: A day or two after meeting Lou's parents, our manager came and told me that Lou had quit the band and gone back to Long Island with his parents.

REED: There were a lot of things going on that summer. Internally, within the band, the situation, the milieu, and especially the management. Situations which could only be solved by as abrupt a departure as possible once I had made the decision. I just walked out because we didn't have any money, I didn't want to tour again – I can't get any writing done on tour, and the grind is terrible – and I'd wondered for a long time if we were ever going to be accepted on a large scale. Words can't do justice to the way I got worked over with the money. But I'm not a businessman. I've always said, 'I don't care about it,' and generally I've gotten fucked as a result of that attitude.

CUTRONE: In the end I just think that Lou had what he thought was his job to do, which was to continue making music in the best way that he could do it. Maybe back track a little to catch up with the general public and at the same time expand.

● "LOADED"

"Loaded" was released in September 1970 on Atlantic's subsidiary Cotillion label. They had changed labels but not escaped being stuck on a subsidiary of their company. This record is controversial among hard core Velvets fans for a number of reasons. After it came out Reed complained bitterly that "Sweet Jane" and "New Age" were tampered with after his departure and sapped of their strength.

REED: On "Sweet Jane" towards the ending it had a minor melody which was so pretty it made sense, but they edited it out. That was sheer stupidity, blatant stupidity. On "New Age" it goes: 'something's got a hold on me and I don't know what/it's the beginning of a new age.' That was supposed to go on for a full minute, that was the powerful part of the song, they have it go on for one chorus. How could anyone be that stupid? They took all the power out of those songs. Secondly, I wasn't there to put the songs in order. If I could have stood it I would have stayed with them and showed them what to do.

The album lacks The Velvet Underground trademark of a series of songs setting up questions and answers and working like a series of connected stories that become comparable to a picaresque novel. The album was a blatant attempt to make it and some feel it suffers from this commercial aspect.

REED: I gave them an album loaded with hits, and it was loaded with hits to the point where the rest of the people showed their colors. So I left them to their album full of hits that I made.

"Loaded" contains some of Reed's greatest rock songs ("Sweet Jane", "Rock & Roll") and it was hailed by the critics as a masterpiece. This was annoying to Lou since not only were they responding for the first time with unanimous praise to an album he knew was flawed, but his name was listed third on the credits below Doug Yule's and Sterling Morrison's and the whole group was credited for authorship of all the songs, a matter which was cleared up when Reed sued and was then granted full rights to all the material. "Loaded" is in fact many people's favorite Velvets album, probably because it is their most easily accessible. It does work well as a way into the group.

DOUG YULE: I had a significant influence on Lou. Lou and I had significant influence together on the group. I, of course, did no more than Lou – he was doing the writing, I was arranger, musical director. I was handling my half, he was handling his. Many said Lou was The Velvet Underground, and in the sense that it was his brainchild he was, he was the main force behind it, but it was a band, and like any band its totality is made up of all its members, not just one person with side musicians. At the time it was going on it was all very crazy, we all had visions of riches and fame and success and general acceptance, but it was kinda warm and dark, lotta late nights, and we had a lot of fun and met a lotta nice people across the country.

Side One:

● **"Who Loves the Sun"** makes a surprisingly acceptable pop sound at the beginning of this last Velvet Underground album, but its irony cannot be lost on any hardcore Velvets fan.

● **"Sweet Jane"** is one of the most successful and influential rock & roll songs composed by Lou Reed during his Velvet Underground period. The lyrics are a further step in Reed's development as the poet laureate of New York City.

● **"Rock & Roll"**. It is hard to ignore the possibility that this may be a strictly autobiographical song in which Reed, to whom gender has never made much difference, is writing directly about his own experiences as a child. It would not be going too far to say that Lou Reed's life was saved by rock & roll.

● **"Cool it Down"**. The message of this song, which fits very nicely into the mosaic of the album, is take life at a more relaxed pace.

● **"New Age"** ends the first side of the album with an attempt to present some encouraging statements to a confused audience as the Seventies began.

Side Two:

● **"Head Held High"** is a straightforward story about a son whose parents advised him from the age of six to hold his head up high.

● **"Lonesome Cowboy Bill"** is a song about William Burroughs.

● **"I Found A Reason".** Lou Reed walks hand in hand with himself. Doug Yule does not understand what he is singing about.

● **"Train Round the Bend"** is the travel weary plaint of a group that had probably been on the road for too long and missed the true inspiration of their urban roots.

● **"Oh! Sweet Nuthing"** is a lament, in the tradition of folk-blues, in which the singer mentions a number of characters cataloging their poverty and asking the listener to say a prayer for each of them. Coming as the final song on The Velvet's final album, it also stands as a statement of their own situation.

L-R: Steve Sesnick, Sterling Morrison, Lou Reed and music journalist Dick Nusser listening to the tapes of "Loaded" in 1970. (Henri Ter Hall)

BOCKRIS: "Loaded" seems to have gotten an outstandingly better reception than the other records. Why do you think that was?

FIELDS: The Velvets always had the critics by the balls, but so what?! They didn't expect much commercially in terms of airplay, but they hoped for it. They always did. And they tried to make very catchy songs. I was so appalled at the cover of "Loaded". In retrospect it's so beguiling.

SESNICK: It was accumulative. The times were catching up to what we represented. A lot of things had fallen by the wayside, in terms of groups and acts that fell apart, who had far more support than we did, enormously more support than we did. They had charts, they had things that record companies could relate to. But they broke up and we were still going, so it was a cumulative thing and it really was culminating very excitingly.

THE CULT OF THE VELVET UNDERGROUND

In 1970 Nico recorded her third solo album and performed one concert at London's Roundhouse. Cale released his first solo album *Vintage Violence* and collaborated with Terry Riley on *Church of Anthrax*. Morrison and Tucker continued to play in The Velvet Underground with Yule and a replacement. Warhol produced 'Trash', directed by Morrissey, and did the cover for The Rolling Stones' *Sticky Fingers*: a zipper on a pair of jeans that unzips to reveal a pair of jockey shorts, it was reminiscent of the banana that peeled.

BOCKRIS: Do you remember hearing about Lou's quitting the group?

TUCKER: Yeah, I was at Max's in fact.

MALANGA: What was your reaction at Max's and how did you feel when you saw someone else up on stage playing drums?

TUCKER: Glum.

MALANGA: You were pregnant at the time?

TUCKER: No, when I went there I wasn't. I had had the baby already. And here she stands right next to me 12½ years old.

MALANGA: What's her name?

TUCKER: Kerry.

MALANGA: Were you married at the time?

TUCKER: No.

MALANGA: Did you go more than once?

TUCKER: The night I went was the last night Lou played. He had told Sesnick he

Sterling Morrison at Max's Kansas City on August 23, 1970. (Dustin Pittman)

Billy Yule at Max's Kansas City. August 23, 1970.
(Dustin Pittman)

Doug Yule and Billy Yule at Max's Kansas City, August 23, 1970.
(Dustin Pittman)

was going to quit and Sesnick told me, then I went and found Lou and talked to him for a little bit. He was really really upset and I was upset too, of course. He didn't say much. He didn't say, 'Well here's my reasons.' He said he felt bad about it, but he had thought about it for a long time and had just decided that he had to go on his own. He was pretty quiet and obviously upset. When I went to go find him he was sitting on the upper section of the stairs at Max's where people didn't walk, alone in the dark, and I sat down next to him on the stairs. As I recall I put my arm around him and I said, 'Louie, what's the matter?' There was nothing I could do. I was really saddened by it, but he was not getting along at all with Sesnick at this point. I don't know really if he just felt Sesnick wasn't doing anything for us, or if the personalities were just rubbing the wrong way. I think some of each. Lou and Sesnick were real close for quite a while. I basically said if you really feel that strongly about it, obviously you have to do it, and I told him I was real sad about it. I think I said something like, 'have you really thought about this?' I had gotten the feeling, and I'm sure this is true, that Doug was really getting on Lou's nerves. And the little combo of Yule and Sesnick was becoming too much. Doug was getting on my nerves a little, too. Doug's a very nice guy, okay, but, at the time anyway, he was starstruck, and began to think he was a lot more important than he was and was becoming a pain in the ass. Being pushy and prima donnaish and just a general pain in the ass, and affecting Lou in a whole different way.

BOCKRIS: How could Doug Yule have had such an effect on Lou Reed?

TUCKER: That's what I meant when I said before about going to hear Doug rehearse and Lou being real excited and saying, 'Wow! This guy's great!' I didn't know this guy at all, but I just had this feeling, I sensed it somehow, and I said to myself, 'Holy shit! Take it easy, Lou, you're going to blow up this guy's head and we're going to have problems.' And that isn't my usual M.O. But it was just very obvious to me for some reason. And that's what happened. I remember saying to Lou on the stairs, because I had sensed that Doug was a big part of the problem, 'Why the hell don't we just throw Doug out? What the hell are you bothering with this fool for if he bothers you so much?' I can't remember if he even answered . . .

REED: And if it's true that you can't live up to everyone's expectations, and if it's true you cannot be all things to all people, and if it's true you cannot be other than what you are (passage of time to the contrary), then you must be strong of heart if you wish to work the problems out in public, on stage, through work before "them" who fully expect and predict in print their idol's fall.

'Passion – REALISM – realism was the key,' Lou Reed wrote five years later on the sleeve notes to "Metal Machine Music". 'The records were letters. Real letters from me to certain other people. I'd harbored the hope that the intelligence that once inhabited novels and films would ingest rock. I was, perhaps, wrong.'

REED: If you play the albums chronologically they cover the growth of us as people from here to there and in there is a tale for everybody in case they want to know what they can do to survive the scenes. If you line the songs up and play them, you should be able to relate and not feel alone – I think it's important that people don't feel alone.

TUCKER: I guess really I'm just glad I was part of it all, and very proud to have been part. I do have two regrets: 1) We didn't stay together, and 2) A rather selfish regret, that we never taped our concerts.

NICO: It was all very exciting. That's all I can say.

MORRISON: It was fun. It was not "Mein Kampf, My Struggle", it was a good time. When it got to be not fun then I didn't want to do it.

BARNEY HOSKINS: Do you think there is still a cult of The Velvet Underground?

CALE: Yes, and it's distasteful to me. I mean, all the promise we showed in those two albums, we never delivered on it. I'm sure Lou feels the same way. He's as stubborn and egocentric as I am.

REED: It was a process of elimination from the start. First no more Andy, then no more Nico, then no more John, then no more Velvet Underground.

WARHOL: It was great. But it's over.

Lou Reed at Max's Kansas City, August 23, 1970 playing his last gig with The Velvet Underground.
(Dustin Pittman)

● THE VELVET UNDERGROUND 1993/4

When our story left off in August 1970, with Lou Reed's surprise announcement that he was quitting The Velvet Underground, it left many people suspended. Apart from our readers and the more than a million hard-core Velvet Underground fans, Sterling Morrison, Maureen Tucker and Doug Yule found themselves in the reptilian clutches of Steve Sesnick. John Cale and Nico had both embarked on strong solo careers, but they were not unaffected by Reed's dramatic move. In a way everything about The Velvet Underground seemed left unfinished.

And indeed, the remnants of the band – dubbed by Danny Fields The Velveteen Underground – continued to tour. They even recorded a new Velvet Underground album, *Squeeze* (1973), before they themselves finally quit and all but virtually disappeared from the public eye.

Ironically, or perhaps fatefully, the very year this book was published, 1983, marked the rumblings of early conversations between members of the original band – including Cale – which centered around a restructuring of the vague business contracts that existed, particularly in the matter of song writing royalties – the vast majority of which had over the years accrued to Lou Reed.

These new arrangements were overseen by a New York based British lawyer named Christopher Whent, who was at the outset John Cale's lawyer and in time came also to represent Morrison and Tucker in matters concerning The Velvet Underground. By 1986 new contracts had been signed and all four members of the band were communicating with each other again, if sporadically. "The band went into the black with the record company in about '83," Whent told the British reporter, Richard Williams "That's when they started spitting out royalty checks. It's not a bad chunk of change. Not enough to live on. But a comfortable supplement."

While the laborious healing of deep wounds proceeded there had, from 1972 onwards, grown a critical recognition of The Velvet Underground's seminal contribution to rock and roll and along with it a growing world wide audience. *Uptight* was not only published in the UK, but in Germany, Japan, Spain, Switzerland, Czechoslovakia and the USA, and continues to find publishers in other territories. The Velvet Underground's albums have been repackaged countless times in countless countries and continue to sell steadily around the world. Simultaneously, numerous bootleg albums have also appeared.

Since *Uptight* was published, the consensus of critical opinion about The Velvet Underground has swung as severely as Poe's pendulum in their favour. "The Velvet Underground were so far ahead of their time that hearing them now it seems scarcely believable that they're not a contemporary group," wrote Lynden Barber in *Melody Maker*.

"They irrevocably changed rock and roll, igniting the avant-possibility in pop with a primal-shriek guitar tumult, harrowing balladry and Reed's candid lyrical discourse on sex, drugs and salvation," wrote David Fricke in *Rolling Stone*.

"If The Velvet Underground were not the best rock band of all, they may well have been the most influential," wrote Richard Williams in *The Independent*.

Steve Mass, founder and proprietor of the Mudd Club, the most famous rock and roll club in the world from 1978-1983, had befriended Cale and recalled several discussions with him about getting the band back together.

STEVE MASS: To me, John Cale was this giant catalyst on the rock scene. He'd put the whole avant garde and traditional rock together and that stuck in my mind. And the more I got to know John the more I felt that he was like a Mozart. He couldn't express himself vocally. He expressed himself through music. As I got to know John I said, 'You've got to get back with The Velvet Underground.' And he'd say, 'That's utter nonsense. That's bullshit.' We'd be sitting in a bar and I'd keep harping on it. Obviously there were no royalties coming from The Velvet Underground and Lou Reed controlled the publishing. It was the last thing he wanted to consider. I said, 'John, you have to do this, you were the resident genius.'

All these disparate strands of growing interest in the band were gathered together under the umbrella of The Velvet Underground Appreciation Society, established in 1978 by a certain Philip Milstein who produced an irregularly published but excellent magazine documenting the group's history, *What Goes On*. After running the organisation successfully and with some appreciation from band members, particularly Morrison and Tucker, Milstein had passed it into the capable hands of one of its major contributors, MC Kostek, under whose auspices it has continued to thrive. Anybody interested in getting in touch with The Velvet Underground

John Cale.
(Renaud Monfourny)

Appreciation Society can write to MC Kostek c/o The Velvet Underground Appreciation Society, 5721 SE Laguna Avenue, Stuart FL 34997-7828 USA.

As the 1980s proceeded, hope grew among the fans and some members of the band that a reunion of some sort might occur in the spirit of that time, during which the Sixties, and particularly the Warhol Sixties and The Velvet Underground's contribution, was scrutinised and presented in a new, altogether more positive light. Furthermore, in the mid-Eighties, two studio albums, recorded in 1968 and 1969 and culled from the vaults of MGM were released to critical acclaim and steady sales.

This growing interest was capped in 1986 by an excellent BBC Television documentary on the band made by Kym Evans and Mary Harron. It was the most comprehensive visual documentation of their history, including several interviews with all the members except Reed, who simply gave permission for a brief clip of excerpts from some other interviews he had recently given to be used.

Of all four original members of the band, Reed always seemed the most reluctant to consider, indeed the most troubled by the concept of, a Velvet Underground reunion. Reed became increasingly morose as he was repeatedly questioned about it during yearly publicity tours promoting his most recent solo record. He finally snapped at one journalist that he didn't like high-school reunions.

Lou Reed.
(Rex Features)

However, just as he had picked the band off the sawdust floor of the Café Bizarre and transported them into his Cinderella realms of magic and multimedia in 1966, Andy Warhol once again unexpectedly brought the band – or more specifically Reed and Cale – together again by suddenly and very unexpectedly dying on February 22, 1987, a day that will go down in infamy in the history of the American medical profession. Warhol had gone into hospital for a routine gall-bladder operation, but due to a lack of care during the post-operative recovery period, had been allowed to drown in his own fluids.

Brought together by ex-Warhol Factory manager and photographer Billy Name at the Warhol memorial service luncheon on April 1, 1987, and inspired by the artist Julian Schnabel at the same event, Cale and Reed joined forces in 1988 to collaborate on a suite of songs which were released in 1990 on an album called *Songs For Drella* (Warhol's nickname when they had worked with him). An attempt at a new form which Reed dubbed Biorock, the songs covered Warhol's life chronologically, mixing fact and fiction to portray the relationship between Warhol, Reed and Cale. More than anything else it gave Reed an opportunity to apologise to Andy for turning his back on him in the early Eighties, after a long love-hate relationship that had raged through the Seventies. It also allowed him to have the last word on the cutting remarks about him in Warhol's posthumously published diaries.

Andy Warhol.
(Rex Features)

John Cale.
(Rex Features)

Songs For Drella was an artistic success, garnering a large amount of attention in the international press. Coming on the heels of *New York*, Reed's finest solo work in years, and Cale's outstanding recent album, *Words For The Dying*, *Songs For Drella* solidified and brought into focus both of their careers and reputations at the beginning of the 1990s.

It did not, however, appear to build a bridge to a Velvet Underground reunion. If anything Reed became more irritated by the constant questions about it. Unbeknown to the public, the new collaboration between Cale and Reed had actually resulted in a decision on both their parts never to work together again under any circumstances. By the time the album was completed they were, like Mick Jagger and Keith Richards in the mid-Eighties, barely speaking to each other.

However, something stronger than Reed's will, or the conflict between Reed and Cale, continued to pursue them in the growing idolatry of Warhol, whose fame multiplied in death like Marilyn Monroe's and James Dean's, particularly in Europe where a necrophiliac relationship with American icons has been an established tradition since the end of World War II. In June, 1991, the Cartier Foundation in France staged an enormous Warhol event to inaugurate the opening of his retrospective in Paris and all four original members of The Velvet Underground were invited to attend, all expenses paid. Nico had died in an accident on the island of Ibiza in 1988. Reed and Cale had agreed to give a brief performance of some of the *Songs For Drella* at the event. At the last moment, Lou decided that it would – under the circumstances – be churlish not to invite Maureen Tucker and Sterling Morrison to join them on stage for at least one song.

LOU REED: We were scooting around that morning, going 'Hmmm, we could... It's possible... No, no... Oh, life's too short.'

MAUREEN TUCKER: Me and Sterling turned up for the show, it got all emotional and five minutes later we were on stage playing "Heroin", totally unrehearsed. I remember thinking, 'Shit, that's Lou Reed out there, that's John and Sterling and this is still the best band in the world.

It was not, however, until November to December 1992, when the band convened in New York for the first ever business meeting to oversee a growing roster of VU product, that the story of their reformation really begins.

MORRISON: What distinguished the business meetings in the past was that they were attended by our lawyers... But this was one we actually convened, in the flesh, and that to me was unprecedented. That was the first time we'd ever done that, John, that was historic!

CALE: Paris was a surprise, inasmuch as it actually happened. Nothing would have gotten done without Lou thinking it was a good idea There was nothing happening for him in 1993 so he decided to try it. So we put together a couple of days' rehearsal in New York just to see if we could keep time. It was very interesting – there was the sound all over again. It turned out to be fantastic. All the original enthusiasm was there.

MORRISON: So we concluded that we could play. The next question was do we want to?

A four week rehearsal period was scheduled in New York for May, 1993. There was some trepidation as to how matters would flow between them once they passed through the initial euphoria of discovering each other again, but things started well. Lou and Sterling, who had talked least during the interim, initially found great joy in re-igniting their guitar partnership. And the combination of Sterling and Maureen served as a buffer between John and Lou that seemed to click perfectly into the emotional engine of the group. Yet to visitors it was obvious that, as one put it, "It's Lou's world. We just live here." It was undisputed that the reunion would never have happened had it not come from Reed's desire. And it also appeared that Lou, not John, was now the musical as well as lyrical conductor of The Velvet Underground.

Reed repeatedly said that he was there to have "fun." Perhaps the others had forgotten what "fun" was for Lou Reed. For the director in Lou, for example, it was fun to pit his wife – and *de facto* band manager – Sylvia, against the other members of the group, encouraging her to treat them like dogshit. It was "fun" to cut into Sterling in front of the others when he had a tuning problem. As the rehearsals neared their end, Morrison was heard to express the emotion that had he known it was going to be like this he would have stayed home.

What saved the day, perhaps, certainly what brought the band through rehearsals that could have ended the reunion, was the fact that, whilst part of Lou had proudly remained fifteen years old, the other three had matured in the intervening two years. Maureen was a mother of five. John, who like Lou had abstained from drugs and alcohol for years now, and

(Rex Features)

Lou Reed, Sterling Morrison, Maureen
Tucker and John Cale.
(Renaud Monfourny)

was weathered by working on *Songs For Drella*, had discovered how to pacify rather than
pander to Reed's little chess moves. Both Sterling and John were able to empathise with the
psychodrama of Reed's daily life and thereby handle, rather than strangle, him.

Even Lou appeared to have changed on the surface. On the day he berated Sterling so
nastily, for example, he had later apologised, astonishing his long-suffering friend. But
the nerve of Lou's "fun" was inescapably present in the persona of Sylvia, who had by now
transformed into what her husband had once been famous for being – a rock monster. She
went out of her way to belittle the other members of the band, particularly Cale. Treating him
like a know-nothing twerp, she constantly compared John to Lou, pointing out to highly
amused observers – since the opposite was so blatantly true – how much better than John Lou
now looked. Sylvia made it as transparent as hydrochloric acid that in her opinion John,
Sterling and Maureen were simply Lou's band, and all owed their lives to Lou's generosity
without which none of them would have existed. In this Sylvia betrayed, for someone in the
music business, an astonishing lack of understanding of the mechanics of a rock band and a
blind spot about the essential collaboration between Reed and Cale, which had played a larger
role in Lou's life as a musician than any other single force. As Cale would regretfully conclude
after the whole "reunion" crashed to an abrupt end later that summer, from the outset
measures were taken to separate Lou from the band. As a result, the sad truth is that although
Lou played with The Velvet Underground through that June and July in Europe, he never
really *re-joined* the band.

**Sterling Morrison, Maureen Tucker,
John Cale and Lou Reed.**
(Renaud Monfourny)

Lou Reed.
(Rex Features)

As soon as it was announced that The Velvet Underground would undertake a European tour in the summer, requests for interviews poured in from numerous publications in every country they would play, primarily in the UK, where the VU had their most loyal following, with France a close second. This series of interviews was organised with steely control by Sylvia Reed. She refused to allow any access without a guarantee that the band, or Lou, would be featured on the publication's cover. The results were impressive. The following montage of quotes sets the stage for the drama that was to unfold.

LOU REED: Delmore Schwartz wrote this great poem called *The Heavy Bear That Walks With Me*, and The Velvet Underground is going to play with this giant bear coming along with it called *Myth*, and we will confront the *Myth*. The critics are going to have to compare it to the records, then see whether they like hearing it live, or if they think it doesn't hold up. We will confront the *Myth*... and we will show them something of the human side of it all.

JOHN CALE: It was early February when we first showed up to play together – in this room. We've got together over the years in every possible permutation: me and Lou, me and Sterling, Moe and Sterling, Moe and Lou, me, Sterling and Lou, but never with the four of us. So now we are. Straight away in rehearsals, the sound was there – basically a very good garage band that doesn't spend a lot of time trying to balance out the instruments. When we tried "Black Angel's Death Song", everybody was running around trying to get rid of the whistling harmonics on the viola, but with all the technology in the world you won't tame this thing. When it works, it's fun. It sounds majestic. When the songs click and we're just getting our teeth around them, then you remember the great things about being in the band. So we're in the process of loosening up. Internally we are the same, but externally it isn't the same.

REED: It's not a reunion, it's a continuum. It feels better now than it did then. We're all wiser. It just sort of happened. I don't recall anybody saying 'Hey, let's play,' it just kinda came about. We just mutually thought in our own little worlds that it might be a hell of a lot of fun to do.

MOE TUCKER: This reunion is basically happening because all four of us really wanted it to, even if it's just for this one tour. I guess you can expect to hear all of those wonderful Velvet Underground hits! I personally don't think it's either necessary or expected that we play any new material, but I kind of suspect that John and Lou won't be happy with just playing old songs. We haven't made any decision about exactly what we'll be playing yet. If this was five years ago or seven years ago, I think it might not work. But we've all had a lot more contact in the past few years and we realise we all like each other. It sounds remarkably the same, which I'm very happy with.

Maureen Tucker, John Cale,
Lou Reed and Sterling Morrison.
(Renaud Mofourny)

MORRISON: People have wanted us to play for a long time and there was no real reason not to, if the four of us felt like we wanted to play together. We decided that we did, so let's do what's right. We'd never talked about doing it before. Everybody was too busy doing other things. But certainly it was something that could be contemplated since 1990.

CALE: That's always kinda the way things happened with us, anyway. There was no massive agenda and there was no great determination... It was like these four people wandering around in a daze and suddenly they decided to do something.

MORRISON: What's unique about this is that, in the past, the fact of our playing wasn't newsworthy in itself the way this is. Now, I would rather play well than be "significant!" But the attention is nice – it would be misdirected or ill-timed or useless unless we actually do accomplish something musically. Whether it turns out to be a good idea or a bad idea, we'll find out. It won't leave me crushed either way. So many bands are playing Velvet Underground material, why the hell can't The Velvet Underground once in a while if they feel like it?

Maureen Tucker, Sterling Morrison, Lou Reed and John Cale.
(Rex Features)

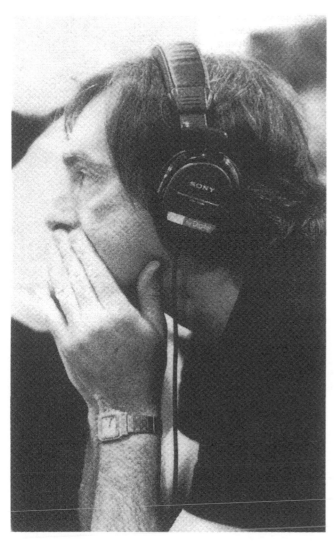

Sterling Morrison.
(Renaud Monfourny)

Maureen Tucker.
(Renaud Monfourny)

JOHN CALE: We're going to attract a lot of ambulance chasers, people who want to see us fail. I read this thing in England which said: "Here are some bands who shouldn't even think about re-forming." We were one of them. The British press was always like that. I'm just having a little pokey. "Oh, look, The Velvets are re-forming and they didn't even bother to ask anybody." There were four distinct personalities always. I was worried for a while... But one thing that Lou's doing and he doesn't normally do in his own work is he's going to wail a lot on guitar – he's going to have fun.

We can take it anywhere we want. There are plenty of ideas floating around. But, for a start, I've had to learn a lot of those songs, because I never played them originally. That was the work of the first week. This week we're starting to perform groups of songs: four, five, six songs in a row, until we've built it up and it's become like a second skin. Then we can throw away the ones that don't work. And I expect that when we get out on the road we'll start trying new things – an improvisation, a song we haven't rehearsed.

TUCKER: My vision of what the audience is going to be is what keeps me from getting glum about all the hoop-la and the machine. I want them to go away happy. I think we all feel that way. There's just so many people who have loved us for such a long time and have continued to buy our records and think so much of us. To me, this is a little bit of thanks.

REED: How long do you need to have it demonstrated that this was for real, completely sincere, above-board and meant in exactly the way it seemed to be meant? Look at the records. They speak for themselves.

As much as they enjoyed playing together, as the time of their departure approached the tensions that faced all of them became apparent. Old wounds open as easily between collaborators in rock as between lovers. Also, there was the undisputed fact, as one British scribe, Terry Staunton, pointed out, that "The Velvets have more to lose than any other band. No other band in history has been surrounded by so much mythology, no other band has had such far-reaching influence on the music that followed them. It could all be forgotten..."

On May 25th, The Velvet Underground flew first class from New York to London. They spent a few days in London rehearsing, then travelled to Edinburgh to face their first commercial audience as a band together since 1968, playing for the first time outside America. Luna were to open for them on the majority of the dates. The group's Dean Wareham kept a diary of the tour's progress.

Nerves were understandably strained to an edge by the time The Velvet Underground stepped out onto the stage in Edinburgh at 8:45 p.m. on June 1st. The five minute standing ovation they received before playing a single note appeared to do little to relax them. The first show was by all accounts uptight.

CAROLINE SULLIVAN: The surrealism of watching rock history come to life is heightened by the sense of expectation. Can four upstanding, middle-aged citizens still whip up any menace? The world will be watching.

ALLAN JONES: There's a sense of a band playing with a gun to its head, hostages of their own legend.

JOHN HARRIS: John Cale is dressed in a close-fitting black suit, awkwardly hammering at bass guitar and looking like Peter Cushing with a wedge haircut. Lou Reed's face, as ever, shows the wounds of his trawl through low-living, and he has the dress sense of a middle-aged suburban professional. Both ooze an inanimate, po-faced academic cool; the kind that comes from knowing you're a genuine elder. Sterling Morrison looks nothing other than ancient, and so long are the intervening years that Moe Tucker is now a mother of five – and you can see the maternal wisdom in her face.

PAT KANE: The first thing you notice as The Velvet Underground stutter and stumble through their first few numbers – deliberately? incompetently, who's to know? – is the inappropriate rude health of Lou Reed. He bulges out of his black T-shirt and blue denims like a cross between Bryan Adams and Nosferatu; the pebble glasses make him look more like a pop professor than real pop professors do. Rock's junkie royal has turned in every detail of his choreography, into an aerobic MTV act.

DAVID BELCHER: Cale was a masterpiece of thespian understatement, deploying the twitchy, upright manner of Peter Cushing as Professor Van Helsing in a Hammer Dracula movie. Cale also took the departed Nico's vocals on "All Tomorrow's Parties" and "Femme Fatale", investing both with a bluff grandeur.

ALLAN JONES: At the end, they line up like chorus girls in the cast of *The Mousetrap*. Cale puts his arm around Lou. Lou jumps. You get the impression that the last time Lou touched him, his fists were probably clenched. There's still a long history between these two. Lou smiles, and puts his arm around Maureen. Sterling taps her on the head.

JOHN ROCKWELL: Those who attended both Edinburgh shows found the second, on Thursday, far superior to the first... Certainly the audience loved it, standing throughout the two-hour set and cheering wildly.

Indeed, there was much to cheer. Mr. Reed still sings with the same ominous distinctiveness; Mr. Cale is still the same multi-faceted musical saboteur; Mr. Morrison still contributes a guitar sound of weight and solidity. The revelation on Thursday, though, was the diminutive Ms. Tucker's drumming.

BEN THOMPSON: Lou Reed seems to be the most invigorated by not having to be "formerly of The Velvet Underground" any more – he's even got rid of that nightmarish Michael Bolton perm in honour of the occasion. Which would you rather play? "Black Angel's Death Song" or "Magic & Loss"?

DEAN WAREHAM: The Velvets' June 2nd show is very different. They play the same songs, but it is apparent that Lou is going to do a fair bit of improvising, playing with tempo and structure. Sterling Morrison is playing bass on some songs, rhythm guitar on most (and he's a great player, all upstrokes), and a couple of great guitar solos on

Lou Reed.
(Rex Features)

Sterling Morrison.
(London Features International)

Nico.
(London Features International)

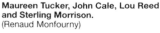

**Maureen Tucker, John Cale, Lou Reed
and Sterling Morrison.**
(Renaud Monfourny)

"Rock And Roll" and "White Light/White Heat". After the show we meet Sterling, Moe and Lou, who are all very friendly. Lou is especially funny in a very New York way, with a very dry sense of humour.

From Edinburgh they travelled down to London where they were booked to play the Forum, capacity 1,200, and Wembley, capacity 13,000. Debbie Harry, Chrissie Hynde and Peter Gabriel were among the celebrity audience at the Forum.

MARK SATLOF: After the stage went black, a roar of the crowd was quickly silenced by a husky "1, 2, 3, 4" count and the immediate, furiously strummed musical greeting of "We're Gonna Have A Real Good Time Together". "It just seems like yesterday," said Lou Reed.

Reed especially transformed his songs with radical new phrasing. He repeated lines, or jumped into vocal lines a few beats later than expected, spitting the words out rapidly to catch a later groove. Moe Tucker validated Reed's quote from a few years back that there are two kinds of drummers – Moe Tucker and everybody else.'

The next night, at the sold out Wembley Arena, The Velvets turned in a far more intense performance. They worked together as a band, comfortable with each other, with the audience and with their songs. Seemingly energised by the sell-out crowd, they shrugged off their earlier nervousness and toyed with the songs even more. Cale and Reed, who had traded glares and scowls the previous evening, competed instead with duelling viola and guitar, and faced off on songs like "Some Kinda Love".

Ironically, in Amsterdam – which had become one of Reed's solo strongholds and in which the Dutch music critics had as recently as 1988 voted *The Velvet Underground and Nico* as the greatest record of all time – there were more doubts about the group's ability to meet their myth than anywhere else.

BERT VAN DER KAMP: People are excited about The Velvet Underground re-forming and coming to Holland, but there is also a lot of negativity. They don't want their illusions shattered so they don't want to go. Also, because they play a large venue and they play a small venue they're charging a great deal.

DEAN WAREHAM: On June 8th we played Amsterdam's Paradiso with a capacity of 1,200. I watched the Velvet's show from the balcony right on the side of the stage. Lou was wearing a white cotton headband, and keeps pouring ice over his head. We briefly attend the after-show party. Lou exits via boat.

**The reformed Velvet Underground
performing on stage at the London
Forum.**
(Rex Features)

On June 9th they played Rotterdam, then travelled to Hamburg for two shows. From there it was on to Prague where their show was attended by Lou's friend, the writer and politician, Vaclav Havel, who invited the band to a private reception following the concert. By now, however, it had emerged, as critics were increasingly wont to point out, that "what you hear is not always The Velvet Underground of legendary repute. For about a third of the 90-minute concert we are here in the less demanding presence of the Lou Reed Band."

The tour climaxed in Paris with a three-night stand, June 15-17, at the famed Olympia Theatre where The Beatles, Stones and Dylan had caused riots in the Sixties and where The Velvets surely would have done it too if Warhol had taken them there as part of his 1967 European tour.

IRA KAPLAN: "Sweet Jane" is followed by a highly tongue-in-cheek little ditty, maybe called "We're The Velvet Underground", in which Reed sort of introduces the band and claims the reunion is Morrison and Tucker's idea, that he and Cale think it's "pretentious shit". As the audience roared and roared, The Velvet Underground gathered centre stage and bowed in unison. Show biz! Cale made that hokey clap-for-the-audience gesture, Reed raised his arms in triumph like an athlete; Tucker waved shyly, seemingly to individuals in the crowd; and Morrison looked both ecstatic and like he'd like to disappear. For the encore Cale sang "I'm Waiting For The Man" from the piano, upstaged (for me) by Tucker's one-handed eight snare whacks to the measure. Next was "Heroin". The members of the VU bowed some more and departed, returning again for a lovely "Pale Blue Eyes", marked by Cale's viola. Finally came a new song, "Cayote". "Could you please repeat that name?" asked one audience member. "Of course," replied Reed. "We're The Velvet Underground, we can do anything!"

All three nights were recorded for a live album and one was also filmed for an accompanying video. Reed told the American rock writer Lisa Robinson that this was the best show ever. It really was just one of those magical nights.

After Paris, they were scheduled to play the tour's last two nights in Berlin.

Lou Reed.
(Rex Features)

DEAN WAREHAM: Tonight, June 20th, is the last show, at a club called Die Halle, capacity 2,500. The VU are really good tonight. "All Tomorrow's Parties" sends shivers, and Lou plays a great eight minute guitar solo to begin "Some Kinda Love".

The Velvet's passage through Europe was outwardly smooth but inwardly bumpy. Although the shows sold out and the press was for the most part over the top positive, there were many older fans who were disappointed by what they saw as a cheap attempt to cash in on their accrued fame (ticket prices were high, astronomically so when they played clubs like the Forum in London and the Paradiso in Amsterdam). In their defence one associate pointed out that few critics had any sense of the immense cost of touring Europe in the 1990s. Apart from a technical entourage of guitar roadies, the expense of putting on the shows and the massive hotel and transportation fees combined with the tax laws of six different countries, did not leave anything like as much money for each musician as some critics imagined.

The real problem was the increasing separation between Lou Reed and the other members and the 'iron butterfly' – Sylvia – who stood between them, barely troubling to approach them civilly, let alone allow them into Lou's private and heavily protected world. The separation between Reed and the band, which harked back to the days in which Steve Sesnick had come between Reed and Cale in 1968, was emphasised by various representatives of Sire Records, who would be releasing the live album recorded in Paris. They never once spoke to any members of the band during the entire tour, except Reed. By the time The Velvet Underground reached Italy to play five opening dates for U2, Lou's uptightness and the constant tension on stage was something that shocked even Cale – who was further upset in Rome when Lou facetiously gave the crowd a Fascist salute. It was clear to John that Lou was not representing the band, and that he had come to see them simply as his umpteenth back-up band.

There had been a lot of criticism of The Velvet Underground's (read Lou Reed's) decision to open for U2. "The Velvets opening for U2?" queried Jeff Curtis in a letter to *Rolling Stone*. "Wouldn't that be like Jimi Hendrix opening up for The Monkees?"

JOHN CALE: I look on it as a real gesture of gentility on their part. I see them as supporting us in a way. I've always understood them to be big fans of ours and I can't think of anybody better than U2 to play with.

John Cale, Lou Reed and Sterling Morrison.
(Renaud Monfourny)

John Cale, Maureen Tucker,
Lou Reed and Sterling Morrison.
(Renaud Monfourny)

John Cale.
(Rex Features)

STERLING MORRISON: We talked about it a bit, and if we were going to precede a band we decided it had to be one whose major strength is their material, which would be U2 – who pretty much live or die by their material and performance. There's not a great emphasis on theatricals.

LOU REED: U2 are supporting us, actually. It's just that the playing order's reversed. It was their idea, not mine. We're here to have fun. That's been the driving force for me, the bottom line is I just want to get off. Turn it up to 11.

From Italy they returned to the UK in July to play a short set at The Glastonbury Festival where reviewers, having gotten over their initial wonder at a reincarnation comparable to a Beatles reunion, caught up with them.

PAUL MOODY: As they survey the biggest open-air bedroom in Europe with dull dollar bills in their eyes, it all becomes too obscene to be believed.

S.P.: Before he's struck a note, Lou Reed's scrapping with a roadie. "Leave it," he instructs with headmasterly impatience, "leave it, LEAVE IT!" The audience, as one, makes a mocking "oooOOOoooh!" The Velvet Underground should never have done this, of course. It's an atrocious idea.

KEITH CAMERON: The Glastonbury Festival appearance was often simply embarrassing, not least when Lou Reed began punching the air and leading the crowd in a ludicrous call and response routine during "Rock And Roll".

Part of the critics' cynicism was due to the fact that throughout the tour "Venus In Furs" had been running on British TV as the soundtrack for an ad for Dunlop Tyres.

At the end of July the band returned to the States and immediately separated to recover. At first it looked as if the hard work was going to pay off big. Not only was the live album and video scheduled for Fall release, but an American tour, an MTV *Unplugged* show and album, and possibly a new Velvet Underground album were all being discussed. Sylvia Reed even went so far as to start setting up US dates. However, as August plodded into September Lou, who suddenly found himself at a loose end, went into a post-tour nose-dive, and launched a fax war with Cale that would shortly bring the whole operation once again to a thundering halt. Reed laid out in some detail why he never wanted to perform on stage with Cale again under any circumstances. Cale, as hurt and dismayed as he had been over the disappointed-with-John comments Lou had passed after completing *Songs For Drella*, had learned by now that the way to respond to Reed's attack was by deflecting it with quiet understanding. This did little to soothe Reed's seething paranoia, however, and he immediately embarked upon another line of attack. He refused to sign any contracts or proceed with any further VU business until it had been agreed upon in writing that he would have total control over the production of the MTV *Unplugged* album as well as any other future VU product. Cale, who pointed out that the band had always worked as a team, was justifiably horrified, and replied in a flat negative. The battle continued through September into October, but by the time the Live album and video were released, Lisa Robinson had already announced in her *New York Post* column – carrying detailed explanations from Reed and Cale as well as some concluding remarks from Maureen which harked back to the Reed-Cale split of 1968 – that The Velvet Underground reunion, if it had actually ever happened, was now undoubtedly over. Sire Records executives were extremely disappointed and the live album, *The Velvet Underground Live 1993*, which could have, along with the band's entire back catalogue, benefited greatly from a US tour, made little commercial impression. It was a sad fall in more ways than one for the band, its audience and its history. Rather than growing up and bringing rock into its maturity, which Reed had been claiming was his goal since the early Eighties, Lou had reacted like the fifteen-year-old he was at times so proud to remain. It was his ball, and if they wouldn't play by his rules there would be no game.

Both *The New York Times* and *Rolling Stone* awarded The Velvet Underground first place in the comeback of the year category that December, but the album received reviews ranging from over the top positive to over the top negative with comparisons between Cale and Reed that were bound to rankle.

KENNY MATHIESON: John Cale's subverted anthem "All Tomorrow's Parties" is the first highlight on disc one (Reed's "Venus In Furs" dirge is on the dull side).

AMY LINDEN: What's most striking in 1993 is how immediate the band and their songs sound, particularly John Cale on the haunting "All Tomorrow's Parties". Reed's scattershot guitar shines on the cacophonous "Hey Mr Rain", though his terse monotone often swells into excessive singing that undercuts the brutal simplicity of the material.

(Renaud Monfourny)

John Cale and Lou Reed.
(Rex Features)

KEITH CAMERON: Anyone who saw The Velvets this summer and thought they were great will hear this mammoth 23-track set and swiftly realise that the emotional impact of actually seeing them – The Velvet Underground playing those songs competently – overrode the fact that much of this was a travesty. Reed's vocal readings of "Venus In Furs" and "Beginning To See The Light" have begun to overstep the line dividing artistic licence from wilful pisstake. "Rock And Roll" is hammered to oblivion; "I'll Be Your Mirror", though badly bruised, just about survives; but "Pale Blue Eyes" is tossed to the floor and stomped on as if to prove that, hell, Lou wrote it and he can murder it if he wants to. No, it's the contributions of John Cale that time and time again boot *Live MCMXCIII* out of karaoke-land and into the realms of respectability.

DAVE MORRISON: Plus points are John Cale's cadaverous cool, Moe Tucker's minimal pounding and some great versions, full of spiky improvisation. Negative point is Lou Reed cramming ad-libbed rubbish into the vocals. "Wooh yeah oooh" doesn't sound right in "Venus In Furs". Put a sock in it, Lou.

The fallout came in a series of interviews published in late 1993 and early 1994.

MOE TUCKER: Lou made it clear that all other (band) activities hinged on his being able to produce the MTV project. It's just so infuriating, because we had such a good time together on the tour last summer.

JOHN CALE: Lou likes to obsess over things. I have different production values than Lou does in that Lou will go for the audiophile situation and I will go for the excitement. I have a lot of respect for the way he produces his own albums, but when it comes to The Velvet Underground's music, that's a different matter altogether. The idea of handing the reins of The Velvet Underground sound to Lou was like putting the fox in to guard the chicken house, which became a problem when I realised the partnership idea was no longer in existence.

LOU REED: I said I could no longer continue doing it unless I did the production for any records that were going to come out of it. John Cale didn't want to do that, so that was the end of it. I've told them, I told John I cannot and will not be involved unless I'm in charge of the production, because everything has to sound up to a certain level and there's only one way that's going to happen. I want to get off. And if I can't then it's not fun, so that's the end of it. And there were things coming up where John wanted to write songs, wanted to do this, wanted to do that. There were opportunities to make albums and everything, and I said, "I can't do any writing at all for any future records unless I do the production, because that's the way it has to be."

On January 19th, 1994, Dennis Barrie, Director of The Rock and Roll Hall of Fame Museum, was quoted in *The New York Times*: "Someone said that we would run out of great people to induct. I think that's nonsense. You haven't seen anything yet. When I think about the people who didn't get in this year, people like Frank Zappa, The Velvet Underground, all these amazing people who just became eligible and will surface again in years to come. There's a wonderful breadth and depth of people to choose from."

(Rex Features)

ARI DELON is apparently completely out of his mind but, we are sure, in a good way. His dad, Alain Delon, should not have ignored him all these years. Best bet: open a restaurant in London called Nico.

AL ARONOWITZ remains one of the many unheralded geniuses of the scene.

BETTY BARZINO remains, as always, one of the great, twisted like Giacometti beauties.

VICTOR BOCKRIS: His books on Andy Warhol, William Burroughs, Keith Richards and Lou Reed are internationally acclaimed stone classics. Fuck you!

JOHN CAGE died and went to musical heaven where he is now conducting rigorous rehearsals in silence with the archangels. They should all shut up with their constant wailing.

JOHN CALE, bless his good heart, has two children and tours the world with his beautifully lyrical, emotional, solo work.

MIKE CURB always wears a nice pair of shoes.

RONNIE CUTRONE remains among the most brilliant painters of comic book dreams in America.

WALTER De MARIA made the right choice in leaving the VU. He is now among the biggest men in the art world.

BOB DYLAN: In the 1980s Lou finally started saying that he dug Dylan and Dylan started saying that he dug Lou, and Lou actually appeared at a number of Bob events, culminating in his incendiary rendition of *Foot Of Pride* at Bob's big Madison Square Garden 50th anniversary project.

FEDERICO FELLINI passed on in a big coffin on the grand canal in Venice where he was undoubtedly filming a movie in his coffin. He was a motherfucker.

NAT FINKELSTEIN appears to have disappeared.

HENRY GELDZAHLER continues to be among the most intelligent influences on Lou Reed.

ALLEN GINSBERG photographed Reed in 1982 and said that Lou, along with William Burroughs, had been a major influence on punk rock.

BILL GRAHAM died in a fiery helicopter crash off the coast of nowhere, prompting Keith Richards to exclaim, "That's the end of night helicopter flights for me, baby," and he was probably right. The Velvets hated Graham but Graham was as great as the Velvets.

ALBERT GROSSMAN was...

PEIRO HELCZER died, not coincidentally, in an automobile accident in France in 1993. God rest his tormented singing soul.

BETSEY JOHNSON bla bla bla... she continues to reign as the Queen of the Negative Girls.

BRIAN JONES bla bla bla... he will never be forgotten.

BILLY LINICH recently reunited with the VU and continues to take divine photographs.

GERARD MALANGA bla bla bla... his star shines brightly.

STERLING MORRISON is currently a tugboat captain on the Gulf of Mexico. His family lives in Poughkeepsie, same town as Billy Linich.

PAUL MORRISSEY lives in New York City and continues an illustrious career of brilliance.

BOBBY NEUWIRTH recently collaborated with John Cale on a series of songs.

NICO died from a heart attack after cycling up a steep hill in savage heat on the island of Ibiza in 1988. Her soul lives on among us all.

ONDINE died in 1989 after a prolonged illness. He gave his life to art. He was the Pope of NY from 1966 until his death. This book and all our books are in reality dedicated to him. Ondine was the spirit of the VU.

BRIGID POLK has been reincarnated as Brigid Berlin.

LOU REED is currently living apart from his wife and attempting to continue his solo career after having destroyed the reunion of the VU. God rest his soul.

INGRID SUPERSTAR went out for a pack of cigarettes one day and, like the character in a Raymond Chandler novel, *never* returned; no, she never returned.

LYNN TILLMAN is a major novelist of the angst-ridden humour of New York.

MAUREEN TUCKER'S solo career is booming now as she tours the world as the Maureen Tucker Band, occasionally accompanied by Sterl.

ANDY WARHOL was murdered in a NY hospital by mange-ridden running dogs for the underground fascist régime that really operates the monopoly game of America. He was a genius and a Saint and a "bad" man. Without him, no Lou Reed, no Nico, no Velvet Underground. Point. Set. Match. Fucke★ everybody who killed him. May they suffer long and hard in the hot sun.

FRANK ZAPPA, decent, humane and a genius, carried on his work until his truly untimely death from cancer in 1993. Even Lou really dug him though he would never admit it. Rock'n'roll war is bullshit. Rock'n'roll is about love and celebration. Who gives a shit what anybody thinks about anybody else?

[★Medieval spelling]

Nico.
(Rex Features)

Maureen Tucker.
(LFI)

Andy Warhol.
(Rex Features)

● DISCOGRAPHY

● SINGLES (US)

● Loop
December 1966
(Seven minute one-sided 7" flexidisc, included in *Aspen* magazine, No. 3, New York)

● Untitled
(7" flexidisc included in "Andy Warhol's Index Book" as a picture disc with portrait of Lou Reed on one side. Features the Velvets discussing the book while their first LP plays in the background.)

● All Tomorrow's Parties/I'll Be Your Mirror
Verve 10427 October 1966
(Promo copies exist in picture sleeve; it is uncertain whether this single was ever issued commercially)

● Sunday Morning/Femme Fatale
Verve 10466 December 1966

● White Light White Heat/Here She Comes Now
Verve 10560 March 1968
(Promo copies exist; probably not issued commercially)

● Here She Comes Now/I Heard Her Call My Name
Verve 10560 March 1968
(Promo copies exist; probably not issued commercially)

● What Goes On Now/Jesus
MGM 14057 1969

● Who Loves The Sun/Oh Sweet Nuthin'
Cotillion 44107 1970

● SINGLES (UK)

● Who Loves The Sun/Sweet Jane
Atlantic 2091 088 April 1971

● Candy Says/Waiting For The Man/Run Run Run
MGM 2006 283 June 1973

● Sweet Jane/Rock And Roll
Atlantic K 10339 August 1973

● White Light White Heat/Heroin/Venus In Furs/Waiting For The Man
Polydor POSPX 398 (12") 1981

● Heroin/Venus In Furs/Waiting For The Man/Run Run Run
Polydor POSPX 603 (12") October 1982

● Waiting For The Man/Heroin
Old Gold OG 4049 (12") March 1988

● Venus In Furs/All Tomorrow's Parties
Old Gold OG 4051 (12") March 1988
(All Tomorrow's Parties is an alternate mix, also available on the CD release on the Velvet's début album)

● Venus In Furs (live)**/Waiting For The Man** (live)
Warner Bros W 0224 (7") February 1994

● Venus In Furs (live)**/Waiting For The Man** (live)
Warner Bros W 0224C (cassette) February 1994

● Venus In Furs (live edit)**/Sweet Jane** (live)**/Heroin** (live)**/Waiting For The Man** (live)
Warner Bros W 0224CD (CD) February 1994

● ALBUMS (US)

● The East Village Other Electric Newspaper
ESP Disk 1034 1966
(One track contains a Velvets backing track with a TV interview with Lucy Byrd Johnson on her wedding day superimposed over it)

● The Velvet Underground And Nico
Sunday Morning/Waiting For The Man/Femme Fatale/Venus In Furs/Run Run Run/All Tomorrow's Parties/Heroin/There She Goes Again/I'll Be Your Mirror/The Black Angel's Death Song/European Son
Verve 5008 March 1967

● White Light/White Heat
White Light White Heat/The Gift/Lady Godiva's Operation/Here She Comes Now/I Heard Her Call My Name/Sister Ray
Verve December 1967

● The Velvet Underground
Candy Says/What Goes On/Some Kinda Love/Pale Blue Eyes/Jesus/Beginning To See The Light/I'm Set Free/That's The Story Of Life/Murder Mystery/Afterhours
MGM SE 4617 March 1969

● Loaded
Who Loves the Sun/Sweet Jane/Rock And Roll/Cool It Down/New Age/Head Held High/Lonesome Cowboy Bill/I Found A Reason/Train Round The Bend/Oh Sweet Nuthin'
Cotillion 9034 September 1970

● Live At Max's Kansas City
Waiting For The Man/Sweet Jane/Lonesome Cowboy Bill/Beginning To See The Light/I'll Be Your Mirror/Pale Blue Eyes/Sunday Morning/Femme Fatale/Afterhours
Cotillion SD 9500 May 1972
(Recorded at Max's on August 22, 1970, by Brigid Polk on a Sony cassette machine)

● Velvet Underground
Candy Says/Sunday Morning/Femme Fatale/White Light White Heat/Heroin/Beginning To See The Light/Here She Comes Now/Afterhours
MGM GAS 131 1972

● Squeeze
Polydor 2383 180 February 1973
(A Doug Yule solo project credited erroneously to the Velvets)

● Lou Reed And The Velvet Underground
That's The Story Of My Life/Sister Ray/Lady Godiva's Operation/Heroin/Sunday Morning/All Tomorrow's Parties/There She Goes Again/White Light White Heat/Femme Fatale
Pride PRD 0022 1973

● Live 1969
Waiting For The Man/Lisa Says/What Goes On/Sweet Jane/We're Gonna Have A Real Good Time Together/Femme Fatale/New Age/Rock And Roll/Beginning To See The Light/Ocean/Pale Blue Eyes/Heroin/Some Kinda Love/Over You/Sweet Bonnie Brown/It's Just Too Much/White Light White Heat/I'll Be Your Mirror
Mercury SRM 2-7504 (double LP) April 1974

● VU
I Can't Stand It/Stephanie Says/She's My Best Friend/Lisa Says/Ocean/Foggy Notion/Inside Your Heart/One Of These Days/I'm Sticking With You
Polygram 823 299 February 1985

● Another VU
We're Gonna Have A Real Good Time Together/I'm Gonna Move Right In/Hey Mr Rain (Version 1)/Ride Into The Sun/Coney Island Steeplechase/Guess I'm Falling In Love (Instrumental Version)/Hey Mr Rain (Version 2)/Ferryboat Bill/Rock And Roll (Original Version)
Polygram 829 405-1 1986

● The Best Of The Velvet Underground
Waiting For The Man/Femme Fatale/Run Run Run/Heroin/All Tomorrow's Parties/I'll Be Your Mirror/White Light White Heat/Stephanie Says/What Goes On/Beginning To See The Light/Pale Blue Eyes/I Can't Stand It/Lisa Says/Sweet Jane/Rock And Roll
Polygram 841 164 1989

● LIVE MCMXCIII (2 CD Set)
Disc 1: We're Gonna Have A Real Good Time Together/Venus In Furs/Guess I'm Falling In Love/Afterhours/All Tomorrow's Parties/Some Kinda Love/I'll be Your Mirror/Beginning To See The Light/The Gift/I Hear Her Call My Name/Femme Fatale
Disc 2: Hey Mr Rain/Sweet Jane/Velvet Nursery Rhyme/White Light White Heat/I'm Sticking With You/Black Angel's Death Song/Rock'n'Roll/I Can't Stand It/Waiting For The Man/Heroin/Pale Blue Eyes/Coyote
Warner Bros 9362-45464-2 October 1993

● LIVE MCMXCIII (Single CD)
Venus In Furs/Sweet Jane/Afterhours/All Tomorrow's Parties/Some Kinda Love/The Gift/Rock'n'Roll/Waiting For The Man/Heroin/Pale Blue Eyes
Warner Bros 9632-45465-2 October 1993

● ALBUMS (UK)
Track listings as US albums unless otherwise stated

● The Velvet Underground And Nico
Verve SVLP 9184 October 1967

● White Light White Heat
Verve SVLP 9201 June 1968

● The Velvet Underground
MGM C 8108 April 1969

● Loaded
Atlantic 2400 111 March 1971

● Andy Warhol's Velvet Underground Featuring Nico
Waiting For The Man/Candy Says/Run Run Run/White Light White Heat/All Tomorrow's Parties/Sunday Morning/I Heard Her Call My Name/Femme Fatale/Heroin/Here She Comes Now/There She Goes Again/Sister Ray/Venus In Furs/European Son/Pale Blue Eyes/Black Angel's Death Song/Beginning To See The Light
MGM 2683 006 December 1971

● Live At Max's Kansas City
Atlantic K 30022 August 1972

● Squeeze
Polydor 2383 180 February 1973

● Lou Reed And The Velvet Underground
Waiting For The Man/Sister Ray/Lady Godiva's Operation/Who Loves The Sun/All Tomorrow's Parties/There She Goes Again/White Light White Heat/Femme Fatale
MGM 2315 256 October 1973

● The Velvet Underground
White Light White Heat/What Goes On/Venus In Furs/That's The Story Of My Life/Here She Comes Now/Beginning To See The Light/Jesus/Run Run Run/Some Kinda Love/The Gift/I'm Set Free/I Heard Her Call My Name
MGM 2354 1976

● Live 1969
Mercury 6641 900 February 1979

● VU
Polydor POLD 5167 March 1985

● The Velvet Underground Box Set
Polydor VUBOX1 1986

● Another VU
Polydor POLD 5028 February 1987

● The Best Of The Velvet Underground
Polydor 841 164-1 1989

● Live MCMXCIII (2 CD Set)
Warner Bros 9362-45464-2 October 1993

● Live MCMXCIII (Single CD)
Warner Bros 9632-45465-2 October 1993